Nabil R. Adam   Bharat K. Bhargava
Milton Halem   Yelena Yesha   (Eds.)

# Digital Libraries

## Research and Technology Advances

ADL'95 Forum
McLean, Virginia, USA, May 15-17, 1995
Selected Papers

Springer

Volume Editors

Nabil Adam
Computing and Information Systems
MS/CIS Department, Rutgers University
180 University Avenue, Newark, NJ 07102, USA
E-mail: adam@adam.rutgers.edu

Bharat K. Bhargava
Department of Computer Sciences, Purdue University
West Lafayette, IN 47907, USA
E-mail: bb@cs.purdue.edu

Milton Halem
Goddard Space Flight Center, NASA
Greenbelt, MD, USA
E-mail: milton.halem.1@gsfc.nasa.gov

Yelena Yesha
Computer Science Department, University of Maryland Baltimore County
Baltimore, MD 21228-5398, USA
E-mail: yeyesha@cs.umbc.edu

Cataloging-in-Publication data applied for

Die Deutsche Bibliothek - CIP-Einheitsaufnahme

**Digital libraries** : research and technology advances ; selected
papers / ADL '95 forum, McLean, Virginia, USA, May 1995.
Nabil R. Adam ... (ed.). - Berlin ; Heidelberg ; New York ;
Barcelona ; Budapest ; Hong Kong ; London ; Milan ; Paris ;
Santa Clara ; Singapore ; Tokyo : Springer, 1996
  (Lecture notes in computer science ; Vol. 1082)
  ISBN 3-540-61410-9
NE: Adam, Nabil R. [Hrsg.]; ADL <1995, McLean, Va.>; GT


CR Subject Classification (1991): H.2.6, C.2, E.4-5, I.4.1, J.1

ISSN 0302-9743
ISBN 3-540-61410-9 Springer-Verlag Berlin Heidelberg New York

© Springer-Verlag Berlin Heidelberg 1996
Printed in Germany

Typesetting: Camera-ready by author
SPIN 10513047    06/3142 – 5 4 3 2 1 0    Printed on acid-free paper

# Lecture Notes in Computer Science

Edited by G. Goos, J. Hartmanis and J. van Leeuwen

Advisory Board: W. Brauer   D. Gries   J. Stoer

Springer
*Berlin*
*Heidelberg*
*New York*
*Barcelona*
*Budapest*
*Hong Kong*
*London*
*Milan*
*Paris*
*Santa Clara*
*Singapore*
*Tokyo*

# Preface

ADL '95, the Forum on Research & Technology Advances in Digital Libraries, held May 15-17, 1995 in McLean, Virginia, reflects substantial growth of interest in the field. There were 350 attendees from a wide diversity of institutions worldwide, nearly twice the previous year. The forum was privileged to have Dr. France Cordova, NASA Chief Scientist; the Honorable James Billington, the Librarian of Congress; and Dr. Larry Smarr, Director of the National Center for Supercomputing Applications, as keynote speakers. In addition, Dr. Michael Nelson, Special Assistant to the President for Information Technology, presented an Administration overview of the National Information Infrastructure (NII).

Cooperating institutions included the Advanced Research Projects Agency (ARPA), the Association for Computing Machinery (ACM), AT&T, Bellcore, the IEEE Computer Society, the University of Maryland at Baltimore County, the National Science Foundation (NSF), the National Institute of Standards and Technology (NIST), Purdue University, and Rutgers University CIMIC (Center for Information Management, Integration, and Connectivity), with NASA Goddard Space Flight Center as the primary sponsor.

A brief background perspective on what motivated this forum, its structure, and the issues it was designed to address is the purpose of this introduction.

To begin with, one might ask, why is NASA playing such a prominent role in the federal digital library program? For more than a decade NASA has been developing digital information systems to provide on-line access to its many observational images and data sets, both to assist our scientists as well as to share this information with local and state governments, universities, other national and international organizations, and the general public. Early in 1993 Congress first considered a bill (H.R. 1757) to create an NII, a bill in which NSF and NASA were assigned lead roles in helping develop digital library technologies. In particular, NASA was singled out to make its remote sensing data available to the public.

ADL '95 is the third meeting on digital libraries sponsored by NASA over the past two years. The first took place in August 1993 at Goddard Space Flight Center and was limited to about 30 invited participants mainly from the information industry, academia (both computer and library science departments), and other government agencies. Discussants explored arenas in which federal agencies might involve the broader community in addressing the critical issues. The meeting also brought to the surface the notion of a digital library foundation. Coming out of that gathering instead, however, was a consensus that the government could play a significant role by organizing a forum for grappling with the rapidly evolving technologies and standards in digital libraries.

A workshop subsequently was held at Rutgers University in May 1994, attended by approximately 180 people. Coming into being at this time were new initiatives sponsored by NASA, NSF, and ARPA. These initiatives attempted to reach the community at large and support a digital library information infrastructure. It is noteworthy to observe the large interest on the part of the international community, evidenced by their strong participation in that meeting. As before, a broad community recommended that a broader-based conference be convened, a notion that found its expression in ADL '95.

In structuring this conference, the steering and program committees focused on three main areas:

1. Defining the research issues associated with digitizing information.
2. Exploring the economic and social issues.
3. Addressing the expansion of the program to global digital library access.

The forum's structure and content, as presented in this volume, reflects these concerns. Nearly twenty selected papers cover topics in digital library visualization, network-based information and resource discovery, document handling, information retrieval, design issues for prototyping, and related areas. Complementing these papers, prominent government and university scientists share their views on dealing with the broader questions arising from this national initiative.

Finally, to address the economic, social, and global digital library issues, panel discussions engage industry, academic, and government leaders on how the rapid expansion of digital libraries will affect the U.S. economy, society, and global relations. It is also appropriate in light of today's constrained resource environment to begin to reexamine the role of federal programs in supporting technologies and the relevance of those programs to our society.

June 1996

Nabil R. Adam
Bharat K. Bhargava
Milton Halem
Yelena Yesha

# Contents

## II   Document Handling and Information Retrieval

# III  Network-Based Information and Resource Discovery

## 12 Data Discovery in Large Scale Heterogeneous and Autonomous Databases
### by Athman Bouguettaya and Stephen Milliner        149

## 13 An Intelligent Agent for the K-12 Educational Community
### by Mark E. Rorvig, Mark W. Hutchison, Robert O. Shelton, Stephanie L. Smith and Marwan E. Yazbeck        167

## 14 Interface Issues for Interactive Multimedia Documents
### by Robert B. Allen        179

## 15 Searching and Discovery of Resources in Digital Libraries
by Nahum Gershon, William Ruh, Joshua LeVasseur, Joel Winstead, and Adrienne Kleiboemer                                191

# IV   Design Issues and Prototyping

## 16 The Almaden Distributed Digital Library System
by David M. Choy, Richard Dievendorff, Cynthia Dwork, Jeffrey
B. Lotspiech, Robert J. T. Morris, Norman J. Pass, Laura C.
Anderson, Alan E. Bell, Stephen K. Boyer, Thomas D. Griffin,
Bruce A. Hoenig, James M. McCrossin, Alex M. Miller, Florian
Pestoni and Deidra S. Picciano                                  203

# Chapter 1

## Communicating NASA's Science to the Public

France Cordova*

## 1.1 Introduction

In the preface to their 1993 book Supercomputing and the Transformation of Science, Bill Kaufmann and Larry Smarr write, "Ultimately most of human knowledge will be stored in a common digital library." How we develop and utilize that library to educate, inspire, and otherwise benefit all people is the real subject of this forum.

The field of digital library research and prototyping has undergone explosive growth nationally, and at a recent (G-7) meeting of heads of state in Europe its international relevance became clear. ADL '95 has brought together many of the world's leaders in exploring and overcoming the technical and societal issues of making digital libraries a widespread means for public access to information. A large part of the technical agenda is shaped by the need for robust methods of storage, organization, and dissemination of digital materials. Technological advances–in storage, computing speed, and networking–play a vital role here, but content-based searching and resource discovery are emerging as equally important research areas for serving user needs. Visualization, multimedia, and hypermedia as well as newly developed document formats, friendly user interfaces, and artificial intelligence will combine to make digital information readily accessible and geared to a broad range of presentation levels.

Digital libraries will have impact on our society, necessitating changes in our laws and the ways we learn and do business, with consequences and benefits for such areas as economics, intellectual property, and medicine. Prototype digital libraries are providing a glimpse of a future Global Information Infrastructure that will make our world even smaller by bringing the sum of its intellectual and cultural assets into people's homes. Already today, communication technologies are providing nearly instantaneous coverage of events across a whole spectrum of areas. On that crowded stage, science has to compete for attention, support, and relevancy.

Science is especially under pressure today to justify investment relative to other critical investments, such as health care, poverty reduction programs, and

---

*NASA Chief Scientist, Code AS, NASA Headquarters, Washington, DC 20546-0001

national defense. With the end of the Cold War we are seeing a diminution in support of the science base. Scientists are perceived by many as just another special interest group. No longer is it obvious to the public that science and technology automatically equate to real benefits. It is becoming increasingly clear that most people do not know what science the federal government is doing or why it is doing it.

The Administration has therefore made science literacy and the communication of science national priorities. In its policy document last August called Science in the National Interest, which was the first White House science policy document enunciated in fifteen years, it listed a few long- term goals for the nation. Two are particularly relevant here:

- Raise the scientific and technological literacy of all Americans.

- Produce the finest scientists and engineers for the twenty-first century.

Science communications are critical for achieving the first goal and can play a decisive role in enabling the second. The Administration has a mandate in the NASA Space Act of 1958 to "provide for the widest practicable and appropriate dissemination of information concerning its activities and the results thereof."

In the last two years we have taken a new look at how well we are fulfilling this mandate at NASA. We formed a cross-agency group under my leadership and set out to make a more effective plan for communicating NASA's science to the public. We examined every aspect of how we communicate and to whom. In a free-wheeling forum on the public communication of NASA science, facilitated by an excellent public communicator, Dr. Carl Sagan, we asked a diverse group of NASA customers (including textbook writers, journalists, teachers, movie producers, scientists, and school children) how we could develop products that would serve them better, products that would ensure that they could get their own unique kinds of messages out to a much larger group of customers. In other words, our approach was to leverage our communication by identifying the specific needs of intermediate customers who would bring the information about NASA's science to the general public, our ultimate customer, through their own unique channels. As a result of this effort we have adopted a variety of approaches to widen the public's knowledge about the science that we do.

First, utilizing the scientists: Through NASA research solicitations, also known as NASA Research Announcements, and announcements of opportunities for missions, we are encouraging scientists to do public outreach as a part of their scientific proposals and to take responsibility for science training, not just for the next generation of scientists and engineers but the next generation of Congress men and women, for example. Science proposals for research and even instruments are graded now not just on a science research plan, but also on a communications plan. This is a very new paradigm for scientists, but one that is right in line with the Administration's recommendation in Science in the National Interest that "federal agencies will encourage research scientists to use their research experiences in support of public understanding and appreciation of science."

Also with respect to the practitioners of science, special supplemental grants to scientists' research grants are being awarded for unusual public outreach initiatives. Some of these initiatives are digital in character. An example is "Ask Dr. Sue," which is an opportunity for students to send electronic queries about astronomy to scientists at NASA's Goddard Space Flight Center.

Another example is "Live from Antarctica," which takes students to this frozen continent where, arguably, the most science per capita on this globe is being conducted. Scientists in Antarctica are searching for dark matter and antimatter using balloon technology, studying changes in the ozone layer and other environmental indicators, understanding the origin and development of cellular life from microbes under the ice crust, and testing closed environmental systems in preparation for long human voyages in space. It is important for the public to know the value of Antarctica for research that will have broad applications.

For the educator intermediaries: We have extended the existing Teacher Research Center network that enables teachers to be more informed communicators of the science we do in space.

For textbook writers: We are providing for the first time archival digital images of early space missions and their scientific results. Before we started this initiative we were only providing the most recent images, but those archival images from our past missions going back to the early 1980s and 1970s were not easily available. Providing archival images allows new creative approaches to introducing students to the latest discoveries in science and space. It is appropriate that the educators and publicists who are close to the cognitive base of education- -how students learn–have the information they need to develop the most useful learning tools.

For the media: We are collaborating more closely with television, utilizing talk-show formats with space scientists discussing their latest results and answering the public's questions live. We have more scientific press conferences using a variety of venues to inform the press of what we are doing in science. The results are paying off. Astronomy in particular has made the front page of premier newspapers at least once per month this year and recently graced the covers of prominent news magazines as well. The challenge, of course, is to get on the front of the smallest town newspapers.

One aspect of the plan we adopted is to utilize cyberspace more effectively. We are expanding the use of new communication technologies, including digital libraries. Proactive electronic distribution of NASA information has increased dramatically over the past year: NASA Spacelink has been upgraded to full Internet connectivity. Our Public Affairs Office has created a homepage and is cooperating with the Internet, Compuserve, and E-World. The World Wide Web has become a highly effective means for our communication.

The following are a few examples of how we are presently building up a gallery of science information to inform the public of what NASA is all about and to engage them, sometimes interactively, in our missions. All of the images can be accessed on the World Wide Web.

NASA has a homepage through which one can access the content of the research and discoveries at all ten of NASA's Centers dispersed around the country. A U.S. map showing the locations of the Centers was made from a mosaic of Landsat satellite images. Hypertext links to each of the Centers are clickable, and the images come, for the most part, from those Centers. The examples, however, are framed by NASA's Strategic Plan, which shows the five Enterprises that represent to the country what NASA does in air and space.

The first Enterprise I will illustrate is Space Science, one of our most active areas. The discoveries here go to the heart of one of the nation's most fundamental values, that of inspiration.

Figure 1.1: NASA is organized along five Strategic Enterprises, as shown on a NASA Public Affairs Office World Wide Web page

Let us start with last summer's once in a millennium cosmic event: the collision of the fragments of Comet Shoemaker-Levy with the planet Jupiter in July. An animation shows the near infrared observations of the impact of just one fragment using the Keck telescope, which is sited on Hawaii's Mauna Kea volcano. The comet impact caught the public's attention like few other science events in recent history. The Jet Propulsion Laboratory (JPL) Comet-Jupiter homepage alone has experienced more than four million accesses since the first impact. The log-ons to JPL and the University of Maryland site have continued almost unabated, long after the encounter. The scientific information from these images and other data, from observatories all over the world, including the Hubble Space Telescope, has led to new understanding about the nature of comets and Jupiter itself, and a new awareness of the potential of Earth hazards.

In 1987 the nearest supernova in 400 years was discovered by an amateur in Chile. The supernova took place in one of our neighbor galaxies, the Large Magellanic Cloud. The event is important because of the information it can give us about the nature of supernovae. It is thought that a long-ago, much closer supernova created the conditions that stimulated the evolution of our solar system. SN87A happened just before the worldwide digital revolution, and although it had wide publicity, including cover stories on major newsweeklies, it garnered nowhere near the attention of the public as more recent, cosmically humbler events that can be accessed digitally.

Figure 1.2: The Space Telescope Science Institute has put together a gallery of some of the most significant images taken by the Hubble Space Telescope.

For instance, there is NASA's recent Astro-2 shuttle mission, our first on-line space shuttle mission. Launched this March, the activity and results of this astronomy mission would, in a pre-World Wide Web world, have been available to only a privileged few–the mission control people at NASA Houston and Marshall and the scientists who acquire and analyze the data. But, by putting the mission on the Internet from prior-launch to shuttle touchdown, 2.6 million pairs of hands (from 59 countries) stepped "on board" the shuttle, causing mission control to say that the shuttle, designed for only eight astronauts, was "getting very crowded." Here are some of the responses of the virtual participants: "Allowing

Internet users an opportunity to directly communicate with the Astro-2 team is a great idea. I think it will really help to boost the interest in the space program by making the general public feel not so detached from what you people are doing." Another response: "It is fun to be part of history." From a teacher: "My fifth grade class is really enjoying this unique opportunity to be so up-to-date with a space mission." A common sentiment: "What you're doing is the only way I enjoy having my tax dollars spent."

A brief tour of the gallery provided by the refurbished Hubble Space Telescope gives clues about the origin and evolution of the universe and the galaxies and stars within it. The Cartwheel Galaxy represents a head-on collision between a spiral galaxy and a smaller galaxy. The contact sends out a wave of energy that triggers the birth of new stars, forming a ring around the bull's eye collision.

In the belt of Orion is a brightly lit nursery of newly born stars. Fifty percent of these young ones are surrounded by large disks of gas, perhaps solar systems in the making. These observations lend more weight to the idea that many suns may host orbiting planets like our own.

Hubble sees the galaxies in the Virgo supercluster at the time that dinosaurs roamed the Earth. Galaxies like M100 harbor pulsating stars that can be used to decipher the age and size of the universe.

An image of a planetary nebula foretells the fate of the Sun. In about four billion years or so planet Earth will be enshrouded in the envelope of the expanded Sun, on its way to becoming a Red Giant star. An ensuing catastrophic collapse will compress much of the Sun into a white dwarf star, with a giant remnant envelope of gas and debris expanding outwards at high velocity. The large, complex nebula is a fossil record of the late stages of the star's evolution.

Hubble serves as a weather satellite for conditions on other planets. For example, 3.5 billion years ago our nearest neighbor Mars might have looked very similar to the Earth and may have hosted life. It is too cold and dry now to harbor life, but in its mantle is the evidence to determine the fossil record, if it exists. Knowledge of extreme and relatively rapid weather changes on Mars, which were noted recently in images taken by the Hubble Telescope, will make us better prepared for choosing sites and optimum conditions for our planned program of landers on Mars, to begin in the next few years.

Scientific studies on the Earth, its environment and natural resources, and how anthropogenic and natural factors are affecting them are themes of the U.S. Global Change Research Program. NASA's part of this program is to provide the scientific spacecraft for remote sensing. Its Earth Observing System (EOS) comprises more than two dozen satellites that will examine all aspects of climate change. This program is part of a large NASA Enterprise called Mission to Planet Earth. The data from one of our present spacecraft, the Total Ozone Mapping Spectrometer, is giving Internet users a good picture of the changing ozone hole. Now the public can view the changes themselves, nearly in real time, and have a more informed dialog with their elected representatives. This program is all about giving the public–the salmon fishermen in the Pacific Northwest, the forester and logger, the farmer in the Midwest, the wine grower in California–the information they need to help make decisions about their industries.

Digital information about natural events on a global scale is informing the public better about the origin, nature, and effects of natural disasters. An example is that of Hurricane Andrew, which may be viewed on the World Wide Web from different angles in a simulated flyby (MPEG and QuickTime formats). This was done by obtaining the cloud heights from an infrared sounder on a National Oceanographic and Atmospheric Administration (NOAA) satellite.

An important aspect of the national environmental initiative is education through the information highway. NASA is a participant in GLOBE, an international K-12 program that seeks to implement Vice President Gore's vision of putting the problem of the care and feeding of the planet in everyone's backyard. Presently 200 schools are linked to project GLOBE, and thousands more schools will be linked up in the next few years. In this program school children take environmental measurements in their schoolyards and transmit these measurements over the Internet to a common database, where they are analyzed and interpreted and sent in the aggregate back to the participating schools. These students are learning about the environment and are using the scientific method to improve our understanding of the factors that affect it. This appreciation of the planet and an appreciation of the contribution of science towards its betterment will probably remain with these students even as they pursue many diverse careers. The digital approach of GLOBE–its roots in education through scientific experiment and understanding–is allowing them to face a "grown-up" problem and take some measure of responsibility for its solution.

Another of NASA's principal Enterprises is the Human Exploration and Development of Space. Web users can view the astronauts who serviced the Hubble Space Telescope and learn something about just how complex that mission was. They can learn as well about the many technologies that go into human space flight and the various kinds of science one needs to do in space to understand how humans can live and work there.

Our shuttle missions are preparing us for the science of the International Space Station. This science makes use of the special condition of low gravity, or microgravity, in space. This dramatic change in the fundamental parameter of gravity allows us to do all sorts of experiments that cannot be done effectively on Earth–unique experiments in combustion, materials, fluids, and biotechnology. An example is growing protein crystals in space. Human cells produce about 75,000 different proteins. These proteins play important roles in the functioning of many aspects of the body. On Earth, buoyancy-induced convection and sedimentation may damage growing proteins because these crystals are loosely bound aggregates of thousands of atoms. The environment of microgravity that the shuttle flies in, however, is conducive to growing large and well-ordered protein crystalline structures. This is of great interest to the pharmaceutical industry, which uses the structure of proteins to develop drugs to interact with protein functions. Penicillin is a well-known drug that works by

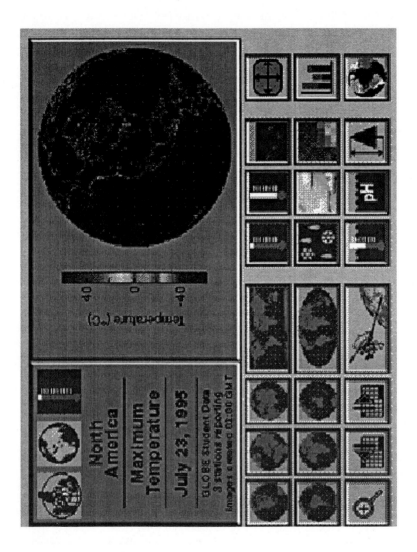

Figure 1.3: Students in the GLOBE Program collect environmental data, which is compiled, visualized, and made available through this interface at Goddard Space Flight Center

Figure 1.4: The plans and progress of the International Space Station can be monitored from Johnson Space Center.

blocking a protein's function.

A fourth major Enterprise of NASA is that of Space Technology. Its new centerpiece activity is access to space, specifically the Reusable Launch Vehicle. This program is a partnership among NASA, the Air Force, and industry for world leadership in low-cost space transportation. This activity is essential if we are to remain a viable space- faring nation. The objective of this program is to develop and demonstrate new technologies for the next generation of reusable space transportation systems that can radically reduce the cost of access to space. This will require a combination of ground and flight demonstrations. The experimental flight (X-vehicles) portion of the program will be used to verify operability and performance in "real world" environments.

The fifth and final NASA Strategic Enterprise is Aeronautics. Information about NASA's research and development on the high-performance aircraft systems of the future can be accessed through its three Aeronautics Centers: Langley, Lewis, and Ames. An example of aeronautics research that can be obtained through the Internet is the Numerical Propulsion System Simulator. This is an interdisciplinary project to unite the various disciplines used in gas turbine engine design. The Simulator can be represented by three main concepts: "Zooming" enables the simulation of complete engine systems at a level of analysis required by the physics. "Coupling" refers to the joining of the various disciplines in a single analysis, and "integration" refers to the integration of the various engine component simulations. These techniques are being developed for a series of engines, including the Energy Efficient Engine for validation and the High Speed Civil Transport and Advanced Subsonic Transport demonstrators.

Aeronautics' Flow Analysis Software Toolkit, or FAST, is a software environment for analyzing data from numerical simulations. It examines, among other things, the distribution of the boundary layer flow around aircraft. It is representative of the close union between supercomputers, computational fluid dynamics, and wind tunnel testing in designing and testing the environmentally safe and economically viable aircraft of the future.

The need for new, bold means of electronic dissemination is clear. As can be seen from the foregoing examples, NASA research is producing unprecedented amounts of data, with startling temporal, spectral, and spatial resolution. In addition to accessing raw remote sensing data and images, digital library technologies are making available animations, multimedia, and interactive multimedia. Availability of so much diverse data on the Internet facilitates interdisciplinary studies that were not possible only a few years ago.

To be effective digital libraries will have to organize these data and products in such a way that they can be obtained, understood, and integrated by specialist and interested public alike. The images hold value for the scientific information they provide to the specialist. Yet the feedback we have been getting from the public logging onto our on-line science missions shows that these images also hold aesthetic interest for the non-specialist. These images inspire curiosity in the science underlying the image. They inspire youngsters to learn and perhaps

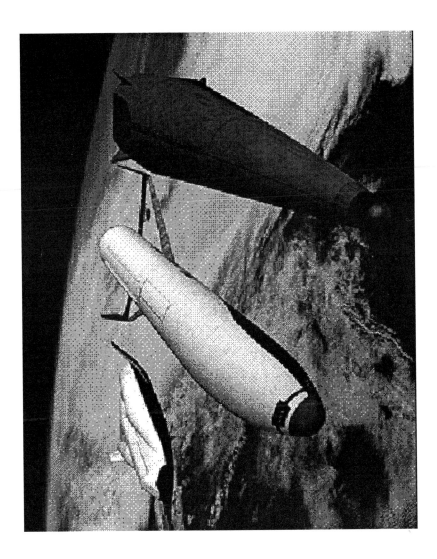

Figure 1.5: The Reusable Launch Vehicle program is developing the follow-on to the Space Shuttle. This picture, from Marshall Space Flight Center, shows several experimental (X-vehicle) designs.

to think about careers in science and technology. And they make people feel like they are getting a return on their investment.

Another aspect to digital communications that is becoming more and more critical is the fact that our space missions are increasingly international in scope. The International Space Station, EOS, the Stratospheric Observatory for Infrared Astronomy (SOFIA), and the International Solar Terrestrial Program are among the many international efforts in which NASA is a partner. In fact, most of NASA's missions are international in character. We are edging towards a world in which partnerships in science and technology can help sustain peace on Earth. The themes of these partnerships–science, technology, and education–are universally valued. In a time when the world must come together to solve many of its most profound problems of sustainability, we need to have global means of telling people everywhere how we carry out research, where the research is going, and why it is important to the world.

To help make these goals a reality, NASA is funding twenty-six digital library technology and applications development teams from across the country, in addition to a Remote Sensing Public Access Center. Focused on facilitating public use on Earth and space science data over the Internet, a wide variety of organizations are involved, including industry, educational institutions, non-profit organizations, NASA Centers, and federal, state, and local government agencies, in various combinations.

The Digital Library Technology project is emphasizing technologies to develop tools, applications, and software and hardware systems that are able to scale upward to accommodate evolving user requirements and order-of- magnitude increases in user access. These technologies encompass integration of multimedia data, wide-area networking, resource discovery, and intelligent information retrieval. This project is a collaboration led by the National Science Foundation and including the Advanced Research Projects Agency (ARPA) and NASA.

Another project, the Public Use of Remote Sensing Data, is designed to encourage the development of innovative applications of Earth and space science remote sensing data. Potential applications include atmospheric, oceanic, and land monitoring; publishing, agriculture, tourism, transportation, libraries, cartography, and education, especially K-12 science and its applications.

One example is called "Creating the Public Connection: Interactive Experiences with Real-Time Earth and Space Science Data." Project Director Dr. Patricia Reiff of Rice University creates interactive displays of real-time science data. The project is a collaboration with the Houston Museum of Natural Science. Dr. Reiff describes her project as providing an "off-ramp" on the information superhighway for people who are not part of the "information elite." It facilitates learning about science with minimal training in information access techniques. It has both museum and school versions. With advanced kiosk technology, people can view automatically updated imagery such as hourly weather maps from satellite data and daily images of the Sun in X-rays from the Yohkoh space satellite. Scientific modeling of the Earth's magnetosphere at Rice makes

Figure 1.6: Ames Research Center's Flow Analysis Software Toolkit (FAST) is allowing engineers to analyze aerodynamics simulations

use of the latest data on the Sun's active magnetic field from the University of Alaska to relay real-time space weather information to students, as well as museum-goers.

Figure 1.7: Part of the Digital Library Technology project, Rice University's "Creating the Public Connection" makes Earth and space science data accessible to the layperson.

Another example is Washington, D.C.'s WRC-TV's program "Public Access to Earth and Space Science Data Via Television." This project, a partnership between JPL, NASA/Stennis, NOAA, and the television station, will develop visualizations of current Earth and space science data to be included as part of the daily weather and news reports for WRC-TV and other NBC affiliates. More importantly, the data will be available over the Internet for use in science classes.

An "Earth System Science Community Curriculum Testbed" has been developed in an agreement between NASA and industry. This effort is developing Internet access and curriculum materials for investigation-based science instruction. Gonzaga High School in D.C. is an associate. The project is working successfully as demonstrated by its early results; one of the Gonzaga student teams recently published a scientific study of clouds and their effect on the Earth's radiation budget. There are many examples of this kind involving schools across the country, enabled through grants and cooperative agreements between NASA and industry. These partnerships facilitate the utilization of imagery and remote sensing data for applications to forestry, volcano monitoring, and even tourism dependent on natural resources.

Based in West Virginia, the purpose of the Remote Sensing Public Access Center NASA funds is to integrate the technology and application efforts and to serve as a demonstration and testing center and technology-transfer focal point.

One of the funded digital library projects involves the University of Wisconsin and Baltimore's own Space Telescope Science Institute. This team will improve the rate at which large digital images, like those produced by the Hubble Telescope, can be transferred across the network. This technology is key to having the widest possible dissemination and enjoyment of the wealth of digital information available.

These projects are part of the Information Infrastructure Technology and Applications component of NASA's High Performance Computing and Communications Program. This program has the goals of developing the technology base underlying a universally accessible National Information Infrastructure. Reaching communities traditionally unserved by the current Internet will lead to gains in education, economic growth, and ultimately the quality of life for all citizens.

I am reminded of the recent Congressional testimony of a young University of Texas astronomer, "Federally funded scientific research is a contract with the U.S. taxpayer not only to create new products, but to satisfy the national curiosity about the world in which we live. It is a fundamental element in the federal investment portfolio that ensures our leadership in the world." The government's participation in seeding digital library initiatives is key to satisfying that national curiosity. It enables a communication between public investor and scientist, the likes of which we have not seen since early in the last century, when science was directly funded by private citizens, in response to very personal appeals by the practitioners of science.

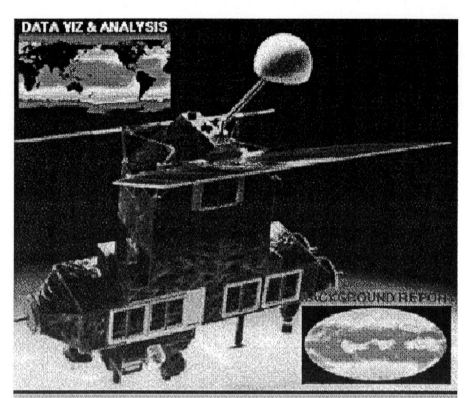

Figure 1.8: Students in the Earth System Science Community Curriculum Testbed learn by becoming scientists, which includes publishing their findings on the World Wide Web. This effort is one of NASA's Public Use of Remote Sensing Data projects

# Chapter 2

## The Library of Congress's National Digital Library Program

James H. Billington[*]

## 2.1   Introduction

It is crucial to realize that in the competitive world in which we live the new technologies may not favor our kind of democracy. They may favor the more authoritarian, Confucian-based societies of East Asia with whom we are friendly on the whole, but with whom we have very competitive relations. In this chapter we attempt to take a closer philosophical look at the new technologies and their impact on our society.

American society, probably more than any other, has taken an aggressively optimistic view of impending technological change. So it was with the first technological revolution, with television almost 50 years ago, which many predicted would vastly enhance education, bring culture and the arts to everyone, and create a better informed, more engaged citizenry. The reality, measured by voter registration and other social statistical indicators, such as student test scores, has been considerably less impressive. Television, except as a marketing device and the family babysitter, is no longer widely touted, even by its practitioners, as a genuine engine of American progress.

The fact is that our kind of democracy and our entrepreneurial open economy depend on the type of active, creative mind that the print culture produced and that the television spectator habit has not. A key question today in America is whether the information superhighway will reinforce the best values of our society. This new interactive multimedia world would seem to offer some promise to do that. It engages the active mind in a kind of intellectual calisthenics. It creates an interplay with useful information. But the answer becomes less clear when we move beyond the technical capabilities provided by the superhighway and ask ourselves what it is bringing and to whom.

Do we want this new technology simply to provide movies on demand, video games, home shopping, telephone services, telebanking, data bases for individual customers? There is nothing wrong with providing entertainment and high

---

[*]The Library of Congress, Washington, D.C. 20540

priced information on demand, but if the highway provides only that, the gap will widen between the information haves and have nots in our society. Americans will lack inexpensive access to the knowledge they need to learn, prosper, invent, refresh themselves, and renew their own creative participation in this society. In fact, we may all forfeit the technology's potential for the renewal of our kind of society. And if America misses this opportunity, the rest of the world is likely to do no better.

Right now we seem to be present at the creation of some important new possibilities where old institutions can play an important role in a new national renaissance. Together with others, libraries in general and the Library of Congress in particular can and should be a powerful force for this national renaissance at the end of this century, just as they were at the end of the last century with the beginning of the Carnegie revolution in public libraries and Congress's decision to underwrite cataloging through the Library of Congress. Since it costs more to catalog a book than to buy it, this decision enabled the entire library system to flourish.

The Library of Congress expects soon to be receiving and organizing vast amounts of material in already digitized form. The material will include films, music, encyclopedias, maps, scientific papers, legal records, government documents, and other data. For preservation purposes, periodicals and books will be in digital as well as paper formats. At the same time the Library alone or in joint ventures with the private sector will be, and in fact already is, beginning to digitize a great deal of its existing paper and film collections for dissemination via the information highway to local schools and libraries. Such efforts, if properly organized and supported, can have enormous positive results.

Our current national concern with setting higher national education standards and getting more initiative and more action at the state and local levels will increase the demand for local access to knowledge which the new technology is capable of providing. The Library of Congress is moving in the direction of getting its contents into local communities.

Now the Library is involved in the Administration's National Information Infrastructure Program, which calls for link-ups between the information superhighway and the nation's schools and libraries. Although the Library is not in the business of building the highways or the trucks that will travel on them, it has a keen interest in where the highway goes, who gets access to it, and what cargo is put on it.

The Library of Congress is enriching the existing network by having become in recent months a major presence on the Internet. It was providing by mid1995, free of charge, more than 40 million records on the Internet, including the entire Library of Congress card catalog, summaries and status of federal legislation, copyright registration records, and abstracts and citations from foreign laws. Many have read about THOMAS, which is an on-line, one-stop resource on the World Wide Web about the workings of the U.S. Congress. THOMAS had its debut on January 5 and logged in well over four million inquiries in less than half a year. Its data base now includes the Congressional Record and some sophisticated searching devices. The Library is also making available electronically the images and accompanying texts from all its major exhibits so that they have a continuing educational impact. The exhibits include Secrets of the Russian Archives, Columbus 1492 Quincentenary exhibit, the Vatican Library Treasures, the Dead Sea Scrolls, and the African American Mosaic. By mid1995 the Library was logging in 20 million computer transactions a month, which is up from eight million three years ago. The most rapidly growing are the Internet transactions from remote locations. The Library staff has designed easy-to-use systems for accessing Library of Congress information and connecting to other resources on the Internet. The Library has continued to build new tools to improve access to our resources over the Internet and to make additional information available. Most important for the long run is the core content that the Library is creating for the new national digital library. During the fiveyear test of our American Memory pilot project, we digitized two dozen American history and cultural collections, more than 200 thousand items, including prints and photographs, manuscripts, sound recordings, and early motion pictures. The Library has unique copies of most of these and they are very fragile. Access to some items has changed from almost no one except a few scholars seeing them, to almost everyone having potential access.

The best known items are perhaps the Mathew Brady Civil War photographs, and the turnofthecentury Edison movies of immigrant life in New York City and of other subjects which have rarely been seen until this time. American Memory has been tested in 44 schools and libraries around the country, and a number of the collections are now beginning to get on the Internet. It is designed to bring the values of the older book culture into the electronic environment and to provide a vitamin enrichment for hard-pressed schools and libraries. Teachers mediate the materials and young people get motivated to delve into books in order to answer questions that they themselves ask when confronted with this archival transfer of documents, photographs, and films that they call up on the screen.

In delivering such materials by electronic means, the Library seeks to reinforce learning in the local communities. Rather than supplementing the home entertainment center, the Library will be a benevolent wholesaler to the local institutions, which will retail the knowledge and information in a variety of ways and with a lot of local initiative to students, teachers and the public.

The National Digital Library is designed to provide substantive content, the highvalue cargo for whatever form or varieties of forms the information super-highway may take. Our tests found, contrary to prior belief, that American Memory works with children as early as the fourth and fifth grades. In fact in many cases it works even better at those ages than at the older ages where the most welcome response was originally expected. American Memory also works well in inner cities and in rural communities. In other words, it motivates people who are not already plugged into the reading and educational system, the escalator on which everyone has to rise in our society in order to become productive members of the economy. Ittends to activate their intellects by stimulating the kinds of open questions that hitherto inaccessible primary materials of our history and of our creativity inevitably raiseexposing them simultaneously to new technology and old values, to the memory of the past and to imagination for the future. It exposes students to historical rather than political correctness, to the good as well as the bad in our history, and thus to a mature but heightened sense of our complex yet common, and, on balance, extraordinary positive cultural legacy.

The Library of Congress's National Digital Library Program will be developed in collaboration with the private sector and with materials included from other repositories both large and small. The Library's vast existing collections will provide the base. The Library receives almost a million items in the Copyright Office each year, approximately half of which are retained as part of the permanent research collections.

Today the Library has about 110 million items; of these twothirds are in non-book format collections. These materials are especially rich in the documentation of American history and creativity. For example, the Library has most of the papers of the first 23 presidents of the United Statesbefore special presidential libraries were built. These papers include George Washington's surveyor drawings, Thomas Jefferson's architectural drawings, the two working drafts of the Gettysburg Address, which we recently put on exhibit, and the draft of the Declaration of Independence in which one can see the active minds of the founding fathers at workand how good their handwriting was.

There is an opportunity to use a variety of material that has an extraordinary effect on students. The Library has all of the commercial sound recordings of Duke Ellington, Jelly Roll Morton, the scores of such famous composers as Irving Berlin, George and Ira Gershwin, Leonard Bernstein, and many other unique items. Many of these are in fragile condition and were previously only available to a few scholars who were able to visit Washington. Now digital versions make it possible for citizens anywhere to see the record of the the American experience and such examples of American creativity as Fulton's design of the steamboat or the Wright Brothers' papers.

Core material for the first stage of the National Digital Library Program will be drawn from cartoons, photographs,almanacs, posters, recordings, sheet music, and unpublished American plays. The Library has 250 thousand unpublished plays from before World War I, which are almost entirely in the public domain but which nobody has ever read, in addition to the largest book, periodical, map, and film collections in the world.

The creation of a National Digital Library Program originates in the Library's vision of providing the widest possible access to knowledge and information. The immediate goals for the National Digital Library Program are: to convert 200 Library of Congress collections to digital form; to build a national digitizing program incorporating unique American history collections from the Library and from other institutions; and to provide the widest possible access to this material.

What is the best way to make this happen? The primary participating partners are Congress and the Library of Congress and other great repositories with unique content. Those institutions and others will prepare and provide the materials. The new Digital Library Program will fund the conversion of those materials and coordinate the program into a coherent package that will tell in a comprehensive way the story of America. The private sector will then add value to this unembellished digital archival material, and do the basic distributing in a variety of packages and delivery systems. Finally, the 15 thousand school districts and 15 thousand libraries in America will provide local access for the public and will use this material in a variety of instructional, inspirational, and educational ways.

By the end of the fiveyear launch period we plan to have up to five million American history items from the collections of the Library of Congress and from other institutions accessible either online or in CDROM to schools and libraries across the country. This body of material will provide educational and inspirational content which will tell the multimedial story of America and, in the process of doing so, will create a model for the parallel formation and delivery of other subject matter to advance American education and productivity.

Digitization, as many are aware, is very time consuming and expensive. The current conversion cost for the variety of different things that we are converting ranges from two to six dollars per page of text, but constant progress in technology is likely to cause a price decrease. Nonetheless the Library ofCongress could not do it alone even if we were in a budgetary expansion mode. The federal government itself cannot do it alone. The private sector must be engaged in order to meet the goal of five million items by the year 2000.

We have requested 15 million dollars from Congress over the next five years and seek an additional 30 million from the private sector in addition to the 15 million in private funds we initially raised to start this effort. This represents a program goal of 60 million dollars over the next five years in addition to what we will do through the regular budget of the Library of Congress.

The Library plans to provide access to the basic documents and other materials– the so-called "plain vanilla" or unembellished version, which will be provided either free or at a very low cost negotiated with those who will receive the materials. The "plain vanilla" is simply an extension of traditional access to a public reading room. Unlike the public reading room now in existence, this will be a library without walls. It will provide access to those Americana collections of the Library of Congress which hold the widest interest.

As we do with our printed materials, we will welcome the opportunity to enter into ventures with private companies to digitize and develop some of the collections to enhance public access to the Library's material. We will not, and cannot by law, grant to anyone exclusive rights to our materials. They are the property of the American people and the purpose is to get them back to the American people, in the same "plain vanilla" form that you get books in the public reading room.

The Library hopes to play a leadership role by developing new approaches to organizing, managing and preserving digital materials; creating the necessary procedures for protecting intellectual property; and acquiring resources to convert current collections to digital formats. Several projects are on the way to building a foundation to accomplish these tasks. First of all, our Copyright Office electronic registration, recordation and deposit system, CORDS, will serve as the test bed to evaluate electronic copyright deposit, registration and recordation concepts and issues, and will point towards a totally electronic registration and information system some time in the near future.

Our electronic cataloging and publication people are testing online transmission of galleys from Harper Collins and several university presses over the Internet to facilitate the preparation of cataloging information and to establish the foundation for an electronic library of machinereadable books. Our Law Library has created the global library information network, GLIN, to bring laws, reports, and official gazette texts electronically to the Library from 13 countries. Our specialists will translate the abstracts into English. The project involves language indexing programs developed in conjunction with the University of Massachusetts, which could help the Law Library receive electronic documents in all languages.

There is no question that protection of intellectual property is one of the keys to the success of the new electronic superhighway system. The Copyright Office, part of the Library of Congress, and our legal and technical specialists have been working with all interested parties to develop new systems of protection that the new technology can accommodate.

In our own current digitization efforts we are confining ourselves to the materials which are in the public domain or for which we have received specific permission to convert into digital form. But we are moving ahead to test possible licensing mechanisms for digitized works used for research and educational purposes. There are many possibilities. First, the Library is participating with six other institutions in the two-year educational site licensing project sponsored by the Getty Art Museum. All seven institutions will send designated collections electronically to seven university campuses for use by students and professors. The idea is to test legal and technical mechanisms needed to allow the full educational use of museum collections and to develop model licensing agreements. Second, with the cooperation of the Association of American Publishers and others, the Library will select copyrighted, multimedial American history materials and make them available electronically under a collective licensing arrangement in schools and libraries.

We expect to learn a good deal from these tests. We will not move more broadly until we have worked out all the kinks. But we expect to learn a good deal about the practical solutions for the proper application of copyright protection in the new electronic age.

Finally, the Library of Congress hopes to contribute to the electronic future by being an exemplary catalyst for thelibrary community. The Vice President has said that libraries are "the keys to American success in fully exploiting the information superhighway of the future." As we see it, the Library of Congress's collections are part of the nation's strategic information reserve which will provide intellectual cargo for the information superhighway.

We hope the Library's National Digital Library venture will also serve as an inspiration or perhaps as a de facto standardsmaking model, for the many libraries in America that must begin making, and in a number of cases are already making, unique collections electronically available. The practical experience of the National Digital Library should help guide those who are only now beginning the task of electronic conversion.

During the next century, libraries in America and elsewhere in the world will be more important than ever. They will provide easy, inexpensive access to a vast variety of information services for the public. And librarians will increasingly assume a new function, resembling the function they assumed in the Middle Ages, before modern cataloging and information retrieval was available. They will become navigators. Their judgment, their ability to navigate through this vast sea of information will be even more indispensable in the future than it has been in the past. They will develop new techniques and new skills in guiding users to the information they are seeking. As the electronic information networks become truly worldwide, librarians everywhere will become sophisticated knowledge navigators, and without libraries and librarians, the information gap between the haves and havenots cannot realistically be overcome.

Sustaining the values of universal access depends strongly on the electronic reinvigoration of the library systems that the new electronics can provide. The critical role of libraries has been recognized in the Clinton Administration's NII agenda for action which calls for linking all schools to the National Information Infrastructure by the year 2000. The Library of Congress will be working with other government agencies to make sure that the needs of libraries are addressed, and it will contribute to discussions of critical public policy questions such as protecting intellectual property rights and developing bibliographic standards for the electronic age.

Since we are the main source of cataloging, we also have to become a major source in helping, with the broader libraryand bibliographic utilities community, to develop standards and retrieval methods. We must also provide the knowledge navigators who help us to use libraries in this confusing electronic world that might accurately be characterized as books scattered around without even labels on them, let alone bibliographic entries.

But how do we assure that the values of an open and democratic society are reinforced and sustained? First, by promoting the recovery of memory, by giving back to the people the enormous record of America that was accumulated over 200 years. The Library of Congress has played an important role in this task. It is also important to demonstrate that everything that comes to Washington does not vanish, as is sometimes suggested, but can be given back to the taxpayers who acquired it in the first place. It is also of central importance that the new digitized knowledge be mixed in with the old books. We found, in the American Memory test, that after looking at the Brady Civil War photographs on a computer screen people want to read about the Civil War. Students ask questions of their teachers that can only be answered by going back into the books.

We believe that the book, that most userfriendly communications medium, has a long life ahead of it. We do not believe that future generations will be reading the plays of Shakespeare or Moby Dick on computer screens. We will continue to support local literacy and reading promotion efforts through our own Center for the Book and its 30 affiliated state centers for the book around the country.

Not everything will or should be digitized. So long as there is a substantial portion of the human record residing only in traditional books, books will continue to be important in transmitting and preserving human culture.

The real pay-off lies far beyond all the data, information, even the knowledge we can accumulate and disseminate electronically. The future of our type of open and creative civilization depends on wisdom and creativity. Wisdom is a very practical quality that is developed among those who live with books. Creativity is the special break-through quality that is given to a small number of people in richness and to all of us in some degree. It is found among people who add new ideas to our store of old ones. Books, which are witnesses from the past, are often better guides to the future than talking heads in the present. Alone with a book, one is not bound by someoneelse's picture on a television screen. A book leads us into Keats' world of "silence and slow time," where the only limit is one's own imagination. And letting the imagination take off is the key to the kind of creativity which both renews civilization and makes it economically competitive.

Without books, our type of civilization might never have come into being at the beginning of the modern age. Libraries are temples of pluralism, base camps for the adventure of life-long learning. They are what the Greeks called the great library at Alexandria: healing places of the soul. Most importantly, perhaps, they are a link between what happened yesterday and what might take place tomorrow.

When I was talking about libraries in Nebraska recently, a Native American in the audience suggested to me that the libraries of today are increasingly becoming what existed before the culture of print came to North America. In the ancient oral cultures of the Indian tribes in the past, he said, "we had that older person who was a living repository of memory in the oral culture. We didn't call them gatekeepers, we called them dreamkeepers."

So our purpose is to provide all schools and libraries with greater access to the fullness of America's memory, to yesterday's dreams as well as to tomorrow's new creative possibilities; to provide an electronic vitamin enrichment for the library system. Libraries are special places where knowledge can ripen into wisdom and occasionally break through to new creation. A central core of widely usable materials delivered electronically will free local libraries to develop their collections in customized ways which will be specially relevant to each community of learning, inquiry, or productivity.

A better life will come not just from data and a modem, but from the better understanding of one another that comes from books. When some of the most literate Europeans, Jesuit missionaries, left China in the early 18th century after their nearly successful effort to build a bridge between the most ancient of Eastern cultures and the Western world, they left behind a haunting written epitaph, which illustrates how human understanding has to be developed in a world where we have gotten closer in communication, but not in understanding. The last words they left behind on Chinese soil were:

> Go now, voyager, Congratulate the dead, Console the living. Pray for everyone, Wonder, And be silent.

Wonder and silence are easier for readers than for TV viewers, for adventurers than for spectators, for dreamkeepers more than for image makers. So let us hope that, as we move into this exciting world of new possibilities, we keep alive in the multimedia age the values of the book which favor the active mind over spectator passivity, putting things together rather than just taking them apart. For whatever the confusions of our own minds and the profusion of information on the Internet, things tend to come back together in a book just as the left and right halves of the brain come together in one still amazing human mind, and the hemispheres east and west, north and south come together in a single, fragile planet.

# Chapter 3

## The Universal Library : Intelligent Agents and Information on Demand

Raj Reddy*

## 3.1  Introduction

If the current projections come true we should have a Giga PC by 2000AD, i.e., a PC with a billion bytes of memory capable of executing a billion operations per second and costing about $5000. There are other predictions that show that mobile personal digital assistants of similar power will be available 3 to 4 years later.

At the Mobile-92 conference, I gave a talk on PDAs of the future and I2D2 (Intelligent Information-access on Demand Demon) Knowbots, and their use in information access from The Universal Library. I would like to present to you that futuristic scenario and its implications for the current discussion on design Δand development of digital libraries.

## 3.2  A Future Scenario

You are in bed after a hard day's night. You pick up your personal ThinkBook running Win-Warp-99. It weighs 24 ounces, roughly the weight of a hardback book. It has a 6x8 inch screenwith color and gray scale with a 300 dot per inch resolution. It communicates with your home computer using a home wireless local area network. This in turn is connected to the The Universal Library. The Thinkbook sells for around $99, roughly the cost of manufacturing the device, following the analogy that you give away the razor to sell the blades.

You select a romance novel from your Sony Disk-of-the-Month Club for a single reading privilege. A secure co-process in your ThinkBook queries your home information system and tells you that the cost for read-once privilege is 25 cents. You say "okay" (remember you are in bed - you don't want to type on a keyboard or write with a pen). The secure co-processor then decodes the encrypted novel using a Public-Private key decryption algorithm.

---

*School of Computer Science, Carnegie Mellon University, Email : rr@cmu.edu

You start to read it, but you get bored and ask for a refund. You get 17 cents back. The Digital-Back Book version of the romance novel self-destructs.

You are trying to decide what might be fun to read. You call up the New York Times book review. The abstracts of the book reviews are free, but you get the ads along with the best seller list. A full review of a book costs you 5 cents to read.

You notice that Tom Clancy's new book has been on the best seller list. You check availability in electronic form. It is not yet available on any disk-of-the-month clubs. You ask for availability of an electronic version through the Hard-Back Electronic Book Channel from Random House. Indeed, it is available for a charge of $9.99. You don't want to spend that much and decide to wait until a Paperback Electronic Book Channel version from Bantam with multi-use privilege will become available for only $1.99.

You go back to the New York Times book review and look at the old best-selling paperback list. You find Michael Crichton's Disclosure, which is available for 99 cents. You download it from a local server which has been caching all the frequently accessed books from the Paperback Electronic Book Channel. You get a special discount of 25 cents when you purchase a cached book on a local server rather than accessing it from an international database.

You start to read this book and decide you would like to hear the background music from sound track of the movie Disclosure. You access the Digital Music Library Channel from Time Warner and pay 35 cents for a single use of the Disclosure sound track. Your ThinkBook transmits the music to the Bose Acoustimass speakers on either side of your bed. You read on to the background music.

You then come to a section where there is a description of Virtual Navigation within a data base, and are curious how it is portrayed in the movie. You access the Digital Video-on-Demand Channel from TCI and request the movie Disclosure for a view-once privilege for $1.99. You set your ThinkBook aside and fall asleep while watching the movie.

Now for a few business details. That night, about 0.1population used The Universal Library. The total value of the services provided was $17 million for that day. The Universal Library kept $5 million, paid $3 million to the phone companies, and the remaining $9 million went to a producer's clearing house, which in turn distributed these proceeds to authors, editors, producers and agents in agreed upon proportions. IBM, Apple and Sony sold 50 million intelligent information appliances that year at prices ranging from $99 to $9,999 at a total market value of $30 billion. That year revenues of The Universal Library were about $10 billion and expected to grow to a trillion dollars by the middle of the century.

The above scenario provides an illustration of a future world of Thinkbook, Win-Warp-99 and The Universal Library. Such a vision raises a number economic, technical and legal issues which need to be solved before the vision can be realized. The rest of the paper discusses a number of these issues.

# 3.3   Conventional vs.digital Digital Libraries

To understand how a digital library might impact society, one must first formulate its properties and attributes. In many ways, these will be distinct from
those of a conventional library. For starters, a digital library will not be subject
to the same constraints of a conventional library.

Instantaneous Access. First, you can expect to get instantaneous access to
books and other documents without having to make a trip to the local library. It
will be accessible through the Home Information System which will permit one
to search, select and access the desired document several orders of magnitude
faster than the traditional libraries.

Comprehensive International Coverage. The scope and size of material available to an average citizen through The Universal Library will be unparalleled.
Assuming an international collaborative venture, the diversity of material available in this library should be substantially larger than that of the Library of
Congress. Since every country can be expected to contribute to the collection,
it will also be multi-lingual in scope.

Agents for Search and Selection. Unlike the conventional libraries, where
search is limited to card catalogs and their electronic variations, one can expect
to see on the market a plethora of intelligent search and selection agents capable
of operating on a wide range of digital libraries. Many of these will be domain
specific with the semantics of the domain built-in.

Fee for Service. There will be significant costs associated with creating and
operating The Universal Library. First there is the cost of converting paper based
books and documents into digital form. The technologies for scanning, optical
character recognition, human or agent-based validation and verification, and
indexing for storage and retrieval function at acceptable levels today although
continued research is needed in each of these areas. This cost is estimated to be
around $100 to $300 per book today. Secondly, there is the cost of operating the
digital library : the cost of computing and communication, personnel costs, fees
to publishers, authors, owners of copy-righted material, and finally the cost of
secure transactions and funds transfer. Systems and costing models will evolve
over the next few years, but it is clear that access to digital libraries will not be
free like the traditional ones. One goal is to base the cost of access to documents
on the local standard of living. For example the cost of accessing an out of print
book for one-time only use might be around the price of a cup of coffee.

Another advantage of the digital library is that it does not require travel
outside the home to gain access to it. It is a library that gives global access to
global information which is a different kind of access to information from what
one may conceive of as being the type of access possible in a local library. A
digital library is universally available around the world to anyone that has access
to a personal digital assistant. Its access is not limited to those who go to the
library and know how to look up a catalog which many people surprisingly do not
know how to do. The digital library is also convenient in that it is available 24
hours a day seven days a week producing the desired information within seconds
rather than hours.

# 3.4    The Economic Model

A major question that is being debated is whether a digital library can provide free and unlimited access as a conventional library. In this section, we will attempt to estimate the cost of creation and operation of the library and how various intellectual property providers would be compensated within the context of an international model of instantaneous access.

Cost of Creation. The cost of scanning, optical character recognition, correction, indexing, and storage has been estimated to be anywhere from $100 to $1,000, depending on the complexity of the document. Thus, a digital library with over twenty million volumes would cost between $5 to $20 billion. It is unlikely that any one country would be willing to bear the cost of creating their own digital library. Most likely it would be an international cooperative venture, with all countries contributing to the creation of the library and all countries having unrestricted access. Unrestricted does not mean it is free. It is likely that there would have to a usage fee to compensate the creators and distributors of the intellectual property.

Cost of Operation. An average book of 500 pages would contain about a million characters of text. If it has a substantial number of images, graphs, and formulas,the storage requirement is likely to increase by a factor of 2 to 3. Compression techniques can be expected to yield 2 to 5 times reduction in the storage and/or bandwidth requirements. Thus, a 20 million volume library will require a 5 to 20 terabyte database. It is reasonable to assume that such a database would be globally distributed where the creators of the original content would also operate and maintain their part of the distributed library. However, system design must provide for frequently used books and documents to be cached in multiple locations so as to minimize congestion on the Internet. Further, in order to protect against accidental deletion of documents, duplicates must be maintained at multiple sites. Finally, it will be necessary to keep in some off line storage, the original scanned documents in bit image format for future verification and research. Thus, the system architecture and the associated costs required to operate The Universal Library will be substantial. However, the cost of operating a universal library will be but a small fraction of the current cost of operating libraries around the world.

The following table provides annual expenditures on various forms of entertainment in the United States. Note that the total market size of the entertainment market in the US is on the order of $300 billion/year. This translates to roughly a thousand dollars per every man, woman and child in the country. The digital libraries will be able to store and distribute multi-media documents such as music and movies, as well as conventional books. The cost of creation, operation and access of information would largely fall on the entertainment part of the expenditures, rather than the information part.

| Category | '93 |
|---|---|
| Music, recorded | 20 |
| Spectator sports | 6 |
| Books, magazines., newspapers | 47 |
| Cable TV | 19 |
| Movies and video rentals | 13 |
| Theater | |
| Toys and sporting equipment | 65 |
| Gaming:casinos, racing, lottery | 28 |
| Theme parks | 14 |
| Interactive E. - video games, PC, etc. | 12 |
| | |
| Total | O($300B) |
| Approximate spending per person | $1000/year |

Intellectual Property Issues. Given that the digital library will permit charging users for individual accesses of various multimedia documents, it is interesting to formulate how this would benefit the owners of the intellectual property. One possible model is that 50 percent of the revenues would be available for the operation and communications costs of the digital library, while the remaining 50would be made available to publishers, editors and the authors of the original intellectual property. Since much of the printing, shipping and retailing costs are eliminated in a digital library model, the cost of digital back books ought to be substantially lower hard back and paper back books.

## 3.5    The Content and Infrastructure Model

Multi Media Content. As we discussed earlier, the digital library will have multiple types of information: books, music, movies, broadcast news, newspapers, reports and open source documents such as government publications.

Publishers. In the distributed library system model, it is anticipated that each publisher would have on line all the books and other media that they would like to make available globally. The electronic commerce model on the Internet should evolve to a stage that each provider of information can transact and receive payment electronically. The Commerce Net and a number of other initiatives that are currently being considered should lead to secure and reliable electronic fund transfer infrastructure. It is expected that payments as little as ten cents can be exchanged without significant overhead.

Distribution. A book of a million characters in a compressed representation can be transmitted over conventional modem in one or two minutes and in less than a second over a cable modem. The event of cable modems promises to make it possible to transmit large multi-media documents, such a movies into homes, in significantly less than real time. The issues of scaling to hundreds of millions of users around the globe using the digital library are not yet fully understood. Further research will be needed in network management and congestion avoidance.

Enhanced Capabilities. With an electronic document, it becomes possible to annotate in the margins of documents beyond the limitations of space in the margin of physical documents. One can have verbal and video annotations in addition to scribbles in the margins of arbitrary size. This permits a user to benefit from commentary made by expert critics as well as other readers and viewers of the information, which is not currently possible with the conventional libraries.

## 3.6    The Home Information System Model

The HIS Configuration. The Home Information System is expected to be a giga PC by the year 2000 AD, consisting of a billion operations/second processor, a billion bytes of memory and 32 billion bytes of disc memory costing around $5,000. This capacity is needed to fully permit the use of such a system for multi-media applications.

Wireless Connectivity. It is expected that an average home can be wired to provide a high bandwidth local area network into every room for about $500. Even with such a system, it would still be necessary to use wireless capabilities to interconnect components of the system.

Display Technology. The Home Information System will serve many purposes. In addition to serving as the replacement for the current television set, it will also act as a replacement for the communication elements such as phone and fax and will be usable as a compute server. Thus, multiple resolution, multiple size screens from 72" flat panel wall screens to active matrix displayed on the portable PCs will be interoperable with common, standard interfaces.

## 3.7    The Operating System Model

Real Time Response. There are a number of changes that have to be made in operating system architecture to include features that do not usually exist now. One feature is for the networks to be able to guarantee the service times and data rates. Without such a capability, there will be the extra task of downloading or pre-loading material into the PCs in order to guarantee the service. Such systems have to be able to anticipate expectations and prefetch because they have cycles and bandwidth to burn to enable the preloading of the desired information on an anticipatory basis and still be willing to throw it away, as computers do now at microcode level, if the information is not necessary. The superscalar architectures can execute four or more instructions simultaneously and it often happens that some of what they compute will not be used.

Security and Encryption. If, for instance, executable, active objects become part of your library there is an increased possibility of viruses capable of destroying programs and data in your home or office. This issue has to be worked through very carefully so that the one who is downloading has the source of an executable object being downloaded and can interpret that source, and at the same time others do not use facilities that are off limits to them as part of that executable object. Systems such as Netscape and languages such as Java are attempting to provide this capability. All the security and protection has to be provided in a way with minimal overhead. For example, downloading of a book for 25 cents and refunding of seventeen cents when it is returned should be possible. In order for the model to work, the transactions for accessing and returning cannot cost more than a few pennies.

# 3.8   The Human Computer Interaction Model

Multimodal Interfaces. The ease of use of the interface also impacts the acceptability of the digital library. The systems must be able to use the so called called SILKy interfaces, i.e., interfaces that use Speech, Image, Language and Knowledge, so that one is not limited to typing as the only means of getting access to information. In the commercial world there are already some very interesting interfaces for digital libraries. One example is the Encarta-95 interface. Encarta is a digital encyclopedia. It has a good interface which one ought to peruse before inventing a new one. It will continue to exist and will improve in the future. The same interface technology is easy to use because of its availability as part of the MSDN tool kit library.

End User Programmability. Currently, most programming is done by stating precisely how the task is to be performed. This poses an obstacle for those who know what they want done but cannot program a computer. Next generation systems that specialize in What-to-How programming will be a necessary part of digital libraries solution.

Intelligent Interfaces. It is often easier to learn how to do something by simply watching an example of the task as it is being performed by someone else. Similarly, it would be helpful to a non-programmer, if the computer could watch the person's steps, as she performs a task, and figure out the processes so that it could perform the same task in the future. An example of such a function is if one were to create an agent to monitor the user behavior in managing a bank account such as the user behavior when the account runs out of money. The computer having witnessed a similar situation and following the trail of the user would know what the user did, so that it can do the same thing in the future in a similar situation.The systems must also be able to create surrogate agents of the user so that one can freely gather the desired information.

# 3.9   Conclusion

The vision of The Universal Library represents a powerful idea. It is not a mere electronic equivalent of a conventional library. The scope of this library would involve a combination of sources which will provide video, movies and music on demand, as well as books, newpapers and magazines. Because of the astronomical cost of $5 to $20 billion that is required to create the The Universal

Library is beyond the reach of any one country, the most effective way to attain this goal is likely to be through a truly international collaboration. The projected world wide annual revenues of $20 to $200 billion is likely to make the idea of The Universal Library into a reality.

The technical community has the opportunity to expand on the idea of the conventional library by creating what is now only a vision. There are a number of difficult technical problems we can begin to solve. But to solve the various problems and bring the vision to life will require the enlightened leadership and cooperation from the national leadership.

# Chapter 4

## Building a Scalable America

Larry Smarr[*]

## 4.1 Introduction

Digital library projects are beginning to appear everywhere across the world. They are an incredibly potent force. This chapter illustrates the importance of recognizing that with respect to the information infrastructure, many of the details currently being explored in library research cannot happen unless they are embedded in a much larger infrastructure that enables them to be used by people remotely and that enables collaboration among people who will use them.

It is important first to understand a ten year perspective of how far we have come at this point and where we are going in building not just a scalable America, but a scalable global civilization. It is not uncommon to question the existence of a connection between supercomputers and a discussion on digital libraries, but there is a connection nonetheless.

The national Science Foundation Supercomputer Center Program has been at work for about ten years. In fact, the early 1980s there was a graining of a national consensus of reports in which the supercomputer centers were created as a result of the Cold War and many have been very mission supportive like the NASA centers and the weather centers. The idea was to take this psychology and make it widely available to the university researchers or the research corporations. The problem was that there had been a period of building up the university computer centers in the 1970's, at the end of the Sputnik era. But until 1985, there had been 15 years of federal benign neglect of support for the means of employing high performance computer systems in American universities. That was rectified with the start of the Centers Program, but by that time the pool of people doing advanced applications using the latest in supercomputers had dwindled to the point where there came a need to completely replenish the national human resource pool. In fact, the NSF Centers within a few years brought 20 thousand academic researchers to state-of-the-art high performance computing systems over the Net, which was built as a result of the centers, to do supercomputing. There were no more than a few hundred that were doing it before the centers opened. At that time the perception was that going from

[*]National Center for Supercomputing Applications, University of Illinois

a few hundred to 20 thousand was a big step forward. Yet that was before we reached the age of Mosaic.

Currently there is a coming together of the HPCC idea with a notion of the NII, National Information Infrastructure of the digital libraries and networks, etc. There is a tremendous transition caused by the victory of the microprocessor across the board with a complete restructuring of the computer industry as a result of that victory. There is also a transition in the direction of a kind of lego approach in which the microprocessor is capable of building a scalable America, which is a network infrastructure for information in which the systems from the desktop to the teraflop are built out of the same basic units. There is software and a software transparency across this structure that enables knowledge to go beyond the boundaries that were originally anticipated.

Many think that the High Computing Communications Program is detached from the NII. Such a perception would be a reality expect for one fundamental difference between computing and any other kind of technology. The fact is that computers are exponentially increasing in power every year, while exponentially decreasing in cost per operation (addition, multiply, etc.). This trend has continued for decades and will live on for decades more. The result of such a trend is that the high performance machines that are sold for $20 million today will be in the range of $2000 to $20 thousand in the future. These follow a trend of approximately a factor of 1000 per decade.

We are witnessing the evolution of a single national agenda in which high performance computing is analogous to a time machine where high performance computing makes it possible to see today the capabilities of tomorrow's desktop systems. This eliminates the need of having to wait for the commercial vendors to bring these capabilities to the desktop before starting to develop appropriate applications. And since economic competitiveness comes form expediently moving from a new idea to an application and ultimately into the market, shortening that time scale between the two stages of idea to application can make a considerable difference in the economics of the situation.

Congress recently asked the National Academy to have the National Research Council do a study of the high performance computing and communications initiative. Dr. Larry Smarr was among the participants of that study, which heard a report in which 25 witnesses from all parts of the Federal Government said that a collision is taking place between the HPCC and the NII in which the HPCC has become increasingly supportive and complementary with respect to what is taking place in the NII. The new Blue Book, the Federal Government's blueprint for the HPCC contains many examples of this current materialization. A number of well documented examples have been published with hyperlinks to far more detailed examples throughout the world of the amazing diversity HPCC applications to information technology.

This is the famous image that Donna Cox, computer artist at NCSA, created years ago. It shows the complexity of the 1990 1.5 megabit per second backbone network by visualizing a database of dataflow over the internet. Every dot represents a university, each with thousands of computers hooked into it. The complexity of the Net even as far back as a few years ago is staggering. But the question is the origin of the development and connection of this development to supercomputer centers.

Although ARPA developed protocols with the computer science community for many years, it was only after the formation of the NSF supercomputer centers that there became a need to hook together a fat pipe that would be the backbone of what emerged as the NSF Net from which stemmed the regional nets. These were the catalysts for the campuses digging up the quads and putting in fiber optics. It was a ripple effect that resulted in the Federal Government's investment which was necessary for continued advancement, even though the total sum of the investment was a few per cent of the actual amount that was spent overall to make the plan a reality.

Yet this pipe, the national superhighway, was only 56 kilobits per second which is equivalent to an ISDN connection that can be installed today in any home. This is a good example of the relevance of HPCC to NII, the backbone begun by NSF would not have become a reality, or would have taken many more years to develop, if it had not been for the supercomputer centers. Furthermore, software and protocols developed for that early advanced backbone at that time now make it possible for people to obtain that level of individual performance to their offices or homes. In fact, Ameritech is working with Champaign County as the first community in which anyone who has a telephone can call and get the telephone company to install an ISDN connection with a Motorola modem that makes it easy to use. By 1988 NSFnet progressed from 56 kilobits to 1.5 megabits per second. As the regional nets began to appear, it is clear that the universities were in a competitive race to figure out who could get their campus network up because they did not want to be left behind. By 1991 the NSFnet backbone capacity had gone from 1.5 megabits per second to 45 megabits per second.

We are still in the process of transitioning to the new internet in which there is a new backbone connecting the NSF centers called the VBNS. This new network is now 155 megabits per second and contains network access at four points awarded by commercial bid. In fact, in the US all of the nets have to hook into the commercial providers. Once again, the NSFnet and now all of the NSF supercomputers have their fat pipe in between each other doing experiments evaluating and developing applications, laying the groundwork for the day that this kind of bandwidth exists throughout the internet.

Although the supercomputer centers' systems are much faster than they were ten years ago, the increase in supercomputer speed is nowhere near the 3000 fold increase in bandwidth of the backbone of the internet. This kind of disproportional increase is a true example of exponential growth and what the supercomputer centers worked with to create that situation in every desktop in universities throughout the world. The public and corporations are more frequently hooking into the internet, therefore proving the presence of a relay synergy that historically created the first part of the infrastructure consisting of the data pipes and the connectivity. Yet there is still no middleware and no software that glues it all together.

Since the creation of Mosaic, which was a software tool developed at the NCSA and given to the international community on the internet, the status has changed from what existed at the creation of the first part of the infrastructure. Although the first cross platform Mac, Unix, and Windows version of Mosaic was released only 18 months ago, the transformation has been stunning. The internet itself is a network of networks. There is a new network that joins the internet every half hour somewhere in the world.

There are between 80 and 100 countries that have access to the internet. In fact, Mosaic was introduced as the first multimedia browser for the World Wide Web, which was developed by Tim Berners-Lee at CERN, a particle physics laboratory in Geneva, to help hyperlink information. That the Web and Mosaic were very easy to use in a cross platform environment lead to an unbelievable increase in their use. Now there is a new Web server every two hours thereby creating the need to browse continuously.

Another way of seeing the effect of Mosaic is to translate it into what a physicist would call a phase transition. In the short period of approximately 18 months, from the time the original Unix version of Mosaic was introduced (when Gopher was a dominant internet file organization tool), advancing to the three-platform Mosaic versions were distributed, and ultimately the release of commercial versions, there was a 100,000 fold increase of internet Web traffic.

In fact, World Wide Web traffic has now exceeded all other forms of transmission on the Net. While Mosaic was only one piece of beta or pre-release software that was put onto the Net, it made a significant change in the world and completely altered NCSA. With commercialization, Mosaic created an entire industry of the computer market segment with various companies competing. In March there were 250,000 copies of Mosaic downloaded just from the server at NCSA over the Net. There are currently over 4 million connections per week on the NCSA web server.

The NCSA Web Server Software which is also free from the is used in over 10,000 of the 20,000 to 30,000 Web servers around the world. And just the Mosaic licensees, there are about 45 companies with 120 products and we only started licensing in the summer of 1994. These figures do not take into account the Netscapes, the IBM Warps, the Net Manages, the American On-line book links and all the others that do not license. There is an entire competing industry built up around web software.

The speed of change has been unprecedented. Yet, again arises the question of what connection this phenomenon has with supercomputers. The fact is that NCSA web server growth went from zero to 4 million requests per week. Hewlett-Packard (HP) gave us a million dollar cluster of a dozen HP machines to use as a supercomputer to perform science and engineering calculations using a network of workstations. At that time the Web server was at the beginning of its development, and the fast growth in web traffic lead us to reassemble the HP supercomputer as a Web server. It is difficult to distinguish between high performance computing and the Net in this synergy.

Together, Mosaic and the Web have enabled a mass of information which currently exists online but which on one can find. While Mosaic may be compared to a digital library, it lacks a digital library's minimal requirement which would be to have the capability of finding something. Although the Web has created an interesting diversion, it does not have the capability that is expected of a real digital library. Thus, what is currently taking place and what will hopefully continue is the development of software that will organize the knowledge structure of the Web in a way that will enable one to find the desired information.

This highly technical slide shows that simply employing a Web server, a piece of software and a file system sitting on a Unix workstation somewhere with the HTTP protocol, is not enough. What is most piquant about, for instance, bringing the whole world of database technology and research to be able to help in the searching problem, is the variety of search engines that are being developed. URLs and hyperlinks represent the first stage. They do not have an object characteristic about them. The current move is towards URNs, URCs, metadata, etc. The idea is to get to a point where the user feeds information and the system organizes and indexes that information. The real enigma is in linking a distributed set of these repositories everywhere with enough smarts built around the Web server so that someone can go out onto the Web and request information on whatever topic they are researching. There is a variety of work in the digital library testbeds. There are many provocative ideas about how the world of distributed repositories is going to make it possible to find things. Again, the recurring theme is to understand the connection to supercomputers.

Another testbed being set up at NCSA, is meant for business applications employing databases. The databases that will be required to keep track of all this indexing are fairly large, particularly in the case of multimedia databases. If you have a small database and you do not need the answer back immediately, a workstation is appropriate. In fact, if you have a small amount of data and you need it back promptly, such servers as AS400s, etc. are effective. If there is a lot of data and promptness is not a priority, there is the world wide market for main frames. However, if there is a lot of data and promptness is a top priority, the only choice is to get access to a supercomputer or a large network of workstations or something to that effect. This is yet another area where high performance computing is involved.

The presence of high performance computing is clear in the area of classification. One approach to classification is traditional. It involves using key words and string searches. There is, however, another approach which is the development of the ability of indexing 400,000 abstracts of scientific papers by simply allowing the knowledge structure to emerge from it by examining within the same sentence which words seem to occur together. The result is something very distinct in the way of a classification.

Dr. Hsinchun Chen (University of Arizona), who is working with the digital library testbed in Illinois, was the largest user of the Silicon Graphics supercomputer in the two weeks leading up to the site visit. He used hundreds of hours of supercomputer time to do a concept space creation out of 400,000 abstracts.

This is not a lot of information. Yet it is highly unlikely to find a supercomputer anywhere that is big enough to do a concept creation of the whole space when one starts the process and finds that in addition to the Web servers one also has the repositories which have to be distributed to 100,000 Web servers each of which have many gigabytes of information.

Currently we have the publishing cycle which involves the notion of the user who wants information. A library has a lot of information which it references. There is also an indexer which classifies it and academic journals which ensure sure that only quality science gets published. This leads to the client who sits with the browser while the servers have the knowledge. It is clear that eventually we advance to a point where any computer on the Net can do all of these tasks.

Everyone is going to become a publisher, but quality may be sacrificed in the course of the process because of the lack of quality control. Unfortunately, there is no way to stop that. This is a peer to peer world in which these computers are peer to peer with each other, and once all the indexing and classification has been distributed out into them, a different environment will rapidly emerge.

Looking at the broad picture of the evolution of cyberspace, there is now the ability to retrieve files in a very user-friendly way. This ability stemmed from first getting the net hooked together, followed by Mosaic and the Net which ultimately lead to the current capabilities.

Now the trend is to move into this new world in which searching has become the thing and where Yahoo, Lycos and the like perform the tasks of preclassification for you. The predication, however, is that this trend, although it is extremely useful now, will be short-lived because it cannot possibly scale to the level which is necessary. The Net itself will have to scale to the appropriate level with the peer to peer model. Yet there is still a need for more research on that because thus far the main focus has been on the text, whereas text is not really what is going to be in the library. In fact, words actually occupy a minimal amount of space. Future searching will be required to handle multimedia objects, such as animations in time and space, and much other fine grained, high resolution image data.

NASA has done a lot to point us in the direction of the real issue. We are funded by one of the NASA CAN projects, the goal of which is to develop interfaces to earth observation data appropriate for, among others, school children and the general public. At the back end of are vast repositories, such as the earth observation system will produce. The earth is really big, if you can image it down to a resolution of square meters, and it is always changing. The digital library is going to have to deal with a high level of detail of granularity, in both space and time, which is many orders of magnitude beyond our capabilities today with current systems and applications.

Stepping back and looking at the broad picture of the digital library concept, it is apparent that there has developed a common misconception that it is scientists who do the astrophysics or earth sciences that are behind this. The reality, however, is that the people and society as a whole are the main players. For many decades the scientific and university community has been able to have the luxury of isolation from that real world. That is no longer going to be sufficient for the digital library ideas as is evident by observing the Web. Science is becoming a participatory activity which calls for interaction between the scientific and the real worlds.

There were approximately one billion people that watched in real time as Neil Armstrong stepped onto the moon's surface when the Apollo moon landing took place in 1969. When the latest shuttle was up the ultraviolet telescope was one of the experiments on board. It took scientists 15 years to make that telescope a reality. But the goal of information technology is to achieve a system which makes it possible for the elementary school student, who happens to be on the internet, to get the images and an explanation of what is in the images at the same time and out of the same digital library that the scientist receives this information.

The goal is to build testbeds that will develop computer science to a point where it has practical applications for real people. If such a goal is attained, it will not matter which party is in power or whether there is restructuring of the Federal Government because people will support what they deem to be in their own best interests.

Among the beneficial capabilities of the supercomputer centers is that they can organize testbeds on multiple scales. Thus, we have gone from a machine room to the university campus to our community to large cities to the state to the country to the world and organized testbeds of which many other cities are doing their own versions. Years have been spent working in communities to create one of these testbeds.

Several months ago during a press conference led by the Illinois Governor and Lieutenant Governor, the two clicked their way through the Web world-wide in front of all the assembled representatives of the Chicago press. Last year the White House participated in bringing up in one uniform infrastructure on Mosaic and the Web all of the federal cabinet offices and independent agencies. Now Vice President Gore and his office are incorporating the new capabilities of the technology into the government reinvention and regulatory reform efforts of the National Performance Review. There are cities, towns, states that are using the latest developments in technology in a variety of ways and many countries are doing the same.

In bringing up a map of Germany and its Web sites which are represented by dots, the map is so dense with dots that it is almost impossible to map them all. This illustrates further that Web sites are a world-wide phenomenon and are a part of the notion of building a scalable America which takes place within the context of building a scalable America which takes place within the context of building a global system. Every participating country, of which there are about 80 to 100, is going through similar steps. They recognize that they can take the lead of a knowledge economy without going through the intermediate stages.

Often we have invested several hundred billion dollars into our infrastructure whereas other countries can avoid equal expense because they do not have to undo what we did, or repeat our development steps, rather they can go directly to a wireless communication system, for example. The only advantage from the economic point of view is to be the first to get access to the newest technological advancement and to get the most number citizens involved in using this technology in a myriad of innovative ways to create value, whether it is value in the economy or value in the knowledge or value in arts, and to collaborate to form vast virtual teams which we are now seeing and of which 18 months ago we could not even conceive.

The fundamental building block for progress is the technologies that are being developed. Dreams and goals for the future with respect to digital libraries can be achieved only by using standards and the collaborative process which must interoperate within the other schemes. The current situation is atypical of the situation in regular research and universities. On the other hand, it is a situation where taking the right measures can potentially have far more pervasive support from the society as a whole than anything we have ever done in the past.

# Part I

# Visualization

# Chapter 5

## Video as Scholarly Material in the Digital Library

Wayne Wolf, Bede Liu, Andrew Wolfe, Minerva Yeung, Boon-Lock Yeo, and Daniel Markham*

## 5.1  Moving images as scholarly material

Moving images are well known as visual aids in instruction and entertainment material, largely due to the limitations of current playback devices. The limitations of movie projectors and VCRs become apparent when we consider how we use books. We can browse over an entire shelf of books to find useful material without knowing exactly what we are looking for. We can quickly ascertain a book's contents by several methods, including looking through the table of contents, scanning section headings in a chapter, or skimming a few paragraphs. We can make notes in the book by underlining sentences, writing notes in the margins, etc. A successful multimedia digital library will make moving image material as rich a medium as print and as easy to use as possible.

Moving images serve as primary source material in many fields, despite the limitations of film and video. Political scientists study appearances of politicians on film and video, both to study the politicians themselves and to study how they are covered by the news media. Similarly, they study political commercials as important links between politicians and the electorate. In many studies, the relationship between words and images is a central concern. Psychologists record experiments on video and review the moving image documents to determine their results. Video records are particularly important when reactions of subjects must be judged and classified. Physicists and other scientists may also make visual records of experiments. Students of literature and film may study feature films and television, not only by watching the pieces as a whole but by selecting certain scenes, stopping the film at critical frames or watching them at reduced speeds. In all these scholarly applications, annotation is critical. The ability to dissect the material, select relevant sections, and make notes are all essential to the scholarly enterprise.

We have been working with political scientists at Princeton on digital video libraries [146], since political scientists make frequent and regular use of video

---

*All authors are with the Department of Electrical Engineering, Princeton University.

material in research and teaching and they need the fast distribution of material (news stories, speeches, commercials) which can only be provided by digital video. The video material of interest to scholars comes from many sources, which show as much variability in editorial content and accessibility as textual library materials: news programs, foreign news broadcast, narrowcast video from political parties and other interest groups, governmental agencies, private recordings, etc.

## 5.2    Digital Video Libraries

Moving images present problems to libraries during accession, for storage, and during patron queries. While digitizing the video alone does not solve these problems (and it at present more expensive than analog storage), digital video in conjunction with the proper tools can ameliorate many of these problems. Patrons often find it difficult to search moving image collections for material of interest since they must watch the material. When searching through a single program, which is known in the literature as video browsing, they have no way of perusing the contents of the film or video. Even though the program may use visual clues to demarcate program elements, much as books use typographic conventions to indicate their organization, VCR-style viewers do not allow the patron to view the material except in quasi-real-time. Those problems are magnified during navigation, when the patron is confronted with a large set of programs which may or may not contain the material of particular interest—for example, the set of all accessions whose bibliographic entries refer to Richard Nixon. The patron does not want to watch 10-50 films in order to determine which refer to a particular subject. The patron needs help extracting information on the program's content. Since almost no moving image material has the equivalent of a book's index, and since the query targets of the user population cannot be exactly predicted, the content summaries must be extracted by the digital library system.

We are developing the Princeton Deployable Video Library (PDVL) as a testbed for digital video libraries. As shown in Figure 5.1, PDVL is a client-server architecture; it is designed to be deployable by making use of relatively low-cost platforms and efficient software architectures which provide good multimedia performance on those inexpensive platforms. We believe that many of the important problems in digital video libraries—navigation, browsing, and annotation—can be studied and solved in a classroom-sized system like PDVL.

## 5.3    Methodologies and algorithms for digital video libraries

This section briefly describes two types of tools we are building for PDVL: video annotation tools and algorithms for extraction of hierarchical story structure from video programs.

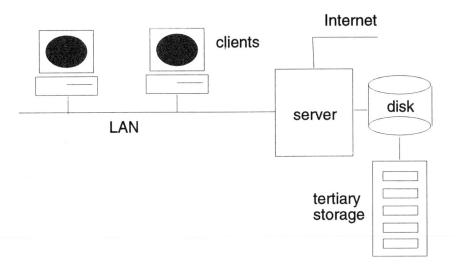

**Figure 5.1** Client-server architecture of a classroom-sized video library.

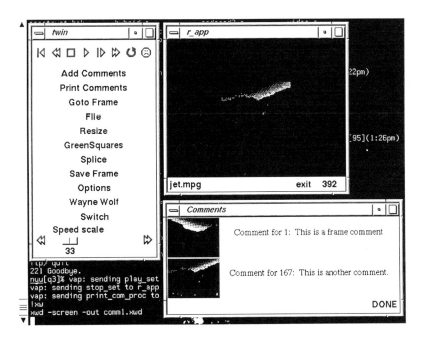

**Figure 5.2** A display from the Princeton annotatable video browser.

Figure 5.2 shows an example of use of an annotatable video browser developed at Princeton. We are developing this browser to serve the needs of scholars, teachers, and students such as political scientists. Scholars often want to annotate video clips which have been selected for study. For example, John Geer of Arizona State University records and analyzes body language of politicians from video clips. Annotations include identification of shots, identification of key frames, pointers to video features and other drawings, text annotations, and voice annotation. It may be necessary to pass on those annotations to other scholars for verification and further analysis. Scholars often want to review particular clips repeatedly to study images, gestures, etc. For example, Roger Masters of Dartmouth has conducted several studies on how people react to nonverbal cues made by leaders [156]. These experiments showed selected clips of speeches and other appearances of political leaders to subjects and measured their responses. The browser supports the playback mechanisms typical of today's video tools: VCR controls allow forward and reverse playback at normal and high speeds, while a slider bar allows the patron to move the playback position along the video timeline. In addition, the patron can enter textual annotation which applies to an interval in the video. The current annotations can be seen in a separate window and the patron can start playback at any one of the currently annotated spots. Developing efficient annotation tools for MPEG-encoded video is particularly hard because MPEG does not represent all frames in the video in the same way. In a motion-encoded video, the majority of frames are represented only as differences from past and future frames. If the patron wants to annotate arbitrary frames, the system may have to process an subsequence of several frames to reach the frame desired by the patron.

We are also working on algorithms for extracting story structure from video programming [239]. Most video programming is organized as a story or collection of stories. Story structure is most evident in fictional material—the traditional hierarchy of story elements in a screenplay moves from the smallest element, a shot, through a scene which conveys a single dramatic point, to a sequence of scenes, and finally to an act [136]. However, news programs, sports, and documentaries also are organized in a manner similar to the shots, scenes, and acts of fiction film.

We are interested in extracting story structure from video programs because the story structure synopsizes the program's content for the viewer. The patron will not be able to view any more than a couple of programs in a search for relevant material. When navigating through a large collection of programs, it is essential that each program be represented by a small amount of information— imagine, for example, presenting a set of nightly news programs for browsing, using one key frame for each story in a news broadcast. Even when viewing a single program, the patron needs help in finding the most relevant part of the program—for example, a talk show can be presented as a sequence of interviews and sketches, with one key frame per segment. Even if searches are performed automatically using advanced algorithms, taking advantage of story structure helps to cull the material which must be processed, greatly reducing the computational requirements of the search. While our methods cannot find all useful types of structure, our analytic techniques can extract many interesting story elements from naturally existing programming.

Story structure is often represented visually—locations and other visual devices are often repeated to signal story structure to the viewer. But to fully understand the story structure, we must relate those visual clues to the temporal relationships of the shots. The story consists in how the shots which comprise the program are interrelated. Extracting story structure requires how shots of different types are used over time in the program; the pattern of usage gives hints about the structure of the story told by the program. In general, the information extracted by our techniques can be augmented by information from the sound track, closed captioning, or other sources; here we concentrate on the relationship between visual and temporal information.

Presenting the program as a hierarchically-organized story, represented by a hierarchy of scene transition graphs, allows the patron to apprehend the program's content much more quickly than a linear viewing or random divines into the program content. We extract story structure from the video in four steps: select a key frame for each shot in the program; cluster the key frames by visual similarity; construct a directed graph where each cluster is a node and an edge connects two nodes if a shot in one cluster immediately precedes in time a shot in the other cluster; analyze the graph to find useful story structure.

We presently use standard techniques for selecting key frames to represent the shots. We can use fairly simple and computationally inexpensive algorithms to classify key frames in the video and identify repetitive visual elements. The key frames from a video of NBC coverage of the 1992 Democratic National Convention shown in Figure 5.3 have been classified using a combination of color histograms and luminance first moment; inspection shows that these simple similarity measures have cleanly separated repeated shots, such as the anchor, from other visual elements like the speaker at the podium. The results in the figure show that, while not perfect, these relatively simple clustering methods provide good results, even though we have no *a priori* knowledge of the contents or meaning of the shots. The quality of the results is due in part to the natural limitations imposed on most video programs: they are shot with relatively few cameras and the cameras frequently stay in roughly the same position for extended periods. These restrictions are due in part to economic considerations and partly due to the fact that many programs are shot and edited in real time, rather than composed from sequences shot separately as is done in motion picture production. However, a major reason for the predictability of shot composition is that too much variation disorients viewers and makes it harder to follow the program's content.

We then build a scene transition graph from the clusters by adding a directed edge from one cluster to another if a frame in the sink cluster directly follows in time a frame in the source cluster. The edges provide temporal information to the patron which indicates the flow of the program's story as indicated by the visuals. A scene transition graph constructed from the Democratic National

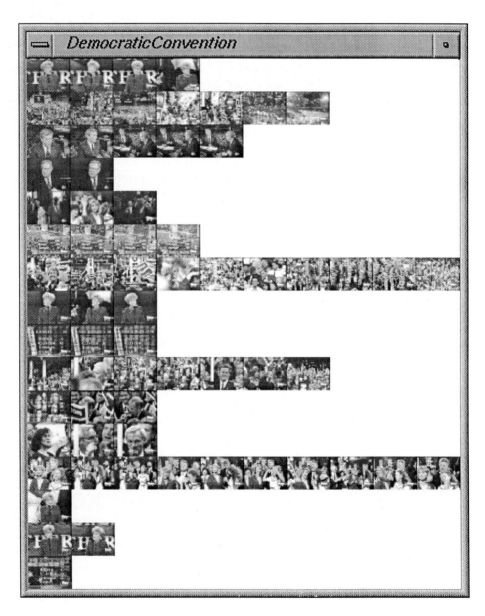

**Figure 5.3** Key frame clustering for video browsing.

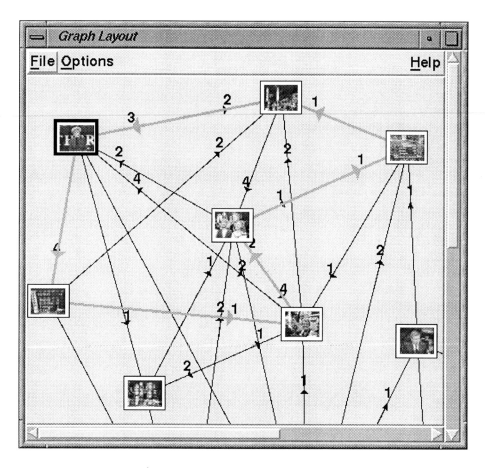

**Figure 5.4** A scene transition graph.

Convention coverage is shown in Figure 5.4. We frequently annotate each edge with the number of transitions from one cluster to the other; the frequency of a transition gives us useful information about the temporal organization of the program.

The scene transition graph is itself a useful summary of the program contents, since is telescopes similar key frames together into nodes and provides a sense of the flow of the story from the graph connectivity. However, we can analyze the graph to find elements of the story embedded in the program. Film and television directors frequently combine shots in well-understood ways; the temporal structure of those combinations may be defined by a scene transition graph fragment. By searching for various types of scene transition subgraphs, we can find the storytelling elements which they represent. By using heuristics, we can handle impure versions of standard directing techniques—for example, a standard interview with occasional inserts of a third party.

Cycles are important structures in scene transition graphs. Cycles of different sizes represent different types of storytelling. The simplest type of cycle is a two-node cycle, which frequently represents an interview. An interview or conversation between two characters is usually portrayed as a sequence of alternating talking heads: character 1, character 2, character 1, etc. Since the key frames have been clustered, this long sequence of shots is portrayed by only two nodes. The cycle itself is a useful summary of the program's content; with additional information, we could further summarize it by, for example, showing the shot of the guest and assuming that the host is known. This type of cycle represents a particular type of sequence. More general sequences or acts frequently form longer cycles in the scene transition graph. For example, the Democratic National Convention coverage includes a long cycle which includes the major shots of the speech made at the podium. Longer story elements form cycles because of the combination of estab- lishing and close-up shots used by directors. An establishing shot covers a broad area, including the major characters in the scene and their immediate physical environment. In the convention coverage, the establishing shot includes the podium and part of the convention floor. Directors frequently interject an establishing shot to introduce a scene, then follow it with close-ups of the major characters showing the major action. In the convention coverage, the program moves between the commen- tators in the news booth and the speech on the floor several times; each time the focus of the program moves from the news booth to the floor, the director uses the establishing shot of the floor to cue the viewer.

A hierarchy of scene transition graphs provides a succession of increasingly detailed views of the contents of a program. A story element identified by analysis can be represented by a single node at the next level of hierarchy. That node can be represented by one or a few frames. We are currently experimenting with heuristics to select one key frame which represents all the shots in a story segment. We believe that a combination of visual and temporal information can be used to find a good key frame which represents the overall contents. One simple but useful heuristic is picking the least common frame in the set as the representative. For example, when summarizing a news story, the anchor appears most frequently and thus provides the least information to the patron about the unique aspects of the story; we prefer to summarize the story with a shot that is unique to that story.

## 5.4 Conclusions

Video is a challenging material for digital libraries because it contains large amounts of data which must be processed quickly and because video programming has not been as conveniently structured for algorithmic processing as text. Since moving images are used as scholarly material in a number of disciplines, digital libraries must be able to support cataloging, browsing, and navigating through video collections. We have shown that computationally tractable algorithms can be used to solve some of the important problems in digital video libraries. While much further work needs to be done, we believe that signal and image processing algorithms will help us solve other important problems in video libraries.

## Acknowledgments

The research on the scene transition graph was supported in part by a Sony Graduate Fellowship, an IBM Graduate Fellowship, Siemens Corporate Research Inc., and a grant from the NEC Foundation. The PDVL project is supported by the ARPA CAETI program.

# Chapter 6

## Digital Libraries for Electronic News

Michael A. Shepherd[*], C.R. Watters[†] and F.J. Burkowski[‡]

## 6.1 Introduction

Research on the use of electronic news as a digital library is a major component of an ongoing research program for the development of an electronic news delivery system that exploits the promised high-bandwidth, switched, interactive communication facilities of the "information highway"[50, 51]. Initially based on a newspaper metaphor (Figure 6.1), the system exploits communication and multimedia technologies to integrate other news sources, such as newscasts and video clips, with the text backbone.[§] The system will provide selective content delivery based on individual and group profiles, hypertext links into archival and external data, continuous coverage of live news events, interactive objects, and consumer-oriented "smart" advertising.

Such an electronic news application is well suited to the promised broadband networks in that:

- the wide distribution of such a communications network is consistent with the mass distribution of news;

- the switched nature of such a network will allow for the customization or personalization of the news format and content;

- the high communications bandwidth is consistent with the multimodal nature of news (text, photographs, video clips, live broadcast, etc.);

[*]Department of Mathematics, Statistics & Computing Science, Dalhousie University, Halifax, Nova Scotia, Canada B3H 3J5, Email: shepherd@cs.dal.ca

[†]Jodrey School of Computer Science, Acadia University, Wolfville, Nova Scotia, Canada B0P 1X0, Email: cwatters@dragon.acadiau.ca

[‡]F.J. Burkowski, Department of Computer Science, University of Waterloo, Waterloo, Ontario, Canada N2L 3G1, Email: fjburkow@plg.waterloo.edu

[§]Newspaper text and phottgraphs are from The Halifax Herald Limited. Television news videos are from Baton Broadcasting Incorporated.

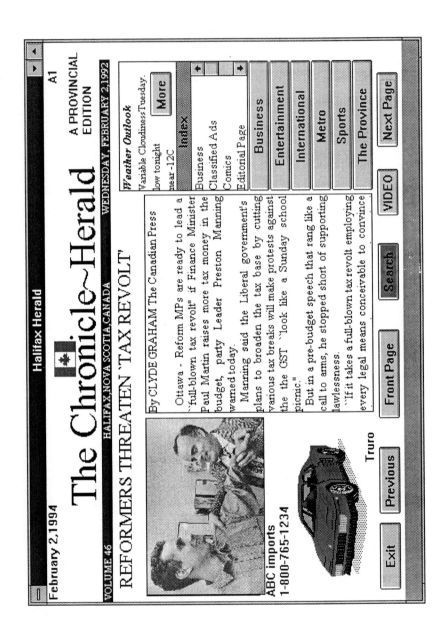

**Figure 6.1** Front Page of Provincial Edition

- the two-way nature of the network opens avenues for interactive and targeted advertising and for interactive items such as bridge hands, crossword puzzles, and classified ads.

An initial prototype client has been developed using data that include television news video clips and newspaper text and photos. An abstract data representation was developed for the integration of layout, syntactic, and semantic information from a variety of sources for the dynamic presentation and manipulation of the news items.

The remainder of this chapter briefly outlines this electronic news project and introduces electronic news as a digital library within the context of this project.

## 6.2 Newspaper Databases

A distinction must be made between newspaper databases and the delivery of electronic news. Generally, newspaper databases with on-line access do not present the news in a recognized "news" format. These systems are essentially document retrieval systems in which individual news stories are treated as discrete units, i.e., stories are treated as documents[173, 180]. In accessing these newspaper database systems, the user task is to satisfy an articulated information need. Retrieval is accomplished by the user formulating a Boolean query or selecting from menus of headings.

## 6.3 Electronic News

Key concepts that differentiate the delivery of electronic news from newspaper databases are; "delivery" of electronic news, a recognizable "news" format, and task. Such news will be "delivered" as a news edition to the home and/or workplace as are today's newspapers and television and radio news. Broadband networks will deliver the news, even to wireless PIAs[96].

These news systems will deliver the news in a recognizable "news" format, initially a newspaper format with integrated video and sound clips. While there is some concern over the acceptability of the newspaper in electronic versus paper form[180], the electronic form appears to be inevitable. Although the newspaper metaphor is likely to be only the initial interface as the paradigm continues to evolve[16], it is a well-recognized and nearly universal platform for news delivery. In addition to this project"[50, 51], the Newspace[23] and is-News[188] projects maintain the newspaper metaphor for electronic news delivery.

Perhaps most importantly, newspaper databases and electronic news differ in the concept of task. The task in accessing a newspaper database is to satisfy an articulated information need, whereas the task in accessing electronic news is to satisfy an unarticulated need, often to simply, "find out what is happening".

## 6.4    Features of an Electronic News System

Our research has focused on the development of a prototype model electronic news delivery system which includes the automatic linking of news items on the same event but from different sources (including different media), the creation of stereotyped editions of integrated news items, client/server architectures, and user interfaces. The system presents news at the user interface in the newspaper metaphor, exploiting broadband communication and multimedia technologies to integrate video, photo, and audio news items with the text backbone. The information content and functionality of such a system, when fully functional, will include; core content, stereotyped content based on group profiles, individual profiles, supplemental content, interactive and real-time objects, and access to digital libraries.

## 6.5    Electronic News as a Digital Library

Electronic news is a particularly interesting basis for a distributed digital library. News is information about events, people, and places. It has a sense of immediacy about it; yesterday's news is old news. Yet, yesterday's news is important in defining and understanding today's news. For instance, a single event such as the Olympic Games is reported on before, during, and after the event. So, a digital library of electronic news must support both electronic news and news databases, whether the news databases are archives of print, television, or radio news. Television and radio news are both read from scripts, so this textual information must be included in the digital library, along with the actual broadcast.

### 6.5.1    Attributes of News Items

Both structural and semantic attributes of news items can be identified and marked up using the Universal Text Format (UTF)[21, 171]. An instantiation of SGML, the UTF is a proposed news industry standard for the interchange of textual material between news agencies and their clients. A UTF marked up item can be embedded in an envelope defined by the Information Interchange Model which can accommodate all types of data, including text, graphics, audio and video. Such papers/organizations as The New York Times, Miami Herald, Chicago Tribune, Dow Jones, and the Mead Data Center are proponents of the UTF.

Structural attributes describe the news object itself, much like a bibliographic entry describes the object of reference. Such attributes include the story byline, headline, subheadings, date and time that the object was created, the source of the object, the news organization, the type of the object (text, graphic, video), keywords describing the content, reference to previous items, etc.

Semantic attributes are drawn from the information within the text of a news item. For instance, the UTF includes markup definition for date and time, location, and the names of people, events, products, companies, etc. It also includes markup for numbers and their units; both within textual news items and within tables such as stock market information and sports box scores.

The UTF markup structure, which is much richer than indicated here, provides a rich information retrieval environment. In addition to retrieval based on such traditional attributes as keywords, names, places, etc., the markup provides possibilities for temporal retrieval and analysis of events and for some numeric processing. In particular, the temporal attributes appear at both the structural and the semantic levels, allowing the user to follow a "time- line" in the reporting of a news item as well as temporal reasoning based on attributes at the semantic level.

## 6.5.2   Integration of News Delivery and a Digital Library

Gladney, et al.[107], suggest that, "[the] document storage and access software [of a digital library] can be implemented in two layers above a base of file systems and database managers." The lower layer is a resource manager which, among other functions, provides a query interface to browsers and retrieves items from the database managers. The upper layer is a document manager which resides in the user's workstation. The term document is used to represent an information item that may be of various media types, possibly a combination of media types. The document manager provides the information model and transforms, combines, and present documents to the user. Where necessary, applications can bypass the document manager and go directly to the resource manager.

As many of the features of an electronic news delivery system are dependent on access to a digital library of electronic news, an architecture is proposed that integrates the electronic news delivery with a digital library of electronic news. Digital libraries are accessed as document retrieval systems, i.e., by user query. The electronic news system as described above requires that news be delivered as stereotyped editions and that the user be able to personalize the edition by retrieval based on user profiles and supplemental queries. This necessitates the integration of the delivery functionality of electronic news with the query functionality of a digital library. The architecture proposed to integrate these functions has three layers (Figure 6.2); the news resource layer, the news management layer, and the news reader layer. The resource management layer of Gladney, et al.[107], corresponds to the news resource layer of the proposed architecture.

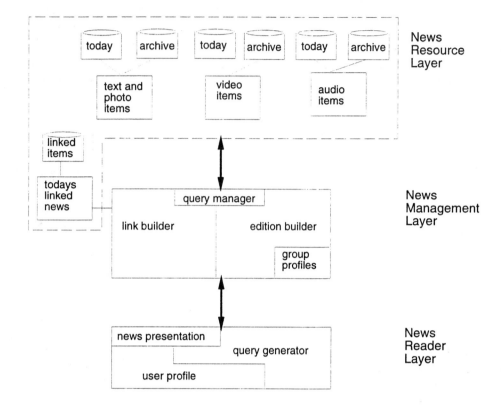

**Figure 6.2** Integrated Electronic News and Digital Library

The functions of the document manager layer of Gladney, et al.[107], are split over the news management and the news reader layers in the proposed architecture. News items are combined into editions at the news management layer, but the information model and presentation aspects reside in the news reader layer at the user's workstation.

## News Resource Layer

At this layer are multiple news providers of each type of media. All such providers, whether they be print, television or radio media, produce news items for immediate dissemination and then store these items in their own archives. Presumably, there will be news items that are generated and stored in the archives but which were never actually distributed. There is usually no cross referencing among news items held in archives by different providers, although there may be cross referencing among items in the same archive or across archives held by the same provider.

Each news resource mounts its archive and the news of the day as a server. The archive and the news of the day can be searched by an information retrieval engine at the server. The use of UTF as a markup language, or even as a switching language, eliminates many problems associated with semantic heterogeneity. Note that today's linked news, linked at the news management layer, is also considered as part of the news resource layer.

### News Management Layer

In the news management layer of Figure 2, vertical lines separating modules indicate that one module does not call the other module for service. Horizontal lines indicate that the higher module calls the lower module for service.

News items of the day are received from the news resource layer. The link builder links together news items which are on the same topic, regardless of the media type or source. These linked items are stored temporarily and used as a resource. The edition builder generates electronic stereotyped "editions" of the news, based on the group profiles, from the linked items in the temporary database. These editions are then sent to the appropriate readers at the news reader level.

The query manager responds to requests from the news reader layer for supplemental information. A query may or may not incorporate the individual user profile at the reader layer. The query manager sends this query out to the news resource layer. Depending on the type of query, it may request service only from today's linked news items in the temporary database or it may go to all of the news resource managers. The query manager calls the link builder to build links among items retrieved from the news resource layer, if necessary. The query manager then calls the edition builder to generate an "edition" of the items retrieved in response to the query. In this instance, the edition builder does not use the group profiles as this is an individual query. These personal query editions are then sent to the requestor at the news reader layer.

### News Reader Layer

The news reader layer resides in the user's workstation. Vertical lines separating modules indicate that one module does not call the other module for service. Horizontal lines indicate that the higher module calls the lower module for service. This layer accepts stereotyped editions of the news and produces personalized editions of the news. This includes dynamic layout of the received news and the requesting of supplemental material based on the user profile or end-user actions.

The news presentation module receives an edition of the news containing core and stereotype news items. In order to personalize the edition, a personal agent based on the user's profile will retrieve items of interest through the query manager in the news management layer. The retrieved items are integrated with the previously received stereotyped edition. In carrying out this function, the news presentation module calls the user profile module and the query generator module.

The user profile module is a dynamically changing profile of the user's interests and preferences in display style of received news.

The query generator allows the user to request information not contained in the initial stereotyped edition. It may or may not reference the user profile module in generating the query. Results of the query are returned as an "edition" for presentation by the news presentation module. The user queries may be classified as requests for news items related to a particular news items in the current edition, either from today's news or from archived news or as requests for news items on a topic, not related to any particular news item, either from today's news or from archived news.

The query manager will retrieve these items from the appropriate news resource servers based on links in the UTF format or will submit retrieval requests to the servers in order to satisfy requests for archived news items.

## 6.6   Summary

Although the delivery of electronic news is well suited to exploit the promised high bandwidth, switched, interactive communication facilities of the information highway, its effectiveness depends on the emergence of digital libraries of electronic news data. Our initial investigations and prototyping experiences indicate that there are many open questions, including appropriate client/server architectures, abstract data representations, the use of personal agents, use of the UTF, amounts of information retrieved, categorization of news content, and automatic updating of personal user profiles.

# Chapter 7

## WebJournal: Visualization of a Web Journey

©Bipin C. Desai[*][†] and Stan Swiercz[‡][§]

## 7.1 Introduction

An increasing number of research institutes, universities and business organizations are currently providing their reports, articles, catalogs and other information resources on the Internet in general and the Web [27, 26] in particular. This is now becoming the accepted method of disseminating and sharing information resources in hyper-media. At this time a number of information sources, both public (free) and private (available for a fee), are available on the Internet. They include: text, computer programs, books, electronic journals, newspapers, organizational local and national directories of various types, sound and voice recordings, images, video clips and scientific data. Also, private information services such as price lists and quotations, databases of products and services, and specialty newsletters are available.

The current trend in the use of hyper-media and many of the documents accessible via the Internet using various browsers are great showcases for the features of the system. The practicality, however, of using links to related documents is both over utilized and a cause of annoyance to the users. A link in a document being perused leads the reader from one document to another, with in turn more links to tertiary documents. The user eventually gets lost and feels trapped in the web.

A number of browsers have been developed which allow ease in accessing this information on the Web. Mosaic[169] is one of the more popular ones. Users, while accessing such information resources, follow links from one document to another. Without a good method of recording their travels on this information highway, they could get "lost". Some of these browsers, record the user's path in a list and allow the user to return to any of these pre-visited documents. However, the relationship among the pre-visited documents is not preserved.

---

[*]Concordia University, Montreal, QC, CANADA, Email: bcdesai@cs.concordia.ca
[†]http://www.cs.concordia.ca/~faculty/bcdesai
[‡]Concordia University, Montreal, QC, CANADA, Email: stan@cs.concordia.ca
[§]http://www.cs.concordia.ca/~staffcs/stan

Nor is it possible to select and save the pointers to only a subset of these pre-visited documents except in a hot-list which may become too large.

As such, there is a need for a system which allows the visualization of a journey through the Web and, furthermore, provides ease in selectively marking documents for later review or sharing with colleagues.

The WebJournal [74] is such a graphical system which provides users with a pictorial representation of their search of resources on the Internet and allows random access to these visited resources. It keeps track of links including figures and postscript documents. In addition, the WebJournal provides direct access to any previously visited resources. Marking interesting resources and collecting these and storing them in a named file for later perusal or sharing is also possible. The marking of selected documents for printing is also possible.

## 7.2   Journaling a Web Journey

WebJournal, in its current implementation, works in conjunction with the Mosaic browser [169]. The latter is modified to allow it to share information with the WebJournal and provide it with a method of displaying the required documents. The WebJournal provides a two dimensional tree of visited hyper-media documents. The nodes could be labeled with the order of its visit, the URL [25] of the resource visited or the title of the resource visited [28]. The user can select any of these labeling schemes. In the latter two cases, however, the nodes tend to be large and the visualization of the journey is lost due to the limited size of the screen.

Figure 7.1 shows the status of the WebJournal beginning with a local home page(node 1). There are two pull down menus labeled *File* and *Options* at the top of the WebJournal window and three buttons, at the bottom, labeled Prune, Mark and Expand respectively. These buttons change their labels to indicate the status of the active node. In Figure 7.1, the unique node one is the active node; in Figure 7.2 node four is the active one. The next node, labeled node 2 in Figure 7.2, is one that is reached when the user directly enters a URL. The third node is reached by following a pointer in the second document. The fourth node is reached from the third node which in turn leads to a fifth node: a Postscript figure in the document corresponding to the fourth node. This Postscript would have been opened by the browser using an external application program such as ghostview, or xv.

### 7.2.1   Layout and Semantics of WebJournal

WebJournal displays each visited hyper-media resource (represented by a URL) as a node in a tree. This tree "grows" from left to right. There are three methods of labeling the displayed nodes. The default mode is to label each node with its ordinal number. The other two labeling possibilities are to use the node's actual

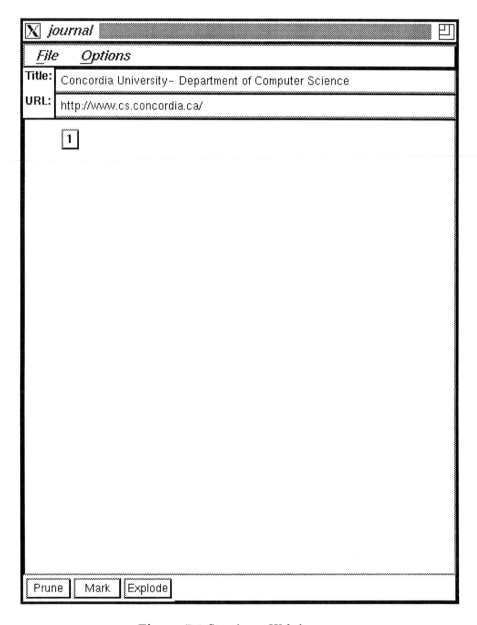

**Figure 7.1** Starting a Web journey

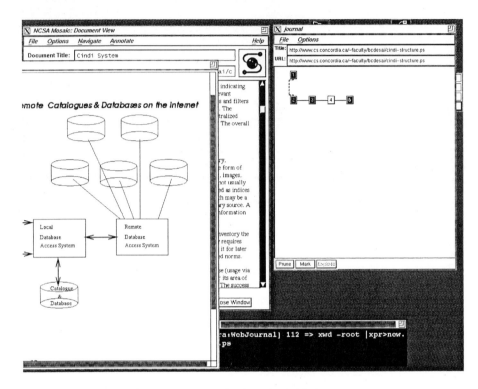

**Figure 7.2** Continuing the Web journey

URL or node's title. However, as the URL's and titles can be rather long, this results in the nodes being rather large. Large nodes use up much of the screen allowing one to view only a small part of a Web journey for a given size of the WebJournal window. As such it is preferable to leave the display in the default mode. The default mode can be changed by selecting the Display menu option in the Options menu.

Besides labeling the nodes, the user can also control how certain nodes are shown. URL's can have hyper-links to other sections of the same document. By default WebJournal does not display these sections as separate nodes even though the URL's are different (there are "#" found in the section URL's to indicate what the anchor is). If the user wishes to display all URL's as nodes then s/he can do so by selecting the Show Self Links radio button in the Options pull-down menu.

It is possible that two different looking documents have the same URL. This happens with CGI executables that send confirmations. The titles may be different but the URL's are identical. WebJournal only takes into account the URL. This implies that the confirmation will not show up in WebJournal.

It is also possible for the same document to have two different URL's. This happens when one WWW site has different names for itself or the document is found in more than one location on the site. As well, in the case of a site home page, the file name may be missing in one instance and if the user selects the "back to home document" anchor, a URL with the file name may arrive. WebJournal will treat these URL's as different nodes.

## 7.2.2  Semantics of Nodes

The node whose URL and title are displayed in the top part of the WebJournal has its label displayed in bold. Single clicking on a previously visited node will change the label to bold and the URL and title information displayed at the top part of the WebJournal will change to show the information of this node. This allows the user to search for a URL or title they had visited earlier and would want to have the corresponding resource displayed again. Single clicking does not change the contents of the browser window.

The node for the URL (active node) that is currently being displayed in the browser window is "highlighted" by using dark label characters on a light background. Previously visited nodes (inactive nodes) are displayed using light label characters on a dark background.

Double clicking on a node will cause a message to be sent to the browser (Mosaic in the current implementation) requesting a reload of the URL associated with that node. The node will be "highlighted" when it is displayed in the browser. Note that Mosaic at this point does not check if the URL is in its cache. It will retrieve the document. In this sense, the graph of the browser's visit of URL's is not the same as that displayed in the WebJournal.

URL's that use an external viewer (gifs, jpegs, mpegs, sound files, Postscript documents, binary ftp'd files for example) do not display in Mosaic's window and thus the nodes associated with these URL's do not get highlighted. The node characters are displayed in bold. Double clicking on such a node will not highlight it even though Mosaic will be sent the request which will open another external viewer. The node for the URL displayed in Mosaic's window will remain highlighted.

## 7.2.3  Semantics of Edges

The tree created by WebJournal is linked together with solid lines. There are also four different types of links denoted by dashed lines that link nodes outside of the regular tree structure. These dashed links "emerge" from the bottom of a node (to indicate where the link started) and go to the top of another node (the destination or new node). Some of these different edges can be seen in Figure 7.3 which represents another Web journey.

- The first type indicates that a user has selected an anchor in a URL to a URL that has already been seen (in the same Mosaic window).

- The second type shows that the user has entered in a URL manually using either the "Open URL" or "Open Local" buttons in the Mosaic's File pull-down menu.

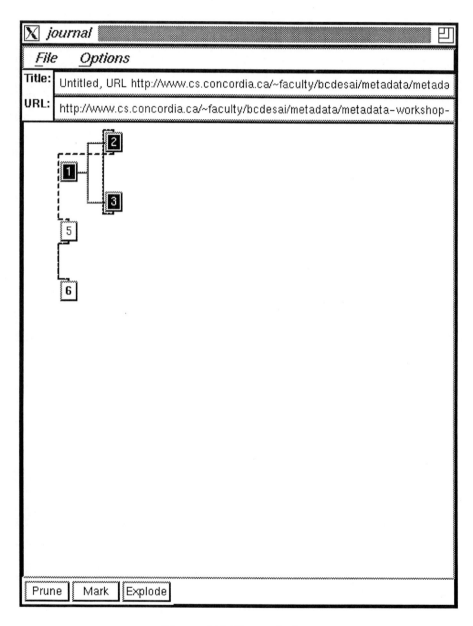

**Figure 7.3** Types of edges

- The third type shows that the user has selected a URL from Mosaic's hot-list.

- The fourth type (clone link) displays that the user has opened another Mosaic window using either the Clone button or using the middle mouse button to select an anchor. If the Clone button was pressed the link will be from the node with the same URL as the new node. If the user pressed the middle mouse button then the link will be from the node where the anchor was selected. If the user pressed the middle button and a node already existed for the new URL in the branch of the original Mosaic window then the link will originate from that node.

URL's that are the same but in different Mosaic windows are distinct. Links of the first three types are only created for nodes in the same Mosaic window.

### 7.2.4  Handling Multiple Browser Windows

Browsers such as Mosaic allow a user to open multiple windows to view different parts of the same document or a number of different documents. Such cloning of the browser windows in Mosaic is done by using the browser's Clone button or by using the middle button of the mouse. Multiple windows allow subsequent independent travel to different parts of the hyper-media hyper-space.

Multiple windows are represented in the WebJournal by designating a highlighted node for each window. The most recent resource visited is represented by displaying the contents of the corresponding node in bold. The cloning is represented by a "clone" edge. Figure 7.4 shows the cloning of a Mosaic window when a hyper-link in node three of the journal in Figure 7.2 was clicked using the mouse's middle button.

## 7.3  Managing the WebJournal Real Estate

WebJournal tries to keep all the branches for a Mosaic window together. If the user for example manually enters a URL and there already exists clone branches, WebJournal will move the clone branches down to make room for the new node.

Double clicking on a node will result in the URL being displayed in the browser window where it originally appeared. In a case where the window has been deleted, the URL would appear in the "oldest" browser window. A warning message would appear in the WebJournal window. A new node would be created in the branch of the tree corresponding to the "oldest" window unless a node with the same URL already exists in the "oldest" window. In this case, that node will be highlighted. In the case where a new node is created, a node containing an ! is placed before this node to indicate that it was previously viewed in a different Mosaic window. All subsequent nodes created from double clicking nodes belonging to deleted windows will appear after this ! node.

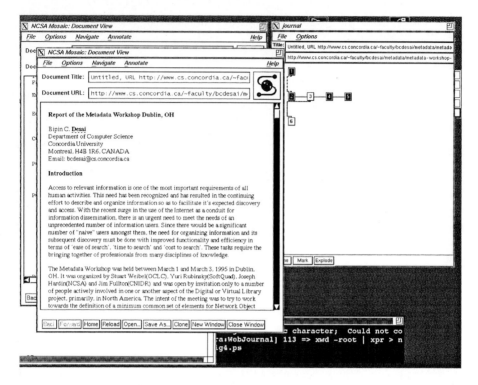

**Figure 7.4** Logging multiple browsers

As the Web journey continues, the tree in the WebJournal grows in size. Such a growing tree can take up a lot of space and the user may find it hard to visualize the recent path. At such points, the user can prune the tree by using the Prune/Expand button found at the bottom of WebJournal window. The label in the Prune/Expand button indicates whether the current node (indicated by the characters of its label being in bold) can be pruned or expanded. The pruned part of the tree, though not displayed, is stored internally and can be recalled by using the "Prune/Expand" button. The pruned branch of the tree is replaced by a graphic representation of a tree as shown in Figure 7.5. This figure shows a pruned node corresponding to the Web journey tree rooted at node 5. The expanded version of this node is given in Figure 7.9. There are four types of pruned nodes. They correspond to the state of a regular node. The significance of the pruned node display is summarized in Table 7.1

Single clicking or double clicking on a pruned node acts on the root of the pruned branches.

If a display node is set to Show Self Links and a node, which is a self anchor to another node, is pruned and then Show Self Links is turned off, that node should disappear but it might have other URL's "under" it. In such a case, WebJournal displays the pruned node but it becomes insensitive to clicks. The lines drawn in this button are fuzzier. Also the Prune/Expand button also becomes insensitive

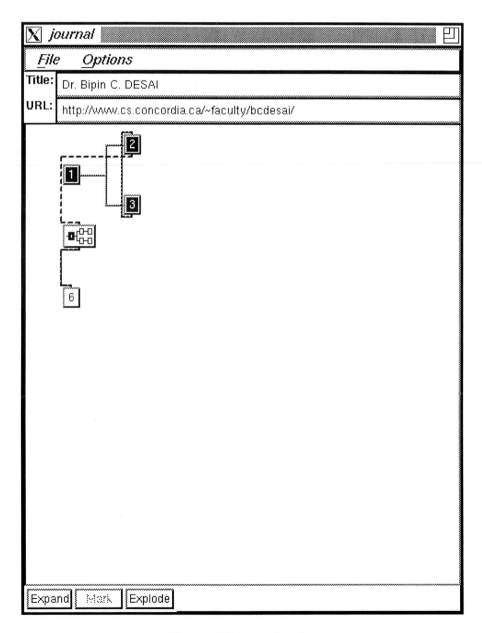

**Figure 7.5** Pruned nodes

| 1) | light character and dark background | visited node |
|---|---|---|
| 2) | dark character and light background | a node in this pruned branch is currently displayed |
| 3) | same as 1 but the first node in the prunded icon is "highlighted" | visited node that has its URL and title displayed at top |
| 4) | same as 2 but the first node in the prunded icon is "highlighted" | a node in this pruned branch is currently displayed and has its URL and title displayed at top |

**Table 7.1** Significance of pruned node display

if this node button is current. The only way to expand such an in-sensitized node is to set Show Self Link and then expand the in-sensitized node using the Prune/Expand button.

## 7.4   Marking Nodes, Saving, Reloading and Printing

A node may be "marked" for later use by using the mark button found at the bottom of WebJournal's window. This button works on the current node (i.e., whose label is in bold). The mark button is insensitive to clicks when the current node is pruned. When a node is marked its label changes to a slanted font. All occurrences of nodes for that document will be marked. If there are any nodes that have the same "root" URL (i.e., if a node is a section of the document or the same URL in a different Mosaic window) they will be considered the same document.

A list of URLs of marked nodes can be saved in a file using the Save Marked option of the File pull-down menu. This file can then be loaded at a future date using the Load option of the File pull-down menu. When URLs are loaded a node is created with the label of an asterisk. This is to indicate that what follows originally came from a WebJournal file. This node is linked with a dashed line indicating a manually entered URL. Such node is associated with the "oldest" Mosaic window. There can only be one asterisk node per Mosaic window. With the deletion of Mosaic windows it is possible to have more than one asterisk node.

An example of such a file list is shown above in Figure 7.6. The order of URL's in the file corresponds to the order in which the nodes were marked. The list is a linear list and the original tree structure is lost. The WebJournal shows these loaded nodes with the first node being marked by an * as shown in Figure

```
WebJournal-format-1
http://www.cs.concordia.ca/~faculty/bcdesai/semantic-header.html
http://www.cs.concordia.ca/~faculty/bcdesai/semantic-header.html
internal
http://www.cs.concordia.ca/~faculty/bcdesai/cindi-system-1.0.html
http://www.cs.concordia.ca/~faculty/bcdesai/cindi-system-1.0.html
internal
http://www.cs.concordia.ca/bcd/semantic-header.html
http://www.cs.concordia.ca/bcd/semantic-header.html
internal
http://www.cs.concordia.ca/bcd/navigate.html
http://www.cs.concordia.ca/bcd/navigate.html
internal
http://www.cs.concordia.ca/w3-paper.html
http://www.cs.concordia.ca/w3-paper.html
internal
http://www.cs.concordia.ca/~faculty/bcdesai/metadata/metadata-workshop-report.html
http://www.cs.concordia.ca/~faculty/bcdesai/metadata/metadata-workshop-report.html
internal
http://www.cs.concordia.ca/~faculty/bcdesai/www3-wrkA/workshop-a.html
http://www.cs.concordia.ca/~faculty/bcdesai/www3-wrkA/workshop-a.html
internal
http://www.cs.concordia.ca/gdep.html
http://www.cs.concordia.ca/gdep.html
internal
```

**Figure 7.6** File of marked nodes

7.7. The figure records a new Web journey followed immediately by loading a file containing previously marked nodes.

Marking nodes and saving them in a file could then be used for later printing the contents of the resources represented by the nodes. This feature would alleviate the current practice of some suppliers of over utilizing hyper-links and making up a document using small sections. Such a practice is also used by many converters. A user wanting to read such a document, off line can mark these nodes. These marked nodes can then be used to down-load the corresponding documents and print them as discussed in section 7.4.2.

## 7.4.1   Exploding a Node

When the Explode button, found at the bottom of WebJournal, is pressed the document corresponding to the URL of the current node is examined to determine the number of hyper-links found within it. Note that the Explode button is only sensitive when a node is both highlighted and current (i.e., the font used is bold). WebJournal examines the source of the selected node to determine the links in it and the number of distinct URLs, therein. Since some of the links could be to anchors to different sections of the same document, WebJournal will consider all these links as a single distinct URL. Once the number of distinct

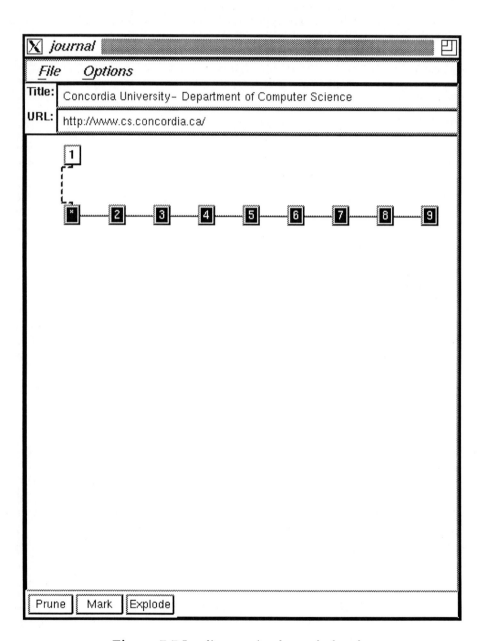

**Figure 7.7** Loading previously marked nodes

URLs are determined, WebJournal informs the user of this number by a pop-up window. If there are some links that point to the same document, then the number of distinct nodes is also shown in this pop-up window. If all the URL's are from one distinct document, then WebJournal will inform the user of it. If the one distinct document happens to be the node that is being exploded, this fact is also mentioned to the user. In this case there is no point in exploding the node. With node five of Figure 7.8 as the current node, if we press on Explode button WebJournal would examine the source document and using a pop-up window ask for confirmation of the action.

The user can either select the YES or NO button. If the user selects YES then another window pops up asking whether the nodes coming from the explosion (fragment nodes) should be marked or not. One reason to mark these nodes would be to print out the exploded set of documents.

Figure 7.9 is the resulting WebJournal display when node five of Figure 7.8 was exploded and marked.

This feature should be used with great care. Exploding a node can cause the creation of several hundred new nodes that will slow down the display. Exploding one of the "fragment nodes" could produce additional edges represented by dashed lines to existing fragments. Such dashed lines would clutter the WebJournal window and could make it difficult to visualize the Web journey.

This feature was designed so that a user who finds an online documentation and wishes to print it, has an easy way of bringing up the individual URLs and marking them instead of requiring a manual visit to each URL. Anyone who has tried to follow these leads know that such manual visitation for documentation having a large number of sections and chapters would be a long tedious task.

## 7.4.2  Marked Nodes and Printing

Marked nodes can be printed from WebJournal by selecting The "Print Marked" option in the pull-down menu under the File option. A dialog pop-up window allows the specification of the printer to be used and the format to use to print the documents. This is illustrated in Figure 7.10. Once these options are set up, the user selects "OK" and the WebJournal opens a new Mosaic window to do the printing. If the URL is for an internal Mosaic document (regular HTML) then when it is retrieved, WebJournal will tell Mosaic to print the document. WebJournal will then instruct Mosaic to fetch the next URL. The user is kept informed of the status of the printing operation via an information pop-up window.

For a URL requiring an external viewer (such as ghostview, xv), a pop-up window informs the user to use appropriate commands available in the external viewer to print the corresponding resource being displayed. Once the user is done with the external viewer s/he should press the "OK" button in this pop-up so that WebJournal can continue. This is done so that the user's screen is not filled with several windows for xv, ghostview, xdvi, etc. Note, that if a marked URL is for a sound file, the user should select "OK" right away. For xdvi documents

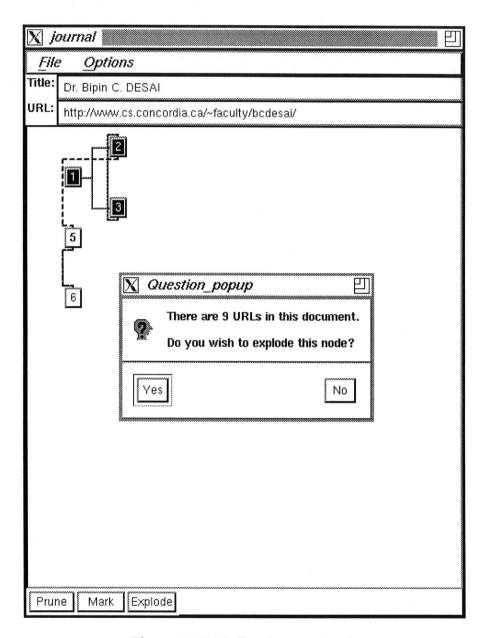

**Figure 7.8** Exploding the current node

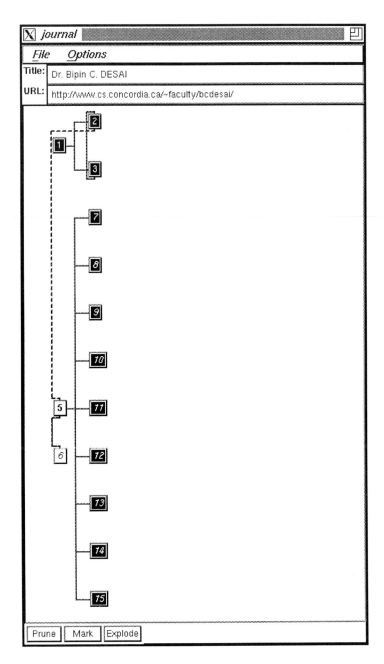

**Figure 7.9** Current node exploded and marked

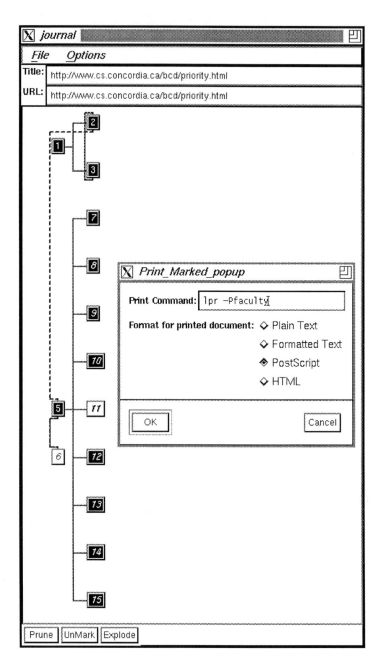

**Figure 7.10** Printing marked nodes

there is no print option available currently. The user however should note the name of the temporary file where the dvi file is down-loaded. This file should be copied to another file. Subsequently, the user needs to employ appropriate dvi-to-whatever converter (e.g., dvips) to print it.

Once all the marked documents are printed the clone Mosaic window used for printing is automatically closed.

# 7.5   WebJournal Internals, communications

WebJournal is written in Motif 1.2.3. The widget used to draw the nodes and edges is a modified version of the Tree widget described in [240] ¶. Extra code was added to this widget to draw the dashed lines.

Communications between Mosaic and WebJournal is through 2 pipes [17]. One pipe is for communication from Mosaic to WebJournal, while the other one handles communication in the reverse direction. Instructions between the processes are very simple instructions such as fetch this URL or such a URL has arrived. X input event handlers are created in both programs to handle their inputs.

# 7.6   Conclusions

Our experience of using the Web as an information discovery tool time and again, and being "trapped" in it, resulted in the conception of our version of a safety net to avoid such a trap. In this chapter, we describe how the WebJournal helps its users find their bearings. The additional benefits of this tool are to record and share the highlights of an interesting journey. The WebJournal's beta version was publicly released in May 1995 and available for **non-commercial** use. It can be down-loaded employing anonymous ftp from:

```
ftp.cs.concordia.ca
```

in the directory

```
/pub/bcdesai/WebJournal/
```

The binaries for the following systems are in their respective sub-directories:

```
Sun Sparc running SunOS 4.1.3
Sun Sparc running Solaris 2.3
Sun Sparc running Solaris 2.4
Dec Alpha running OSF1-2.0B
```

---

¶ A highly recommended text for those interested in X Window applications.

Webers may use the following URL to make this task less tedious:

```
ftp://ftp.cs.concordia.ca/pub/bcdesai/WebJournal/
```

## 7.7   Acknowledgment

WebJournal is a component of the CUILT Project for Developing Virtual Library Infrastructure, supported in part by a grant from Seagram Funds for Academic Innovation.

# Part II

# Document Handling and Information Retrieval

# Chapter 8

## Uniform Structured Document Handling using a Constraint-based Object Approach[*]

Anisoara Nica[†] and Elke Angelika Rundensteiner[‡]

## Abstract

Complex multimedia document handling, including the modeling, decomposition, and search across digital documents, is one of the primary services that must be provided by digital library systems. In this paper, we present a general approach for handling structured documents (e.g., SGML documents) by exploiting object-oriented database technology. For this purpose, we propose a constraint-based object model capable of capturing in a uniform manner all SGML constructs typically used to encode the structural organization of complex documents. We present a general strategy for mapping arbitrary document types (e.g., article, journal, and book DTDs) expressed using standard SGML into our model. Most importantly, we demonstrate that our model is designed to handle the integration of diverse document types into one integrated schema, thus avoiding the generating of numerous redundant class definitions for similar document subtypes. The resulting document management system DMS is thus capable of supporting the dynamic addition of new document types, and of uniformly processing queries spanning across multiple document types. In this paper, we also describe the implementation of our approach on the commercial DBMS system Illustra to demonstrate that the ease with which our approach can be realized on current OODB technology – without requiring any special-purpose constructs. Our DMS system provides support for integrated querying of both structural as well as content-based predicates across arbitrarily complex document types.

---

[*]This research has been funded in part by the joint NSF/ARPA/NASA Digital Libraries Initiative under CERA IRI-9411287, and by NSF under grants RIA #IRI-9309076 and NYI #IRI-9457609. We also thank Illustra Inc. to provide us with the University Innovation Equipment Award.

[†]Dept. of Elect. Eng. and Computer Science, University of Michigan, Ann Arbor, MI 48109-2122, 1301 Beal Avenue, anica@eecs.umich.edu

[‡]Dept. of Elect. Eng. and Computer Science, University of Michigan, Ann Arbor, MI 48109-2122, 1301 Beal Avenue, rundenst@eecs.umich.edu

# 8.1   Introduction

## 8.1.1   Structured Document Management

With the coming of the information age, the amount, complexity and variety of digital documents available on the so-called information super-highway is increasing dramatically on a day by day basis. To cope with this overload of digital information, it is thus critical that we have at our avail a proper set of software tools to aid with all aspects of document handling. This includes tools and techniques for the creation, editing, management, storage, filtering, retrieval and presentation of structured multimedia documents.

One of the primary goals of the University of Michigan Digital Library (UMDL) project [32], funded by NSF, ARPA, NASA as well as numerous industrial sponsorers, is to develop an agent-based software architecture for maintaining such digital information distributed over a large set of heterogeneous collection databases. The UMDL system is being designed to support the management and efficient retrieval of digital information over the internet. This requires techniques for identifying digital material that most closely matches the information needs of individual users – a functionality typically provided by information retrieval (IR) systems. However, documents of the current and future information age are no longer simple sequential pieces of text, mimicking their old cousin – the paper book. Rather, digital documents are complex, highly structured artifacts, that are closely interconnected referring and re-using passages and digital subdocuments in an integrated web structure. The challenge thus remains to not only identify documents as a whole, but rather to find individual document fragments, to search based on the structure of a document, and to compose document fragments into complex, customized documents targeted to meet the particular information needs of the users. DBMSs have been designed to handle such complex structured query and information integration requirements – besides of course also providing other traditional DBMS functionalities such as concurrency control and recovery.

For these reasons, much work has been initiated in recent years in integrating database (DBMS) and information retrieval (IR) technologies for developing structured document management systems [65, 67, 35, 34, 33, 56]. This research has generally proceeded in two directions: either IR systems are extended with structured representation and associated query techniques or DBMS systems are extended by incorporating IR matching techniques into their query language and access structures. It is likely that eventually a true 'marriage' will emerge once both approaches have fully matured. In this paper, we built on this previous work, in particular, we utilize a DBMS system that has been extended with IR techniques as foundation of our document management system (DMS) system.

Our goal is to provide for document management technologies using generic techniques and tools, whenever possible. For this reason, our DMS is designed to handle SGML documents. SGML (Standard Generalized Markup Language) [131] is a recently prevailing standard that has been developed as a means for the generic interchange of digital documents between different platforms and systems. SGML encodes different types of textual documents (e.g., document type definitions - DTDs - for articles, books, journals, etc.) by marking their structural contexts. It has been found that SGML structure can be exploited for guiding the retrieval process over digital documents, by allowing for example queries that incorporate not just content-based information needs but also structural requests. Examples of queries that our DMS can support, by exploiting SGML structuring, include *'Retrieve all figures with associated captions and the names of the sections they appear in for all documents written by Elisa Meister that are on the subject of "Database" and "Information Retrieval".'*

## 8.1.2 The Constraint-based Approach

This paper describes our solution to building a document management system (DMS) that can handle complex mixed queries by exploiting both IR as well as DBMS techniques. Our goals here are two-fold: (1) to build upon previous work whenever possible, and (2) to develop generic solutions that can be quickly adapted by others into their respective document management systems. Our work utilizes SGML as document structuring technique due to the increasing popularity of this standard among publishers[§]. In order to simplify mapping of SGML DTDs into database technology, we propose a constraint-based object modeling and merging approach.

First, we introduce a formal object model which (containing only well-accepted object modeling primitives) can easily be mapped to most of the currently available OODB systems[¶][172]. Rather than introducing special-purpose data types and meta-classes or requiring new query processing techniques for handling particular SGML-constructs, as proposed by other researchers, we introduce a constraint-based object model that provides a generic mechanism for document modeling. We then present a general algorithm for mapping any SGML construct into our formal constraint-based object model[‖]. Finally, we discuss our successful experience of implementing our DMS system on the commercial system Illustra[**]. This effort demonstrates that our formal constraint-based object model can easily be mapped to available OODB technology.

Furthermore, we show that our model is designed to support the integration of multiple DTDs into one integrated system – sharing class definitions among different DTDs whenever possible. Our integrated schema approach is based on the recognition that the textual document types that we are currently considering, such as, articles, books, journals and so on, typically exhibit significant overlap in terms of their document structures. We thus propose to exploit this fact by merging schemata rather than maintaining a distinct schema for each

---

[§]The digital library project at the University of Michigan (UMDL) is getting delivered document collections in SGML format from content providers such as Elsevier and others.

[¶]We have previously identified constraint mechanisms as a powerful object modeling technique[197].

[‖]It is important to note that most commercial DBMS systems provide some form of rule or constraint support, and that active OODBMS technology is increasingly gaining popularity [235, 141].

[**]Illustra is a registered trademark of Illustra Inc.

separate DTD in DMS – as commonly assumed by all the other systems that we are aware of. This not only reduces the size of the schema, but it can also simplify document retrieval by allowing for the structural and content-based queries against the integrated schema – i.e., across diverse DTDs. Specification of queries across various document types becomes possible without requiring special syntactic query constructs or query processing techniques.

To validate our constraint-based approach, we have implemented a working prototype of our document management system DMS. The foundation of our system is Illustra, a commercial object-relational DBMS, which we chose for its support of basic object-oriented features, of SQL and textual query processing, and of rule specification. Given this suitable platform, we were able to rapidly build an initial version of DMS within a few months. In this paper, we describe in detail a realization of the SGML-to-OODB mapping strategy on our chosen platform. Our prototype DMS can handle mixed queries like the one listed earlier. To summarize, key contributions of this proposed approach are its genericity and simplicity, which allow structured document handling to be easily added to any OODBs system that supports constraints.

### 8.1.3   Overview

In the remainder of this paper, we first overview our general approach towards document management (Section 8.2). Section 8.3 introduces the constraint-based object model, while Section 8.4 describes our proposed strategy for mapping SGML model groups into the constraint-based model. Each of these steps is clarified by presenting a detailed example of how it is realized in our current prototype implementation using Illustra. Our model simplifies the task of merging multiple, possibly diverse DTDs into one uniform schema, as described in Section 8.5. Finally, related work is presented in Section 8.6, and conclusions and future work are given in Section 8.7.

## 8.2   Project Background

Our goal is to develop an integrated document management system (DMS) that can handle mixed queries involving both structural as well as content-based predicates. The general architecture of our system is given in Figure 8.1.

**Using SGML for Document Management.** The SGML standard [110, 131], developed to support the representation and exchange of structured text, such as book or article document types, has increasingly become popular with major publishers. We hence have chosen SGML as the formalism for encoding the structural characteristics of our documents. In other words, our DMS system is designed to accept SGML documents as input, to generate SGML documents as output, and to provide support for querying, editing, and filtering of documents based on their structural characteristics as encoded by SGML (Figure 8.1).

Mapping the structure of SGML documents into a database requires that the database model supports (1) the hierarchical structure of the SGML documents, (2) abstract data types such as variable-length ordered lists and tuples, (3) complex data types which can capture the semantics of the expressions obtained using SGML connectors ("|", "&", ",") and SGML occurrence indicators ("+", "?", "*") and (4) ways of defining constraints for the above data types [56]. In Sections 8.3 and 8.4, we present our constraint-based object modeling and merging approach which represents our solution to the problem of SGML modeling.

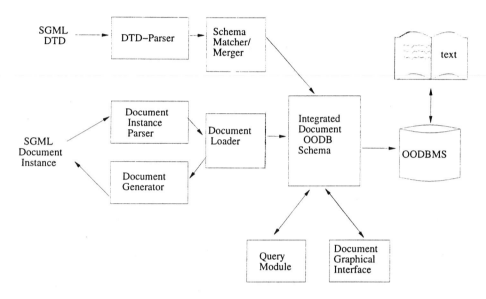

**Figure 8.1** The Integrated Document Management System Architecture.

**Selection of DBMS System as Platform.** Since the complex structure of digital documents requires powerful data modeling, we have chosen the commercial DBMS system Illustra as platform for DMS. Illustra is based on an object-relational model which builds on top of the relational model through its support for objects and abstract data types. Thus, Illustra combines the mature features of relational databases (such as SQL query support) with the object modeling power of OODBs. Illustra provides built-in extensibility of data types, so that we can easily define new abstract data types, such as ordered lists, as required by SGML modeling. Another advantage of Illustra is that it provides support for textual search functions through its "Text Datablade" package, supporting manipulation, storage and retrieval of free form, unstructured text of arbitrary length.

In addition, Illustra meets our project needs by supporting a mechanism for constraint specification and management. This is important since, for example, if we were to use this document database within an SGML editor or composer application, it would be necessary to have a mean to ensure that any object instance modified would still translate into a valid SGML document. Without these constraints being handled within the database, it would be necessary to translate an object back into a SGML document and run a parser on it to determine whether or not it is still valid.

**DMS System Overview.** As depicted in Figure 8.1, the DTD-mapper module of our DMS system translates an input DTD into our internal schema representation. Our schema-merger module merges the newly generated classes with the integrated document schema. Given an SGML document instance, the loader module determines a match between the particular document and the integrated DTD schema. Based on this match, the document will be decomposed and loaded into the DMS repository as a complex document object. A query module is available to process extended SQL queries, while a graphical interface for displaying query results (in particular, structured document fragments) is under development.

## 8.3    The Constraint-Based Object Model

As the foundation of our system, we are assuming a general object model as adopted by most other OODBs [49, 53]. In order to support modeling of all SGML constructs, we extend the model with constraints over the attribute set [172]. As we shall describe, the constraints are used to model properties of a subset of the attributes of a class and they must hold for every instance of the class.

Let $N$ be the set of all classes, $L$ the set of attribute names, and $O$ the set of object instances. We represent a schema $S$ as a tuple $(C, E, G, T)$ where:

1. $C \subseteq N$ is a finite set of classes. For every class $c$ in $C$, there is a collection of object instances in $O$ that defines the content of the class $c$. The object instances are said to be members of (or instances of) their class $c$.

2. $E \subseteq C \times L \times C$ is a finite set of attributes. For an attribute $(p, a, q) \in E$, every instance of the class $p$ has an attribute named $a$ whose value is a member of the class $q$. The class $q$ is called the domain of $a$ for $p$. For all $e_i \in E$, such that $e_i = (p, a_i, q_i)$ for some class $p$, we call $\{a_i | (p, a_i, q_i) \in E, \forall a_i \in L, \forall q_i \in C\}$ the attribute set defined for $p$.

3. $G \subseteq C \times C$ is the specialization relation on classes. For $(p, q) \in G$, we say that $p$ is a specialization of $q$ (or $q$ is the generalization of $p$) which indicates that every instance of $p$ is also an instance of $q$. $G$ is a reflexive, transitive and antisymmetric relation on $C$.

4. $T \subseteq (E \times E \times B) \cup (E \times U)$ is the set of binary and unary constraints over the attribute set $E$, where $B = \{b : E \times E \rightarrow \{True, False\}\}$ is a set of binary constraint functions and $U = \{u : E \rightarrow \{True, False\}\}$ is a set of unary constraint functions. $T$ is defined as a finite set: $T =$

$\{((p, a, q), (p, b, t), f) \mid f \in B, (p, a, q) \in E, (p, b, t) \in E$ and $f((p, a, q), (p, b, t)) = True\} \bigcup \{((p, a, q), g) \mid g \in U, (p, a, q) \in E$ and $g((p, a, q)) = True\}$.

The set of constraints $T$ is defined by enumerating the constraint tuples (argument(s), constraint function) corresponding to the $True$ values of the constraint functions. For the purpose of this paper, we use only binary and unary constraints over the attribute set of the same class. The data model could easily be extended with a more general set of constraints. However, we found this restricted set of constraint types sufficiently powerful to handle all SGML semantics.

An example of an unary function is the non-null constraint denoted by:
$NotNull : E \rightarrow \{True, False\}$.
This constraint is defined, for example, as follows for the class $Person$:
$NotNull((Person, SSN, Integer)) = True$
with the semantics that this is true if and only if any instance of the class $Person$ has an attribute $SSN$ not null, with the later a member of the class $Integer$. This constraint assures that every person instance does have a legal ssn value.

An example of a binary function is the exclusive-or constraint denoted by:
$ExclusiveOr : E \times E \rightarrow \{True, False\}$.
This constraint is defined, for example, as follows for the class $Student$:
$ExclusiveOr((Student, VisaType, String), (Student, Citizen/PermRes, String)) = True$
with the semantics that every instance of the $Student$ class must have either an attribute value for its $VisaType$ or for its $Citizen/PermRes$ status, but cannot have values for both.

In addition, we establish that a schema $S = (C, E, G, T)$ must satisfy the following properties in order to be considered well-defined:

1. If $(p, a, q_1) \in E$ and $(p, a, q_2) \in E$ then $\exists q \in C$ such that $(q, q_1) \in G$, $(q, q_2) \in G$ and $(p, a, q) \in E$.

   This property says that for every attribute $a$ of a class $p$, there exists a *least* one class $q$ that is subclass of all domains of $a$ defined for $a$ in $p$. Since all members of a class must meet *all* constraints defined on the class, this assures that there is ultimately one unique most restricted domain for each attribute of a class.

2. If $(p, q) \in G$ and $(q, a, r) \in E$ then $(p, a, r) \in E$.

   This property, often called the full-inheritance invariant, states that any attribute of $q$ is inherited by all subclasses of $q$.

3. If $(p, a, q) \in E$ and $(q, r) \in G$ then $(p, a, r) \in E$.

   This property states that the attributes are preserved by the specialization relation over $C$.

4. (a) If $(p, q) \in G$ and $((q, a, r), g) \in T$ then for all $r' \in C$ for which $(p, a, r') \in E$ we have that $((p, a, r'), g) \in T$ .

   (b) If $(p, q) \in G$ and $((q, a, r_1), (q, b, r_2), f) \in T$ then for all $r'_1, r'_2 \in C$ for which $(p, a, r'_1) \in E$ , $(p, b, r'_2) \in E$ we have that $((p, a, r'_1), (p, b, r'_2), f) \in T$ .

The last property enforces that the constraints are also preserved by the specialization relation by being inherited from a generalization class to all its specialization subclasses. In particular, 4.a states the constraint preservation principle for unary constraint functions, and 4.b states it for binary constraint functions, respectively.

## 8.4 Mapping SGML Model Groups into the Constraint Based Model

In this section we define a general strategy for mapping SGML basic model groups to a constraint-based object schema based on the model defined above (Section 8.3). The proposed strategy is general in that it could easily be realized on any OODB system that supports the elementary OO modeling constructs, such as objects, classes, attributes, and generalization relationships. In addition, we assume that the target OODB system supports constraints. If this is not provided by the OODB system, then the constraints defined in the mapping process would have to be realized using method encoding.

**The Example Document Type Definition (DTD).** We will use the Document Type Definition (DTD) for documents of type *article* given in Figure 8.2 as source for the examples throughout the remainder of this section. This article DTD example was first defined in [56], and represents a realistic though simplified version of the Elsevier Science Article DTD documented by Elsevier Science Pub. [183]. In order to validate our approach, we also describe in this section how our DMS system realizes the resulting constraint-based object schema for the article document type using the Illustra DBMS engine [††].

The definition of the element **article** (line 2 in Figure 8.2) can be represented as a Directed Acyclic Graph (DAG) where the leaves are the elements of the SGML basic types (e.g., #PCDATA) and the internal nodes are SGML connectors (e.g., "&", "," and "|" ), SGML indicators (e.g., "?", "*" and "+") and elements which are defined using other elements. Figure 8.3 depicts the DAG representation capturing the DTD from Figure 8.2.

**General Mapping Strategy.**

*Step 1: Basic Types.* In the general mapping, every SGML basic type (e.g., #PCDATA in Figure 8.2) is represented by a class of the appropriate type (e.g., **TEXT** or **DOC** in Illustra).

---

[††]Recall that we have chosen Illustra since it supports both content-based queries as well as general constraints.

```
1. <!DOCTYPE article [
2. <!ELEMENT article    -- (title, (author+), affil, abstract,
                               (section+), (bib&ack))>
3. <!ELEMENT title     -O (#PCDATA)>
4. <!ELEMENT author    -O (#PCDATA)>
5. <!ELEMENT affil     -O (#PCDATA)>
6. <!ELEMENT abstract  -O (#PCDATA)>
7. <!ELEMENT ack       -O (#PCDATA)>
8. <!ELEMENT bib       -O (#PCDATA)>
9. <!ELEMENT section   -O ((title, (body+))| (title, (body*),
                               (subsectn+)))>
10. <!ELEMENT subsectn -O (title, (body+))>
11. <!ELEMENT body     -O (figure|paragr)>
12. <!ELEMENT figure   -O (picture, (caption?))>
13. <!ELEMENT picture  -O (#PCDATA)>
14. <!ELEMENT caption  -O (#PCDATA)>
15. <!ELEMENT paragr   -O (#PCDATA)>
]
```

**Figure 8.2** A DTD for a Document of Type Article.

*Step 2: Complex Types.* Each basic SGML model group is represented by a class with its attributes corresponding to the elements of the model group and with the constraints imposed by the connector used in the model group. The name of the class is the name of the defined SGML element if the model group is the content of the element definition. For example, **(title, (body+))** is the model group defining the element **subsectn** in line 10 of the DTD in Figure 8.2 and it will be mapped into a new class with the name **SUBSECTN**. Note, for example, that in Figure 8.3, there exists a subtree representing this model group (T2) which is the only child of the node **subsectn**.

If the model group is used inside another model group then we will generate a unique name for the corresponding class. For example, the **(title, (body*), (subsectn+))** model group is used in the definition of the **section**. Thus a unique class name will be assigned to this model group so that it can be referred to in the **section** class. In this case, the subtree in Figure 8.3 corresponding to this model group (T1) is the child of a node labeled with the SGML connector "|".

**Mapping Algorithm for Model Groups.** Concrete mapping steps based on the SGML connectors and indicators are listed below:

*Case 1: Optional Indicator.* The optional indicator "?" indicates zero or one occurrence of an element. A model group **(a?)** will be mapped into an attribute **a** and no constraints: the attribute **a** can be null.

A definition of an element $p$ in SGML:

```
<!ELEMENT p    -O (... (a?) ...)>
```

will be translated into a new class $p$ with one of its attributes equal to $(p, a, q) \in E$. No unary constraints will be associated with the attribute $a$. $q$ is the class corresponding to $a$'s model group, with the later defined using this mapping algorithm.

*Case 2: No Indicator.* An element with no occurrence indicator must be constrained to be not null using the unary constraint function **NotNull** defined above. A definition of an element $p$ in SGML:

```
<!ELEMENT p    -O (... a ...)>
```

will be translated into a new class $p$ with one of its attributes equal to $(p, a, q) \in E$. We also impose the $NotNull$ unary constraint $((p, a, q), NotNull) \in T$. Again, $q$ is the class corresponding to $a$'s model group.

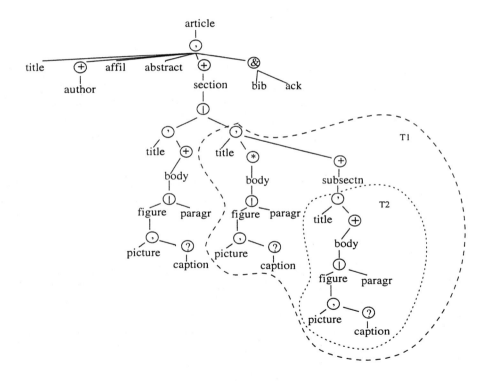

**Figure 8.3** Directed Acyclic Graph Representation for the Element *article*.

To illustrate the previous two mapping steps, we now give the translation of the **figure** definition from the DTD example (line 12 in Figure 8.2):

```
<!ELEMENT figure    -O (picture, (caption?))>.
```

In Illustra, a new complex class **FIGURE** and the corresponding table **FIG-URE_table** are created as following:

```
create table FIGURE_table of new type FIGURE (
    picture DOC not null,
    caption DOC
);
```

Not-null is an unary constraint that is directly supported in Illustra. The constraints imposed by the sequence indicator "," for **(picture, (caption?))** model group, are defined below in Case 5.

*Case 3: Closure-Occurrence Indicator.* The asterisk sign indicator "**\***" indicates zero or more occurrences of an element. The model group (**a\***) is translated into an attribute of ordered-list type with no unary constraint imposed: the list could be empty. The ordered-list type composed of elements of the same type $a$ must be supported by the target OODB system.

A definition of an element $p$ in SGML:

```
<!ELEMENT p    -O (... (a*) ...)>
```

will be translated into a new class $p$ with one of its attributes equal to $(p, a, q) \in E$. No unary constraints are specified for the corresponding attribute $a$. $q$ is the ordered-list class with the element type corresponding to $a$'s model group. Since Illustra does not support any built-in variable-length lists, we model the ordered list in Illustra by using a position field which gives the position of the elements in the list.

*Case 4: Multiple-Occurrence Indicator.* The plus sign indicator "**+**" indicates one or more occurrences of an element. The model group is translated like the "**\***" model group but with an unary $NotNull$ constraint imposed. A definition of an element $p$ in SGML:

```
<!ELEMENT p    -O (... (a+) ...)>
```

will be translated into a new class $p$ with one of its attributes equal to $(p, a, q) \in E$. In addition, we specify the unary constraint $((p, a, q), NotNull) \in T$. $q$ is the ordered list class with the elements of type corresponding to $a$'s model group.

In our example, the model group **(title, (body\*), (subsectn+)))** (part of line 9 in Figure 8.2) is translated as following:

```
create table  A2_SECTION_table of new type A2_SECTION (
    title DOC not null,
    bodys BODY_list,
    subsectns SUBSECTN_list not null
);
```

with **BODY_list** and **SUBSECTN_list** defined separately as described above.

*Case 5: Sequence Aggregation Connector.* The SGML sequence (aggregation) connector "," imposes an order between elements connected by it. In the constraint-based object model, an aggregation model group $(a_1, a_2, \ldots, a_n)$ will be translated into a class $t$, with attributes $(t, a_1, q_1), (t, a_2, q_2), \ldots, (t, a_n, q_n) \in E$ where $q_i$ is the class corresponding to the domain of the element $a_i$. If $a_i$ is a SGML basic type (e.g., #PCDATA) then $q_i$ is the class of the appropriate type (e.g., **DOC** in Illustra). If $a_i$ is another model group, $q_i$ is the class corresponding to $a_i$'s model group.

In order to support the semantics of the aggregation model group, we need to introduce the binary constraint function "$<$" defined by:

$$<: E \times E \rightarrow \{True, False\}$$

where $< ((p, a, q_1), (p, b, q_2)) = True$ if and only if the value of the attribute $a$ is always before the value of the attribute $b$ for every instance of class $p$.

In particular, for the class $t$ defined above, we add the following constraints:

$$((t, a_i, q_i), (t, a_j, q_j), <) \in T$$

for all $1 \leq i < j \leq n$. Remember that $T$ was defined as a set of *all* constraint tuples corresponding to the *True* values of the constraint functions. We currently have no way to infer that if $(e_1, e_2, f) \in T$ and $(e_2, e_3, f) \in T$ then $(e_1, e_3, f) \in T$. Hence we must enumerate all the tuples for which $f$ is *True* even $f$ is a transitive function as in the case of "$<$" function. Once the model is extended with inferencing support, we can optimize the constraint representation by removing redundant constraint tuples whenever deducible.

In our example, the definition of the element **subsectn** (line 10 in Figure 8.2):

```
<!ELEMENT subsectn  -O (title, (body+))>
```

is translated to a new class **SUBSECTN** with two attributes **title** and **bodys** defined as following:

```
        create table SUBSECTN_table of new type SUBSECTN (
            title DOC not null,
            bodys BODY_list not null
);
```

The constraints are supported by creating a rule which for example imposes the order of the attributes when the **select** is executed on **SUBSECTN_table**:

```
        create rule select_SUBSECTN
        on select to SUBSECTN_table
        do instead
        select title, bodys from
        SUBSECTN_table ;
```

The constraints indicated by the aggregation connectors must be explicitly imposed for every operator that accesses a subset of the attributes of **SUB-SECTN_table** in the case of the Illustra system. For example, we have defined a function **GetDocText** for every class in the schema which returns the SGML text of an article instance. The order in which the different pieces are composed into the structured document is imposed by the aggregation connectors used in defining sequence model groups and by the original order of the instances corresponding to "+", "*" and "&" model groups.

We do not introduce a rule for the insert operation, because we want to allow the user to dynamically insert or edit subcomponents of the document's subsections at their convenience. However, if a whole document instance is inserted at a time, we assume that the SGML instance loader (instance parser) will check the constraints imposed by the sequence model groups by utilizing the DTD as grammar.

*Case 6: Alternative Aggregation Connector.* The SGML alternative aggregation connector "&" imposes no order between elements connected by it. In the formal constraint-based object model, an alternative aggregation model group $(a_1 \& a_2 \& \ldots \& a_n)$ will be translated into a class $t$, with attributes $(t, a_1, q_1)$, $(t, a_2, q_2)$, ..., $(t, a_n, q_n) \in E$ and $n!$ subclasses $t_i \in C$, $(t_i, t) \in G$ for $1 \leq i \leq n!$ [‡‡]. A subclass $t_i$ has no attributes and has the constraints corresponding to one of the permutations of the set $\{1, 2, \ldots, n\}$. More precisely, there exists a unique permutation $(i_1, i_2, \ldots, i_n)$ of the set $\{1, 2, \ldots, n\}$, so that for the subclass $t_i$, we have $((t_i, a_{i_j}, q_{i_j})(t_i, a_{i_k}, q_{i_k}), <) \in T$ for all $1 \leq j \leq k \leq n$. The $q_i$'s are the classes corresponding to the model groups of the $a_i$'s. While the class $t$ may not have any direct instances, its instance set will be the union of the instance sets of its subclasses $t_1, t_2, \ldots, t_{n!}$.

In our example, the model group (**bib&ack**) (line 2 in Figure 8.2) will be translated as following:

```
        create table BIB_ACK_table of new type BIB_ACK (
            bib DOC not null,
            ack DOC not null
);

        create table BIB_ACK_12_table of new type BIB_ACK_12 (
) under BIB_ACK_table;

        create rule select_BIB_ACK_12
        on select to BIB_ACK_12_table
        do instead
        select bib, ack from
        BIB_ACK_12_table ;

        create table BIB_ACK_21_table of new type BIB_ACK_21 (
) under BIB_ACK_table;
```

---

[‡‡] To optimize, we will only generate a subclass $t_i$ if it is actually being used — i.e., if it contains at least one document instance.

```
create rule select_BIB_ACK_21
on select to BIB_ACK_21_table
do instead
select  ack, bib from
BIB_ACK_21_table ;
```

The table **BIB_ACK_table** has no direct elements of its own. This can be expressed in Illustra by creating a rule for preventing the direct insert operation:

```
create rule insert_BIB_ACK
on insert to BIB_ACK_table
do instead nothing;
```

It is important to note here that while the SGML alternative aggregation connector "&" does not impose any order between elements, our DMS system still keeps track of the original order in which document instance fragments were loaded into the DMS database to assure that the documents will be displayed in the same manner as before having been entered into DMS. If this requirement of preserving the initial (though, of course, optional) document fragment ordering can be relaxed, then the SGML alternative connector "&" would simply be mapped to the one class $t$ without any constraints.

Like with the "," connector, the constraints defined for "&" must be explicitly imposed to any operator where the order is important (for example, **select** operator). However, for the & connector, the membership of an element instance in one of the subclasses will implicitly define the constraints. For example, two instances of **BIB_ACK_table** are equal if and only if they are both instances of the same subclass (**BIB_ACK_12** or **BIB_ACK_21**) and the values of the attributes **ack** and **bib** are equal. This semantics could be used to define an equality operator for two document instances.

The obvious advantage of the above approach is that our solution preserves document input and output equivalence. Another advantage of this representation is that we can query attributes based on their position. The query *"Find all the articles where the acknowledgement precedes the bibliography"* will be translated into a query which returns the articles for which the attribute **bib_ack** is an instance of the class **BIB_ACK_21** (the class with the constraint "**ack** is before **bib**").

*Case 7: Choice Connector.* The choice connector "|" provides an alternative for which element is to participate in the choice model group instance: $(a \mid b)$ indicates that either $a$ or $b$ is not null but not both. To map a choice model group $(a_1 \mid a_2 \mid \ldots \mid a_n)$ into our constraint-based model we create a new class $t \in C$ with no attributes and $n$ subclasses $t_1, t_2, \ldots, t_n \in C$ , $(t_i, t) \in G$ for all $1 \leq i \leq n$. A subclass $t_i$ has only one attribute $(t_i, a_i, q_i) \in E$ and an unary constraint $((t_i, a_i, q_i), NotNull) \in T$ for all $1 \leq i \leq n$ where $q_i$ is the class corresponding to $a_i$'s model group.

Next, we explain how we would implement this model group in Illustra using the following example. For the **body** element definition (line 11 in Figure 8.2) we define:

```
        create table BODY_table of new type BODY (
);

        create table BODY_figure_table of new type BODY_figure (
            figure FIGURE not null
) under BODY_table;

        create table BODY_paragr_table of new type BODY_paragr (
            paragr DOC not null
) under BODY_table;
```

The supertable **BODY_table** will have no direct instances of its own, but a query over it will return the rows of its two subtables, e.g., the elements of type **BODY**. This construction is one example that demonstrates how our approach allows us to easily specify queries ranging across diverse document types, without having to use special query constructs nor having to worry about which element types are contained in which particular DTD.

# 8.5   Schema Merging Using the Constraint Model

In the previous section, we have defined a general algorithm for mapping a DTD into a constraint-based schema. We now address the issue of how we can represent a collection of SGML documents $\{(DTD_i, file_i)\}_{1 \leq i \leq n}$ where every document has its own DTD. One solution, which appears to be commonly adopted by other researchers, is to map every DTD into a separate schema. This requires the underlying OODB system to support multiple classes with the same class name. Furthermore assuming, for example, that there are several DTDs defining the element **subsectn**, a query like *Q1: Find all the subsections of the documents containing the sentence "electrical engineering"* must be split into numerous subqueries over all the schemas that define the class **subsectn**.

An alternative solution, which we propose instead, is to have an integrated schema representing the collection of all DTDs. This process of DTD integration is similar to the problem of view or schema integration. Our strategy here is that the elements defined in different DTDs having the same name are mapped into the same class even when their definitions are slightly different (This is clearly a simplifying assumption that could be relaxed using several techniques typically applied for view schema integration. One, a table of synonyms could be utilized to identify additional classes that should be merged since they express the same semantics. Vice versa, human input could help to determine when same-named constructs represent distinct semantics and thus should not be merged).

Let's take for example two DTDs: one with the subsection as defined in Figure 8.2:

```
S1: <!ELEMENT subsectn  -O (title, (body+))>
```

and the other one having the **subsectn** defined as:

```
S2: <!ELEMENT subsectn  -O (title, (body*), paragr)>.
```

Our goal is now to define a merged schema representing both DTDs. We thus must address how the two disparate **subsectn** definitions can be mapped to an integrated class definition meeting all constraints. Our solution to this problem is to introduce one general **SUBSECTN** class capturing the common elements and constraints of the two definitions. In our example, this **SUBSECTN** class would have the attributes **title** and **bodys** and the constraint "**title** is before **bodys**".

In addition, we need two subclasses of the class **SUBSECTN**, one **SUB-SECTN_1** with no attributes but with the constraint $NotNull$ for the attribute **bodys** and the second **SUBSECTN_2** with one attribute **paragr** and the constraints "**title** is before **paragr**" and "**bodys** is before **paragr**" corresponding to the definitions S1 and S2, respectively. The two subclasses represent the difference between the two definitions of the **SUBSECTN** concept in the two DTDs. The subsections of the SGML document instances following the first DTD will become instances of the **SUBSECTN_1** class and the subsections of the SGML document instances following the second DTD will be instances of the **SUBSECTN_2** class. But, of course, all of them will be instances of the class **SUBSECTN**. The query $Q1$ from above will thus be able to directly access the extent (the set of the instances) of the integrated class **SUBSECTN**.

While above we described one example of our schema merging strategy, we now present the general algorithm for mapping a set of DTDs into the same schema. It consists of the following three steps:

1. Merge the set $\{DTD_i\}_{1 \leq i \leq n}$ into one $DTD_0$:

   (a) Every element $E$ defined in some subset $\{DTD_{i_k}\}_{1 \leq i_k \leq n}$ of $m$ DTDs with the definitions

   { <!ELEMENT    E     $def_j$ > } for $1 \leq j \leq m$

   is defined in $DTD_0$ as

   <!ELEMENT    E     $((def_1) \mid (def_2) \mid \ldots \mid (def_m))$ >.

   (b) Every element $E$ which is defined only in one DTD has the same definition in $DTD_0$.

2. Map $DTD_0$ into the constraint-based object schema (as defined in Section 8.4).

3. Optimize the resulting schema.

Note that schema merging can be naturally achieved within the confines of our constraint model. As indicated above (step 3 of the merging algorithm), optimization of the generated schema is desirable. However, a detailed treatment of optimization is beyond the scope of this paper. Instead, we enumerate a few optimizations to give the reader a flavor of the type of optimizations that we are considering. One type of possible optimization includes reducing the number of defined classes. For example, for the nested model groups with occurrence indicators "*" and "+", we would not need to define a new class, rather we would only add a new attribute. The choice connector model group can be translated into a superclass with all the common attributes and constraints of the subclasses corresponding to the elements of the group. The above definition of the **SUBSECTN** class would be the result of such an optimization.

# 8.6 Related Work

There is a growing body of literature on proposals for developing structured document management systems by integrating database (DBMS) and information retrieval (IR) technologies [35, 65, 238, 203]. For example, Estrella [67] is one such system, an object-oriented extension of the relational DBMS Oracle extended with a predefined 'text' class. No structural document modeling using SGML is considered.

Another example is the work by Böhm, Neuhold and others [35, 34], who study the integration of the OODBMS VODAK with the IR system INQUIRY. While their system is also designed to handle SGML documents, they take the approach of defining special-purpose meta-classes for realizing specific SGML constructs. We, on the other hand, have proposed a constraint-based object model that provides a generic mechanism for document modeling. Most importantly, our model is designed to support the integration of multiple DTDs into one integrated system – sharing class definitions among different DTDs whenever possible – rather than maintaining a distinct schema for each separate DTD.

Blake et al. [33] propose a mixed system - combining a relational schema with SGML support - to query a collection of SGML files. The SGML files are kept in the file system, while a fixed set of attributes about the documents are stored in the database. In their system, each DTD is stored separately in a file as well, and is reprocessed each time a document is accessed and/or queried. Our DMS instead provides for full document management support by decomposing each SGML document into its individual document fragments as encoded by SGML and then managing the SGML document as a complex document object.

[56] proposed a mapping strategy from SGML into the $O_2$ database. This work requires an extension of the underlying OODB system, namely, the support of new kinds of meta-data types such as paths and union types. We take a different approach to the problem by utilizing a constraint-based model. [56] assumes the mapping of each DTD to a separate schema, while our work introduces the notion of schema integration for integrated document modeling.

[65] propose a system that couples the IR module INQUERY with the func-

tional DBMS IRIS. Their DMBS schema is designed to model one particular document type only. The documents are stored highly redundantly, being stored both in the DBMS as well as in the IR system. The focus of their work is on object retrieval based on a probabilistic inference net model, while our paper address the DTD modeling and merging problem.

The constraint-based object model we present is an extension of the formal object model presented in [49] — namely, it is extended with general constraint specification. Similarly, the merging strategy we indicate in Section 8.5 is based on previous work on schema integration. Our main contribution here is again the focus on the integration of constraint-based schemata. As far as we know, the application of schema merging to complex document handling has not previously been studied.

## 8.7    Conclusions

It has been widely recognized that document management systems that effectively manage structured digital documents should integrate functionalities of both database and information retrieval technologies [35, 65, 238, 203, 67, 33]. Towards this end, we have developed a DMS system that can handle complex mixed queries incorporating both structural as well as content-based requests.

As a foundation of this system, we have introduced in this paper a formal constraint-based object model. Rather than requiring the extension of the underlying DBMS platform with special-purpose data types for handling particular SGML-constructs, as proposed previously, we have developed a general algorithm for mapping any SGML construct into our formal constraint-based object model.

To validate our approach, we implemented a working prototype of the DMS system using our constraint-based approach. In particular, in this paper, we describe a detailed example of applying our proposed algorithm for mapping the article DTD to our formal constrained-based object model, and then to our implementation on Illustra. This experiment demonstrates the ease of realizing the proposed constraint-based object model using current OODB technology. Most importantly, we show that our model easily supports the merging of arbitrary DTDs into one integrated schema. To the best of our knowledge, this is the first work studying the application of schema integration techniques in the context of the document management problem. Our approach allows for the specification of queries across diverse document types, if desired, without requiring special syntactic query constructs or query processing techniques. Our approach towards structured document handling offers genericity and simplicity, enabling any existing OODB system to be quickly extended with structured document management support.

In the future, we plan to investigate strategies for optimizing integrated constraint-based schemata generated by our algorithm. We also plan to experiment with our prototype to evaluate its effectiveness in document retrieval. This includes the integration of the DMS system into UMDL – the digital library system being developed at the University of Michigan – as collection database to allow for experimentation with structured versus unstructured document search techniques over the same document sets. Finally, the issue of query optimization of mixed queries on structured documents remains a largely unsolved problem.

**Acknowledgments.** The authors wish to acknowledge Wu-Chang Feng, Priya Raman, and other students at the University of Michigan for their efforts in helping to implement the *document management system* prototype on Illustra. We also thank John Price-Wilken for introducing us to SGML, and all other members of the UMDL team for providing us with a supporting environment for digital library research.

# Chapter 9

## Digital Software and Data Repositories for Support of Scientific Computing [*]

Ronald Boisvert[†], Shirley Browne[‡], Jack Dongarra[§], and Eric Grosse[¶]

## 9.1  Introduction

Most work on digital libraries has focused on storage, retrieval, and display of digital forms of documents. A number of on-line software repositories have been developed that provide access to software and software artifacts. These document and software efforts have been mostly independent, with little attention paid to integrating the two types of libraries and to developing common principles for organization and operation.

This chapter discusses the special characteristics and needs of software repositories and describes how these needs have been met by some existing repositories. These repositories include Netlib [81, 47], the National HPCC Software Exchange [48], and the GAMS Virtual Repository [37]. We describe new network mechanisms for remote program execution and for software change notification. We also describe some systems that provide on-line access to various types of scientific data. Finally, we outline a proposal for integrating software and data repositories into the world of digital document libraries, in particular CNRI's ARPA-sponsored Digital Library project [140, 134].

---

[*]The work described in this paper was sponsored by NASA under Grant No. NAG 5-2736, by the National Science Foundation under Grant No. ASC-9103853, and by AT&T Bell Laboratories.

[†]National Institute of Standards and Technology, Email: boisvert@cam.nist.gov

[‡]University of Tennessee, Email: browne@cs.utk.edu

[§]University of Tennessee and Oak Ridge National Laboratory, Email: dongarra@cs.utk.edu

[¶]AT&T Bell Laboratories, Email: ehg@research.att.com

# 9.2    Characteristics of Some Existing Software Repositories

## 9.2.1    Netlib

Netlib began services in 1985 to fill a need for cost-effective, timely distribution of high-quality mathematical software to the research community. Some of the libraries Netlib distributes – such as EISPACK, LINPACK, FFTPACK, and LAPACK – have long been used as important tools in scientific computation and are widely recognized to be of high quality. The Netlib collection also includes a large number of newer, less well-established codes. Most of the software is written in Fortran, but programs in other languages, such as C and C++, are also available.

Netlib sends, by return electronic mail, requested routines together with subsidiary routines and any requested documents or test programs supplied by the software authors [81]. Xnetlib, an interactive tool for software and document distribution [80], use an X Window interface and TCP/IP connections to allow users to receive replies to their requests within a matter of seconds. The interface provides a number of modes and searching mechanisms to facilitate searching through a large distributed collection of software and documents. World Wide Web browsers such as Mosaic and Netscape can also be used to access Netlib via HTTP and FTP ‖.

Although the original focus of the Netlib repository was on mathematical software, the collection has grown to include other software (such as networking tools and tools for visualization of multiprocessor performance data), technical reports and papers, a Whitepages Database, benchmark performance data, and information about conferences and meetings. The number of Netlib servers has grown from the original two, at Oak Ridge National Laboratory (initially at Argonne National Laboratory) and Bell Labs, to servers in Norway, the United Kingdom, Germany, Australia, Japan, and Taiwan. A mirroring mechanism keeps the repository contents at the different sites consistent on a daily basis, as well as automatically picking up new material from distributed editorial sites [113].

Netlib differs from other publicly available software distribution systems, such as Archie, in that the collection is moderated by an editorial board and the software contained in it is widely recognized to be of high quality. However, the Netlib repository is not intended to replace commercial software. Commercial software companies provide value-added services in the form of support. Although the Netlib collection is moderated, its software comes with no guarantee of reliability or support. Rather, the lack of bureaucratic, legal, and financial impediments encourages researchers to submit their codes by ensuring that their work will be made available quickly to a wide audience.

---

‖Netlib is accessible from a **WWW** browser at `http://www.netlib.org/`

## 9.2.2   The National HPCC Software Exchange (NHSE)

The National HPCC Software Exchange (NHSE) is an Internet-accessible resource that will facilitate the exchange of software and information among research and computational scientists involved with High Performance Computing and Communications (HPCC) [48]. The purpose of the NHSE is to promote the development of discipline-oriented software and document repositories and of contributions to and use of such repositories by Grand Challenge teams, as well as by other members of the high performance computing community. The target audiences for the NHSE include HPCC application and computer scientists, users of government supercomputer centers, and potential industrial users. A prototype of the NHSE is accessible from a WWW browser at http://www.netlib.org/nse/.

The scope of the NHSE is software and software-related artifacts produced by and for the HPCC Program. Software-related artifacts include algorithms, specifications, designs, and software documentation. The following types of software are to be made available:

- Systems software and software tools. This category includes parallel processing tools such as parallel compilers, message-passing communication subsystems, and parallel monitors and debuggers.

- Data analysis and visualization tools.

- Basic building blocks for accomplishing common computational and communication tasks. These building blocks will be of high quality and transportable across platforms. Building blocks are meant to be used by Grand Challenge teams and other researchers in implementing programs to solve computational problems. Use of high-quality transportable components will speed implementation, as well as increase the reliability of computed results.

- Research codes that have been developed to solve difficult computational problems. Many of these codes will have been developed to solve specific problems and thus will not be reusable as is. Rather, they will serve as proofs of concept and as models for developing general-purpose reusable software for solving broader classes of problems. The development of this reusable software is expected to be undertaken by commercial companies, rather than by academic researchers.

A catalog of the software currently available from the NHSE is accessible at http://www.netlib.org/nse/sw_survey.html.

Although the different disciplines will maintain their own software repositories, users should not need to access each of these repositories separately. Rather, the NHSE will provide a uniform interface to a virtual HPCC software repository which will be built on top of the distributed set of discipline-oriented repositories. The interface will assist the user in locating relevant resources and in retrieving these resources. A combined browse/search interface will allow the user to explore the various HPCC areas and become familiar with the available resources. A longer term goal of the NHSE is to provide users with domain-specific expert help in locating and understanding relevant resources.

## 9.2.3    GAMS Virtual Repository

The Guide to Available Mathematical Software (GAMS) project of the National Institute of Standards and Technology (NIST) studies techniques to provide scientists and engineers with improved access to reusable computer software components available to them for use in mathematical modeling and statistical analysis. One of the products of this work is the GAMS system, an on-line cross-index and virtual repository of mathematical software [37]. GAMS performs the function of an interrepository and interpackage cross-index, collecting and maintaining data about software available from external repositories and presenting it as a homogeneous whole. It also provides the functions of a repository itself (i.e., retrieval). However, instead of maintaining the cataloged software itself, it provides transparent on-demand access to repositories managed by others.

GAMS currently contains information on more than 9800 problem-solving software modules from about 85 packages found in four physically distributed software repositories (three maintained at NIST and Netlib). In addition to most of the software in the Netlib collection, GAMS cross indexes individual components in large multipurpose libraries such as IMSL, NAG, PORT, STARPAC and SLATEC, as well as capabilities of statistical analysis systems such as DATA-PLOT and SAS. Both public-domain and commercial software is cataloged, and although source code of proprietary software products are not available through GAMS, related items such as documentation and example programs often are.

All problem-solving software modules in GAMS are assigned one or more problem classifications from a 736-node tree-structured taxonomy of mathematical and statistical problems developed as part of the project [38]. Users can browse through modules in any given problem class. To find an appropriate class, one can utilize the taxonomy as a decision tree, or enter keywords which are then mapped to problem classes. Search filters can be declared which allow users to specify preferences such computing precision or programming language. In addition, users can browse through all modules in a given package, or all modules with a given name. Each module's abstract lists the retrievable objects associated with the module, such as documentation, examples, test programs, source code and dependencies. (More than 32,000 such objects can be retrieved.)

At the core of the GAMS system is a relational database of information about available software. This database is maintained at NIST, which provides a classification service for the repositories it indexes. The GAMS network server provides this information to network clients using a specialized protocol over TCP/IP connections. In addition, a gateway to the World Wide Web has been developed. **.

---

**Accessible at http://gams.nist.gov/

# 9.3   Indexing and Searching of Software Objects

Cataloguing information for software objects serves two purposes – 1) to supply material from which a searchable index may be constructed, and 2) to supply information needed by the user to select/reject search hits and to obtain and use selected software. The field names and definitions used for cataloging in a particular library are described in the *data model* used by that library. For example, for document libraries, the CSTR project [134] has adopted RFC1357 [58] as its data model.

## 9.3.1   Data Models

Data models used for document digital libraries are not in general suitable for use by software repositories. Although some fields are useful in both settings – e.g., author,title, abstract – software cataloging requires a number of additional fields. A field that appears in most major catalogs is a **requirements** field that lists the hardware, operating system, and other software needed to use the catalogued item. Another important field in the case of public domain software repositories such as Netlib, where software is author-supported, is a **contact** field giving an electronic mail address to which questions and bug reports may be sent. Still another field used by many software repositories is a certification field that tells at what level the software has been certified and possibly includes pointers to certification artifacts such as completed checklists and testing results.

The Reuse Library Interoperability Group (RIG) has developed and approved the Basic Interoperability Data Model (BIDM) as a standard data model for software repository interoperability, and the BIDM has been submitted for balloting as an IEEE standard [5]. The BIDM provides a good starting point upon which to build. However, because of considerable variation in the purpose, contents, and application domains of different software repositories, no single data model will be suitable for all, and important cataloging information may be lost in exporting to the BIDM. An example where such loss occurs is the certification field. This field was not included in the BIDM because of the wide variety of certification and evaluation methods in use at different repositories. The RIG also encountered difficulty in developing controlled vocabulary lists, because again different sets of terms were appropriate for different repositories. The approach now being taken by the RIG is to define a standard for an Extensible Interoperability Data Model (EIDM), which will be a meta-model a repository can use to describe the data model it is using. For example, using the EIDM, a repository will be able to define its certification methods and the meanings of different certification levels. As a member of the RIG, Netlib is participating in development and promotion of standard data models for software repositories.

## 9.3.2   Software Classification

A number of studies have shown that proper classification of software objects contributes to effective location of the objects by potential reusers [61, 185, 102].

Classification is carried out by assigning codes and/or keywords from a classification scheme or thesaurus. Classifications and thesauri developed for indexing documents, such as the INSPEC classification [3] and INSPEC thesaurus [4], are inadequate for indexing software objects. Firstly, these tools cover a broad range of topics and cover software-related topics only superficially. Thus, they do not allow the user to discriminate finely enough among the available software objects. Secondly, effective classification of software objects requires that the function of the object be indexed [44]. Because documents are not used as software is, terms related to function have not generally been included in thesauri developed for document indexing.

A classification scheme that has been developed specifically for use in indexing mathematical software is the GAMS hierarchy [38]. The GAMS scheme has been widely adopted by network-accessible repositories such as Netlib and by commercial mathematical software libraries such as NAG and IMSL. A successor to GAMS is currently under development. The new scheme will refine areas needing better discrimination and will add new categories to encompass recent developments in numerical algorithms. The new scheme will also be reorganized so as to be less cumbersome.

An HPCC software thesaurus is under development as part of the NHSE. This thesaurus uses GAMS categories for mathematical software but defines new terms for other areas of high performance computing. Some of these terms are drawn from an existing HPCC glossary [119] and from a book that gives an overview of parallel computing [101]. Terms from the INSPEC thesaurus [4] are being used for application areas. The thesaurus has a faceted structure with facets for application area, problem area, function, algorithm, and target architecture. The thesaurus will be made available on-line in hypertext form to assist with searching the NHSE, similar to [182]. Hypertext links from terms to scope and definition notes will also be provided.

## 9.3.3   Search Interfaces

Netlib currently provides a search interface [tt] that allows the user to do field-specific keyword searching. For example, the user may search by author, filename, abstract keywords, or GAMS classification. Search results are returned as a hypertext list of catalog records from which the user may select files to view or download.

Searching by keywords or classification codes often returns a large number of search hits, leaving the user to sort through them. Further discrimination often cannot be provided by an overall classification scheme, but requires use of a domain specific knowledge base. Such knowledge bases have been constructed for specialized domains, including differential equations [147, 135, 8] and approximation [112]. We are experimenting with providing on-line hypertext interfaces to such knowledge bases. For example, we have provided a hypertext version of

---

[tt] Accessible from a WWW browser at `http://www.netlib.org/nse/netlib_query.html`

a decision tree for approximation algorithms ‡‡.

We have also developed a prototype expert help system to assist users in selecting software within specific domains [36, 37]. An advisory system for a given problem class helps the user discriminate between problem-solving software modules for that class. For a given problem class, a set of features are partitioned into a small set of feature classes, and information is encoded about how each feature applies to each software module. Prototype user interfaces have been developed that allow the user to interact with choice widgets for the various features. The system provides more specific and effective help in selecting software than a domain-independent search interface.

# 9.4   Retrieval of Software Objects

Once a user has located relevant software objects, he needs to be able to make use of them. Modes of use include the following:

1. Downloading, configuring, compiling, and executing a complete program or package.

2. Downloading routines and combining them with a user-supplied main program and other user-supplied routines before compiling and executing.

3. Using retrieved source code as a starting point for developing software with similar functionality.

4. Downloading templates or archetypes that provide a framework for writing actual code.

5. Using a remote execution service – i.e., shipping input data over a network to a remote execution server and then retrieving the resulting output data.

## 9.4.1   Downloading Files

A user may download files from Netlib by sending an email request or by clicking on the filenames from Xnetlib, GAMS, or WWW interfaces. Netlib files are organized into directories. Some directories contain a single package, such as the LAPACK directory, while others contain programs for a particular domain, such as the OPTimization directory. Each directory contains an index file containing catalog records for the files in the directory. Most directories also contain a readme file giving an overview of the directory. Some directories have subdirectories, for example for the different Fortran precisions available and for test and example programs. A user may initially do a keyword search to locate relevant directories and then browse the index files for those directories to locate relevant files which may then be downloaded.

When downloading a routine from Netlib, a user may make use of a dependency-checking mechanism that allows retrieval of the entire dependency tree for that

---

‡‡Accessible from a WWW browser at `http://www.netlib.org/a/catalog.html`

routine. The user may specify that a subtree be omitted, however, if those routines have been retrieved previously. There is also an automatic tar facility that builds and returns a tar file of any Netlib directory or subdirectory upon user request. Binary executable files for several Netlib packages are also available – for example, for the Xnetlib and HeNCE packages.

Users may download files from the NHSE via a WWW browser. The NHSE provides a searchable catalog of HPCC software, as well as a browseable listing by category (accessible at `http://www.netlib.org/nse/sw_survey.html`). Each entry in the catalog includes either a URL that may be clicked on to retrieve the software or more information about it. Clicking on these URLs connects the user to the software provider's home site – i.e., the NHSE provides an interface to a virtual distributed repository consisting of a large number of independently maintained physical repositories. In the near future, the NHSE will switch from using URLs to using location independent names [46]. Use of location independent names will allow files to be moved without requires references to them to be changed and will permit transparent mirroring and reliable cacheing.

Care should always be exercised when downloading and using files obtained over a network, especially tar files and executables. Although Netlib is regarded by most users as a trusted source, it would be possible for someone to impersonate a Netlib server and make dangerous tar or executable files available, purportedly from Netlib. Because source code is unlikely to be examined closely by the user, deliberately introduced bugs or other malicious modifications might also slip past in source code form. In the near future, both Netlib and the NHSE will use public key cryptography to allow users to authenticate the source of downloaded files.

## 9.4.2   Templates and Archetypes

A template is a description of a general algorithm rather than the executable object code or the source code more commonly found in a conventional software library [18]. Templates may be customized by the user – for example, they can be configured for the specific data structure of a problem or for the specific computing system on which the problem is to run. Templates are written in a language-independent Algol-like structure, which is readily translatable into a target language such as Fortran or C. A collection of templates focusing on iterative methods for solving large sparse linear systems is available from Netlib (accessible at `http://www.netlib.org/linalg/html_templates/report.html`). For each template, the following is provided: a mathematical description of the flow of the iteration; discussion of convergence and stopping criteria; suggestions for applying a method to special matrix types (e.g., banded systems); advice for tuning (for example, which preconditioners are applicable and which are not); tips on parallel implementations; and hints as to when to use a method, and why.

A program archetype is (a) a program design strategy appropriate for a restricted class of problems, and (b) a collection of program designs with (c) implementations of exemplar problems in one or more programming languages and optimized for a collection of target machines. The program design strategy includes archetype-specific information about methods of deriving a program from a specification, methods of parallelizing sequential programs, the program structure, methods of reasoning about correctness and performance, empirical data on performance measurements and tuning for different kinds of machines, and suggestions for test suites. A project at Caltech is exploring the question of whether a library of parallel program archetypes be used to reduce the effort required to produce correct efficient programs (Note: more information is available at `http://www.etext.caltech.edu/Papers2/ArchetypeOverview/ArchPaper.html`).

### 9.4.3 Remote Execution

If a user needs to run a program only infrequently, and if compiling and installing the program involves considerable overhead, the user may prefer to take advantage of a remote execution service if one is available. Netlib has experimented with making remote execution of the Fortran-to-C converter (f2c) and Fortran checking (ftnchek) programs available. We configured the Mosaic WWW browser to invoke the Tcl language interpreter to execute downloaded files of type application/x-safe-tcl. We then made downloaded user interfaces for the f2c and ftnchek programs available on a Netlib server. Users could then download the interface modules and use them to interact with the remote execution services. The user interfaces allowed the user to select files to be transferred for processing and to set various options. Our work on remote execution is experimental at this stage because a safe client execution environment for Tcl has not yet been rigorously defined, although researchers at Sun Microsystems are working on it.

Software for using ORNL's GRAIL and GENQUEST remote execution services for doing DNA sequence analysis, gene assembly, and sequence comparison is available through the NHSE (more information is available at `http://avalon.epm.ornl.gov/`). These services cannot be used from a WWW browser, but require downloading specialized X-Windows client software. In the future, the NHSE plans to support use of such services from a WWW browser by means of a safe execution environment for downloadable Safe-Tcl code, so that the client module may be executed directly from the browser.

Another possibility for remote execution is to allow users to upload executable code to a Netlib server and run it there. For example, the user might want to send an agent that would sift through and summarize computer performance data residing on Netlib. A search service such as Harvest might send an agent that would summarize the contents of Netlib and stream the summary back to an indexing engine. We are investigating the provision of this kind of user-directed remote execution using the Plan 9 operating system developed at AT&T Bell Labs.

### 9.4.4 Change Notification

Some digital document libraries have a notification service that informs subscribers of newly available documents. The notification service for a software repository is somewhat different, because it informs subscribers of changes and bug fixes to the software as much or more than of additions of new software. In the early days of the Netlib repository, when all access was by email and the traffic was mostly from professional numerical analysts, we relied on log files to send out notification of important bug fixes to everyone who had retrieved affected files. Now, because access is more anonymous and a wider spectrum of users are involved, the old scheme has been replaced by explicit subscription. People may indicate interest in specific Netlib directories, using *subscribe* and *unsubscribe* commands. Automatic notification is sent, on a daily basis, when files in the directory are changed. The subscriber lists also give the authors and editors a way to judge what community is particularly interested in a given Netlib collection.

## 9.5    Access to Scientific Data

The Netlib Performance Database provides an on-line catalog of public-domain computer benchmarks such as the Linpack Benchmark, Perfect Benchmarks, and the Genesis Benchmarks [30]. A benchmark code is a program designed to be run on an architecture so as to produce a relative measure of its execution. Benchmarks tend to evolve from individual applications that do not necessarily stress all features of a given architecture. Thus, benchmark numbers do not imply general machine performance but instead describe the performance of a machine on an algorithm or application class.

Although benchmarking has become very popular because of the diversity and competition in the computer hardware business, there was, previous to development of our database, no central repository for benchmark data. The WWW interface to our Performance Database (accessible at
`http://performance.netlib.org/performance/html/PDStop` allows the user to

- view complete benchmark reports that display sorted data from various published benchmark reports,

- browse the performance data tree by selecting the benchmark and machines about which information is desired,

- search the performance database

There are also pointers to benchmark papers and other benchmark and performance-related literature.

Various archives of scientific data are accessible from the NHSE – for example, NASA's Planetary Data System (accessible at `http://stardust.jpl.nasa.gov/pds_home.html`) and Astrophysics Data System (accessible at `http://adswww.harvard.edu`), NIST's Atomic Spectroscopic Database (accessible at `http://aeldata.phy.nist.gov/nist_beta.html`), and NOAA's Environmental Data Centers (accessible at `http://www.esdim.noaa.gov/`). There have been attempts at defining a metadata reference model for scientific data [43, 124]. Metadata standards for specific fields have also been defined [79, 123]. In general, however, there is as yet no uniform cataloging method or search interface for scientific databases, nor a standard way of describing the contents and services offered. Thus, the user has no way of systematically discovering relevant databases and must learn a different interface for each one.

# 9.6 Integration with Document Digital Libraries

The Corporation for National Research Initiatives (CNRI) is working with five major universities (CMU, Cornell, UC-Berkeley, Stanford, and MIT) on an ARPA-sponsored project to develop concepts for digital libraries. As part of this project, each university is placing its Computer Science Technical Reports on-line and providing access to the distributed CSTR collection. Technologies developed for the CSTR project include the Dienst distributed search system [70] and a Handle Management Service for assigning, maintaining, and using unique identifiers for digital library objects [84].

The basic architecture being developed by CNRI for distributed digital libraries includes the following concepts [134]:

- A *digital object* which consists of one or more sequences of bits, including data plus a unique identifier known as a *handle* (the binding between the handle and the sequence of bits may change over time).

- *Naming authorities* who are responsible for assigning unique identifiers within their portions of the handle namespace.

- *Repositories* from which digital objects are available.

- *Information Reference (IR) servers* that provide reference information about collections of digital objects.

The CNRI work is closely related to the IETF Uniform Resource Identifier (URI) Working Group's work on Uniform Resource Names (URNs) [216] and Uniform Resource Citations [68]. CNRI's handle is the equivalent of IETF's URN, and CNRI's IR server serves a similar function to IETF's URC server.

The Netlib and NHSE Development Group has been engaged in a parallel effort to implement a location-independent naming architecture [46]. We provide for two types of location-independent names:

- a Uniform Resource Name (URN), for which the contents it refers to may change – e.g., the "current version of LAPACK".

- a Location Independent File Name (LIFN), for which the binding between the name and the byte contents of the file it refers to is fixed, once assigned. This type of name is needed for unambiguous references when attaching critical reviews or reporting scientific results obtained using a particular version of a piece of software. LIFNs also permit reliable and efficient cacheing and mirroring of files.

At any given time, a URN is associated with exactly one LIFN. By looking up the LIFN associated with a URN and then retrieving the file corresponding to that LIFN, the user is assured of retrieving the most recent copy, even if some mirrored copies are out-of-date. Thus, we obtain consistency of replicated copies without the overhead of a replica control protocol.

We are also developing a URC server that provides support for the following:

- Provision by the publisher of attribute-value pairs for a given URN in the form of cryptographically signed assertions.

- Retrieval and authentication of assertions by users.

- Specification of the data model used for a particular URN.

- Choice of encryption algorithm, including none.

We propose to integrate our software repository naming architecture with CNRI's digital library architecture in the following manner:

1. In cooperation with CNRI and the IETF, we will develop a common framework for resolving location-independent names, including handles, URNs, and LIFNs.

2. Our URC server will be an implementation of CNRI's IR server that may be used for cataloging software and data archives, as well as general Web resources.

3. Similar to the Dienst protocol for document repositories, we will develop service specifications and retrieval protocols appropriate for software and data repositories. In addition, similar to the Digital Library Document Architecture that defines requirements for digital document structure [224], we will define requirements for software and data archive structures.

# Chapter 10

## Semantic Hypermedia Retrieval in Digital Libraries

Stephan Wiesener*, Wolfgang Kowarschick†, Pavel Vogel‡ and Rudolf Bayer§

## 10.1   Introduction

Due to the great progress in networking and multimedia database technologies, digital libraries have evolved from low-bandwidth catalogs to extensive document sources [98]. Today they do not only offer mere attributes which describe author, title, publisher, etc., but also allow retrieval of complete documents which then immediately become available on the users desktop [19, 230]. The pure access hurdle seems to be taken; current digital libraries profit from efficient data searching and navigation procedures.

In the recent years two mainstream approaches to electronic document access have been established: declarative retrieval (e.g., SQL-like query languages) and associative hypermedia retrieval. Both have succeeded in practice, both have characteristic pros and cons.

Declarative query systems expect queries as input (e.g., SQL queries, fulltext queries, reference texts, etc.) which are then used to identify the relevance of documents. The query evaluation process may be fuzzy and if so, it should offer ranking. Context relevant connections to other documents are not modeled by purely declarative library systems, and thus related documents are only accessible if the user knows how to formulate the appropriate queries. On the other hand, declarative systems have the advantage that the user does not need to know where documents are located in the document space.

The hypermedia systems community advocates a very different point of view. Pure hypermedia systems usually offer structured multimedia documents which are connected to others by means of links. Documents and links together form

---

*Bayerisches Forschungszentrum für Wissensbasierte Systeme (FORWISS), Orleansstr. 34, D-81667 München, Germany, Email: wiesener@forwiss.tu-muenchen.de

†Technische Universität München, Fakultät für Informatik, D-80290 München, Germany, Email: kowarschick@informatik.tu-muenchen.de

‡Technische Universität München, Fakultät für Informatik, D-80290 München, Germany, Email: vogel@informatik.tu-muenchen.de

§Technische Universität München, Fakultät für Informatik, D-80290 München, Germany, Email: bayer@informatik.tu-muenchen.de

a network—a hypermedia through which the user has to navigate in order to obtain the information he needs. In contrast to declarative systems, document parts in hypermedia systems are related to others by means of links. That means that hypermedia libraries besides consisting purely of documents also manage relationships which together form a knowledge base.

Although hypermedia information access is efficient within limited document sets, it suffers from the well-known lost-in-hyperspace syndrome when the amount of links and documents grows. Moreover, if links are static, each interconnection is restricted to a fixed context the authors assumed to be useful at link creation time. Unfortunately, many retrieval situations will differ from this special context, and thus hard coded links lose much of their relevance in practice. What is even worse, every time a document is retrieved *all* links are presented to the user. This can cause confusion amongst users and thus entail expensive navigation into many non-relevant documents. Last, but not least, in case of large and dynamic libraries the maintenance of links is very expensive or even not practicable. Think, e.g., of a scientific library containing hundreds of thousands of documents and expanding daily.

Document retrieval can be made **more effective** by means of problem and context sensitive access methods. A first step is to combine both the access techniques described above [138]. This allows both a goal-directed discovery of documents by declarative querying as well as browsing through related information along links. This, however, does not solve the problems caused by static links. These problems can be overcome by replacing static by computed links, which are deduced from a semantic knowledge base. Each such knowledge base does not contain ordinary documents but meta-knowledge of a limited domain. It is structured into semantic nodes representing domain-specific topics. These nodes are connected by labeled edges. With such knowledge bases being made up of nodes and edges they can be regarded as semantic nets.

Semantic nodes include query patterns whose execution yields documents that are concerned with the current topic. Semantic links describe relations between different topics. Thus a semantic knowledge base implicitly defines links between documents that are concerned with related topics (see Figure 10.1).

Documents exist entirely independently of semantic knowledge. They are inserted, deleted, or changed without further efforts of maintaining links. Users choose document servers (which contain documents but no semantic knowledge) separately from the semantic knowledge servers but use them together as one intelligent digital library. Thus, one and the same document may be accessed in many different domains and contexts, each of them offering another variety of links.

The rest of this chapter is organized as follows: Section 10.2 briefly introduces the OMNIS digital library system and gives an overview of its operation in practice. In section 10.3 we describe our efforts in developing OMNIS into a knowledge-based hypermedia system as described above. A summary and ideas concerning further extensions can be found in section 10.4.

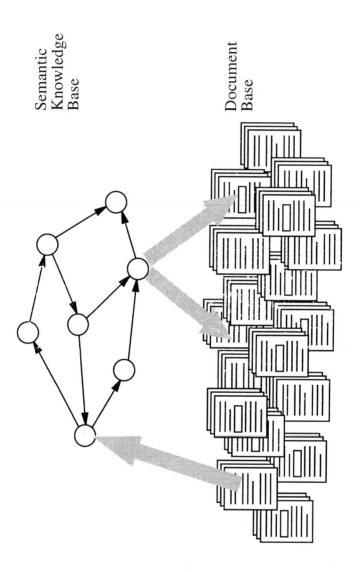

**Figure 10.1** Semantic net connecting documents

## 10.2    The OMNIS Digital Library System

OMNIS is a declarative information retrieval system for the administration of documents in libraries and office organizations [19]. It has been developed by the Computer Science Department of the Technische Universität München and by FORWISS (Bavarian Research Center for Knowledge-Based Systems). Supported by Myriad, a fulltext database system [223], OMNIS runs in a client-server environment and offers a number of economic and functional advantages by consequent utilization of latest achievements in data technology.

The start of the OMNIS project was motivated by the well-known problems in the area of scientific literature. Nearly every research team is confronted with a huge amount of scientific documents. Only a small part of these is subject to the individual cataloging and indexing procedure in scientific libraries and thus open to (mostly manual) literature search. Beyond these "official" documents distributed by commercial channels, a scientist usually works with a lot of "gray literature" like internal reports, preliminary copies, personal notes, etc. Because of high cataloging costs this very interesting class of scientific documents normally is excluded from traditional library catalogs and literature retrieval instruments. Thus, a literature information system had to be developed which combines both cheap document indexing and efficient document retrieval by a comfortable selection mechanism.

OMNIS offers a semi-automatic archiving and indexing procedure, very selective document access through fulltext and relational querying, low response times and a simple user interface. The OMNIS solution became feasible through latest technological innovations like multimedia, scanning, OCR (Optical Character Recognition), fulltext database systems and client-server architecture. The whole OMNIS system is network-based (TCP/IP) and therefore allows worldwide access to documents. Though specially developed for library needs, OMNIS is suitable for many other fields of application where large numbers of documents have to be efficiently stored and made accessible.

### 10.2.1    OMNIS System Architecture

OMNIS has primarily been developed as an administration tool for scientific libraries and other collections of scientific documents in paper form and consists of three components: *archiving*, *searching* and *lending*. The architecture reflects the three classes of systems users: users searching for literature, people archiving documents, and professional library personnel responsible for library management.

#### OMNIS Documents

The basis of the whole OMNIS philosophy is the "document," an atomic unit for archiving and retrieval. Each OMNIS document refers to a paper or electronic document (e.g., book, journal, or even a single conference contribution).

The original information is stored in three different kinds of attributes (see Figure 10.2):

- **Structure Fields** describe the document in a relational way. Fields like *author*, *title*, *document type* (e.g., journal or book), *year*, *publisher*, etc. provide structured information as known from traditional literature retrieval systems. They are the basis of relational queries.

- **Fulltext** contains a good deal of the document's text. It is the basis for fulltext queries. Usually it is generated from image data by OCR.

- **Image Data** provides the document content in its original form. Bitmap image data as well as PostScript data are supported. Image data is displayed to the user but is not subject of queries. Each single OMNIS document may contain an arbitrary number of images. Image data is stored in BLOBs (Binary Large OBjects) of the Myriad database system.

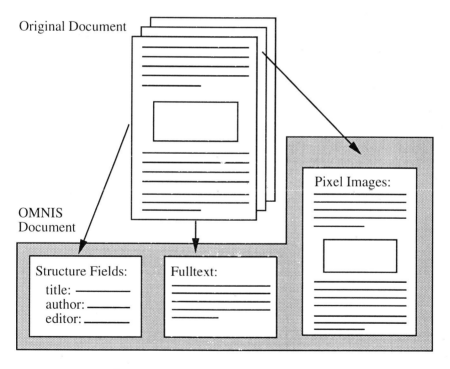

**Figure 10.2** OMNIS document structure

Although the electronic storage of paper documents was the primary purpose of OMNIS, it is also suitable and can be utilized for storing electronic documents as, e.g., man pages, news, and e-mail. In this case the lending module is, of course, superfluous.

## Functional Distribution

OMNIS/Myriad has been designed as a distributed system with client-server architecture [20]. Each server may manage multiple independent OMNIS document databases. A client system offers the OMNIS retrieval and/or archiving functions to the users (recently a WWW retrieval interface was completed [57]). In contrast to some other popular information systems, the process of archiving documents runs fully concurrently without blocking worldwide retrieval. Moreover, OMNIS is capable of handling huge amounts of documents stored in optical storage media jukeboxes without significant performance loss.

## 10.2.2   Archiving and Retrieval

Due to the strict separation of the user groups "archivists" and "retrievers," we have developed two separate tools for archiving and retrieval. This is typical of an information system where few people create documents but many read them.

### Document Archiving

To reduce costs of document indexing, the OMNIS archiving procedure is semiautomatic. In order to disclose the contents of a document to electronic search characteristic phrases and expressions are needed. Instead of using highly trained people like librarians to extract these characteristics by hand, OMNIS utilizes the fact that they are elements of the document text itself or its components, e.g., abstract, table of contents, summary. In case of paper documents the cheapest way to transfer this data into a computer is to scan it in and transform the text from picture format to ASCII characters by OCR programs. Most of the structure fields can be easily supplied from the text by the Cut-&-Paste facility of the window system if desirable. Structure fields, text, and picture data constitute an OMNIS document. PostScript data may be added as well, if it is available. This enables the retrieving user to print out documents in their original quality.

Editorial publications like journals and conference proceedings can be put into archives either on the level of volume or on the level of single contributions. In the former case tables of contents are stored as fulltext, in the latter case either abstracts or even complete contents are archived. Whether the more precise and more expensive level of individual contributions is affordable is an economic question. Full-automatic archiving tools for several electronic data/document interchange formats like BibTeX, PostScript, MAB (Machine Readable Exchange Format for Libraries), EMail and News are in operation.

### Document Retrieval

In order to meet the demands of a broad range of sometimes unexperienced users, the query process must be intuitive. Documents are retrieved by structure and/or fulltext queries. The fulltext query language does not only permit the search for single words, but also for phrases. Phrases may be seen as text patterns enabling the use of wildcards. Moreover, documents can be accessed via relational structure fields. Both, fulltext and relational search can be combined in one query. For instance, the query

```
database ... optimi% & (?year > 1993 | ?author = Ullmann%)
```

would deliver all documents which were published after 1993 or by an author like "`Ullmann, J.`" and contain the word "`database`" at most three words before a word that starts with "`optimi`" (e.g., "`optimization`"). Several user interfaces (VT 100 without picture data, X/Motif, WWW) offer comfortable query masks.

For all query hits, a list of short information (e.g., author and title) is displayed. The user may now decide which hits seem to be interesting enough for further detailed examination. Every document may be opened independently. Structure fields, fulltext and image data are displayed. If available, PostScript can be used additionally to display or print the document.

### 10.2.3  OMNIS in Practice

The OMNIS digital library system is in intensive use at several universities in Germany. At the Technische Universität München more than 600,000 documents from many sources are made available to students and scientific employees. In the DFG-sponsored project "VD17" more than 250,000 catalog entries of historical prints of the 17th century with about 1 million pixel images will be stored in a central OMNIS database using optical storage media jukeboxes. In the DFN-project "Regionales Testbett" (Regional Testbed) OMNIS is in operation as a multimedia pilot application for a regional high-speed network.

## 10.3   Towards Knowledge-based Navigation in Digital Libraries

Though the OMNIS digital library system has succeeded in practice with several thousand users, we have received many suggestions on how to improve OMNIS. A common criticism is that OMNIS document contents are completely unstructured (flat fulltext and picture data) and relationships between documents are not handled by the system, even if evident (e.g., links from a document's bibliography to related works). This, however, is a result of the OMNIS history. It initially was formed by a need for cheapest archiving and indexing procedures for paper-based literature. Until today it is almost impossible to automatically extract all retrieval relevant document features from scanned pixel images.

Fortunately, the latest efforts in electronic document interchange formats and standards (e.g., SGML [109, 45], HTML [122], ODA [15], LaTeX/BibTeX) has made this reconstruction process of document features much easier. By using modern editing tools authors add a lot of meta-knowledge (e.g., structure, classification and correlation knowledge) to their work without much expenditure.

This knowledge traditionally disappears during the transformation process to a paper-based issue.

In hypertext systems the authors express meta-knowledge by linking document parts. As described in section 10.1, this kind of knowledge is not very global, because it only reflects relationships the author knew about and was familiar with at link creation time. A writer therefore often cannot conceive what relationships his document has or will have with others. On the other hand, there are persons who have an extensive knowledge of a special area, i.e., of important topics and how these are related, even if they never have published a document. But even so not one of these experts would ever be able to connect all existing documents with useful links, because the publishing machinery moves much too fast. Summing up, it may be said that in practice it is impossible to maintain a hard coded link space completely and consistently.

A solution to this problem can be achieved by the introduction of three distinct, partly independent knowledge layers, which are characterized by different levels of abstraction and—what is most important—different levels of variability:

- **Document Content and Document Structure** contain very detailed information, which traditionally is published in paper form. The existing OMNIS supports fulltext retrieval (multimedia/multimodal retrieval methods should also be supported; these, however, are not subject of this chapter). For a more precise and realistic retrieval as it must be, the document structure should also be taken into consideration weighted differently whether you hit upon the document's title or abstract than on a subsection of the text.

  Users can have direct access to documents by querying the contents without any navigation. The content knowledge is very dynamic as a (digital) library typically is under steady expansion.

- **Document Attributes** contain meta-knowledge from the document's author's point of view. This may be classification (e.g., degree of difficulty or media type), additional keywords, etc. Attributes are displayed to the user on demand only. They exist optionally and may also be the result of an automatic document content analysis. In OMNIS attributes are realized by means of structure fields.

  Users may have direct access to documents by querying these attributes. Attributes are typically used in queries combined with content search. Attributes play an important role in the process of knowledge-based linking. As to the content knowledge, the attribute knowledge changes with every newly inserted/deleted document.

- **Semantic Knowledge** is separated from documents and exists independently. It may even be stored at a remote location and maintained by different persons. Semantic knowledge represents rather common coherences and interdependencies in a limited problem domain within a semantic network. Semantic nodes describe specific topics of the domain area. They are interconnected by labeled edges, which are used to describe relations between different topics.

Users can query the set of nodes in this network (e.g., to find an entry point for document search) or navigate through it. In contrast to the document knowledge described above, the context knowledge is rather stable. Usually it is not influenced by new documents published in its domain. Maintenance is required only in case of fundamental innovation. Typically such a network is built and attended by a group of experts.

- **User and System Environments** reflect the characteristics of users and the client system (e.g., "beginner who prefers videos to plain text, no audio device available"). This knowledge is stored at the client machine and is automatically taken into consideration at querying time.

The essential advantage of the knowledge splitting described above is the drastically decreased dynamic of link knowledge compared to conventional hypermedia systems. Furthermore, documents may be used in completely different domains and contexts by addressing other knowledge bases. The powerful combination of fulltext queries and navigation along semantic edges offers a very flexible means of document access.

## 10.3.1   System Architecture

The final system will be a distributed application. Contributing components will be located at different sites though working hand in hand (see Figure 10.3). The following components are distinguished:

- **Document Servers** manage multimedia documents with their contents, structure and attributes. Archiving personnel may insert, delete or update documents, whereas retrieval clients have access to documents (or parts of them) via a fuzzy retrieval interface. The clients' combined fulltext/attribute queries are processed at these servers. Document hits are ranked, their IDs and measure of matching are delivered back. If requested by the client, document contents and attributes are provided.

- **Semantic Knowledge Servers** manage domain specific semantic knowledge stored in semantic nets. Administration personnel inserts, deletes or updates nodes. The integrity of the network should be supervised automatically. Semantic servers may receive document parts (see section 10.3.3) from clients, match them against their set of nodes and give back a ranked list of node IDs. Furthermore, nodes can be accessed by clients via fulltext or attribute queries, where the node's fulltext description and their attributes are searched. A client can also access labeled edges, leaving or pointing to a node for navigation purpose. That is, semantic knowledge servers provide hypertext that can be searched by both declarative and associative retrieval [138].

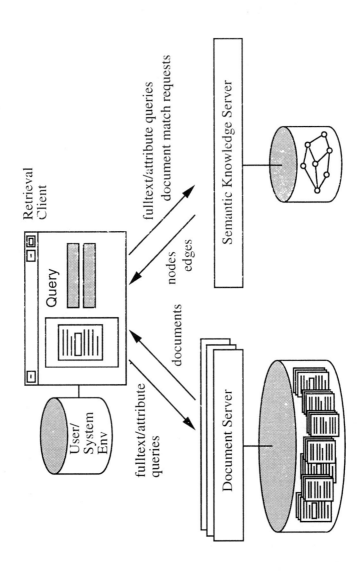

**Figure 10.3** System architecture

- **Retrieval Clients** manage user and system environment parameters. They interact with system users, document servers, and semantic knowledge servers. Based on user model and user interaction queries are generated and sent to servers. Results are interpreted (e.g., ranking, measure of matching) and influence further behavior. Retrieval clients offer various ways of querying document and semantic servers. They may be connected to several of them at a time. Another important task for retrieval clients is the presentation of documents as well as nodes and edges of the semantic nets to the user by means of graphical user interfaces.

## 10.3.2 Documents and Semantic Knowledge Bases

The components—in the sense of [117]—of a knowledge-based digital library system are *documents* as well as *semantic nodes* and *edges*. In this section these components shall be discussed in more detail.

Documents are stored together with their attributes in document servers. Usually they are structured into subcomponents which relate to many others but describe different parts or views of the topic. Typical subcomponents are *title, abstract, table of contents, chapters, sections, subsections, paragraphs, references,* etc. Such components usually contain a fulltext which can be used for searching. Besides, they can, of course, contain attributes, images, audio data, etc.

As the significance of a keyword found in a text document depends on the subcomponent where it is placed (not every book mentioning "database systems" in some subsection has database systems as topic), the structure of a document should be retained when it is inserted into the document database. That, for instance, can be achieved by means of *composite components* [117]. In OMNIS these will be realized by storing each subcomponent as a separate document with special attributes describing its relationship to other components of the main document. Thus it is possible to restrict queries to specific subcomponents of a document and therefore to formulate queries more precisely (e.g., the query `database IN ?abstract` yields all documents mentioning databases in the abstract).

A semantic net [189] is a directed graph with labeled nodes and labeled edges. Figure 10.4 depicts a part of a semantic net for the database systems' knowledge domain, which is to be used both for retrieving information on database systems directly as well as restricting searches in the document base to some specific problem area.

This is achieved by adding additional information to each node and link. Both nodes and links of a semantic network can be looked upon as components of a hypermedia [117, 138]. That is they both contain *attributes, fulltext,* and other hypermedia information just as usual hypermedia components. Thus the semantic net can be used as any other hypermedia for searching and retrieving information. Due to the fact that semantic nets are built by experts to structure millions of documents, such nets are hopefully well designed and relatively small.

| Abbr. | Link Label | Reverse Label |
|-------|------------|---------------|
| isa | is-a | may-be-a |
| ipo | is-part-of | has-a |
| ibo | is-based-on | is-basis-of |
| ist | is-similar-to | is-similar-to |
| iaao | is-an-application-of | has-as-an-application |
| isb | is-supported-by | supports |

Links are represented by labeled arrows. Every link, however, may be considered as a bi-link with a *reverse label*. A *link label* may be adorned by a keyword stating the probabilistic quality of the relationship:

- always (= default)
- often (o)
- sometimes (st)
- seldom (s)

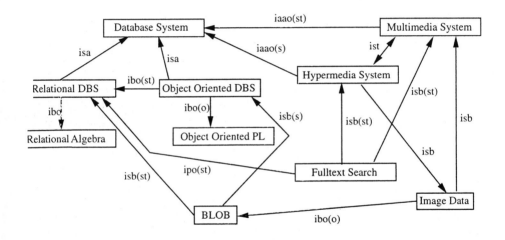

**Figure 10.4** A simple semantic knowledge base

That is, the lost-in-hyperspace problem usually does not occur in such nets.

The structuring of dynamic document bases is obtained by *query patterns* which are part of each semantic node. A query pattern is a standard OMNIS query optionally extended by variables. These variables are instantiated by retrieval clients based on the current user and system environment. Executing such an instantiated query pattern yields documents concerning the node's topic restricted to the users actual context.

The **Database System** node, e.g., should select standard database literature reflecting the users experience. This may be done by the following query pattern:

```
?doctype=(textbook|survey|tutorial) &
USER_EXPERIENCE IN ?experience &
?docno NOT IN USER_HISTORY &
((database%|data....base%)...system% IN ?title |
 (database%|data....base%) IN ?keywords)
```

The above query pattern contains the variable USER_EXPERIENCE which is set to a value out of {novice, intermediate, professional, expert} by the retrieval client. This restricts the search space to documents reflecting the users experience. Moreover, the statement ?docno NOT IN USER_HISTORY excludes all those documents that have been retrieved before. Of course, more complex user models can be employed in practice.

Query patterns should not address documents directly (i.e., by containing their ID) since document bases usually evolve and semantic knowledge bases should be applicable to many document bases. Thus it is possible that, e.g., a special expert team of the database community designs and maintains a semantic net for the domain "database systems" which can be used for any document base in the world containing database relevant literature.

Note that there are two possible extremes. On the one hand, a semantic net could consist of exactly one node with query pattern % (i.e., search all documents). In this case the semantic hypermedia system behaves like an ordinary digital library with declarative retrieval (i.e., fulltext/attribute search). On the other hand, a semantic net could, at least in principle, introduce a single document node for each document of the document base. In this case a standard hypertext would be the result where hypermedia retrieval can be done as usual.

## 10.3.3   Queries and Navigation

Initially users connect to a number of document servers and a single, domain specific semantic knowledge server. As in conventional digital library systems, documents or subparts of them are retrieved by declarative querying. To obtain more precise results document structure and attributes may be taken into consideration as well. The contents of hits are transfered to the user's client on request and presented there. Similar access is possible to the semantic nodes of the knowledge server. By searching their fulltext descriptions and/or attributes context specific nodes may be located. By means of the labeled edges a hypertext navigation to related nodes is possible. Every node of the semantic net restricts the document bases through its query pattern. Executing such a query—be it with or without further refinement from the user—yields current, topic-relevant documents.

Combining the techniques of declarative document access by query patterns and semantic net browsing allows a knowledge-based hypertext navigation through digital libraries. Typically, when a library user is reading a document, the desire to find complementary information will arise at arbitrary document positions. After pointing to such a position, the following steps yield related documents:

1. The component path (or certain parts of it) from the document root to the chosen subcomponent is transferred to the knowledge server. It is matched against the semantic net to assign it to a context. This is done by executing all nodes' query patterns against the component path (which is in fact not a performance problem, as it can be done completely within the main memory). A few good matching nodes with all outgoing edges are returned to the client.

2. The library user now can navigate through the knowledge base by using the semantic nodes obtained in step 1 as starting nodes. Eventually he will reach some related node with a specific query pattern. Note that link labels and node descriptions may, e.g., be presented to users as popups inside the current subcomponent.

3. Finally, executing the query pattern of a node selected in step 2 will deliver a set of documents which are semantically related to the initial subcomponent in a certain context.

This procedure offers a great variety of semantic connections between arbitrary document components to users. Newly inserted or updated documents are immediately integrated without further efforts of link maintenance. Authors and document archiving personnel do not need to know about possible relations between documents which simplifies document handling.

## 10.4   Summary and Outlook

In this chapter we have compared declarative with pure hypertext retrieval methods and pointed out their characteristic qualities. It turned out that the combination of both approaches increases user comfort and practical value. A remaining problem, however, are the static hypertext links created by document authors. They are expensive to maintain, become obsolete and therefore condemn hypertext navigation to incompleteness. After introducing the declarative digital library system OMNIS as it is in operation today, we disclosed our ideas for solving this problem by developing a knowledge-based digital library system, where document contents and semantic knowledge are separated. Declarative document retrieval together with knowledge-based hypertext navigation in different contexts reduce library maintenance and add a new dimension to digital library service quality.

For further extensions this architecture can also be the basis of intelligent document search in digital libraries. A deduction process by the retrieval client then combines user model and knowledge of link servers to generate more goal-directed relations between documents. By rule-based computing of labeled paths instead of single edges the semantic net may be condensed to fit users' individual needs. Thus a more goal-directed navigation and document access is achieved.

# Chapter 11

## Fuzzy Full-Text Searches in OCR Databases

Andreas Myka[*] and Ulrich Güntzer[†]

## 11.1  Introduction

The arrival of the paperless era has been announced many times before. Though this arrival may really happen some time ahead, paper is still used more often than electronic media are, either as storage medium and/or an interface.

The use of paper as a *storage medium* is mainly due to the fact that a huge heritage of paper documents exists that has not been transformed into electronic form. In addition, most books are still published exclusively on paper for several reasons (i. a. dissemination of standard hardware/software, copyright issues), though electronic processes are involved in producing them. In order to make use of the advantages of electronic media, these documents have to be converted into non-coded and/or coded electronic form by those who need advanced individual search and storage mechanisms.

In the context of computers, the use of paper as an *interface* has mainly two aspects: the interface between machine and man, and between machine and machine. In case the information flow via paper is directed from machine to man, the interface can be considered as secure with regard to a possible loss of information. However, if a machine is the destination point of information flow that uses paper as an interface, loss of information has to be expected. This is due to the fact that OCR packages are still far from being perfect in doing character recognition compared to the recognition rates humans are accustomed to.

Though OCR devices are steadily improving [190, 191], the imperfections of these systems have to be dealt with in the near future. In order to cope with these errors, several solutions can be used to improve the situtation, i.a.:

[*] Wilhelm-Schickard-Institut
Universität Tübingen
Sand 13, D-72076 Tübingen, Germany
EMail: myka@informatik.uni-tuebingen.de
[†] Wilhelm-Schickard-Institut
Universität Tübingen
Sand 13, D-72076 Tübingen, Germany
EMail: guentzer@informatik.uni-tuebingen.de

- OCR software delivers sets of characters, in cases where ambiguities exist,

- connection of different OCR packages with an independent voting mechanism that decides on the final "recognition" of a character/word [191],

- improvement of OCR results by means of using dictionaries/thesauri (see e. g. [222]),

- translation of full-text queries into fuzzy queries.

The delivery of character sets instead of a single (uncertain) character is not common in commercial OCR systems. Furthermore, in many cases no additional OCR package (for implementing a voting system) and no appropriate dictionary (for correcting all strings) are available. Therefore, in this chapter we will focus on the fourth aspect of adapting full-text queries to garbled OCR text databases. Thereby, the effects of several methods on recall and precision are examined: while it is trivial to give an algorithm that provides for maximum recall ("deliver each database entry for any query") in such a digital library, increasing recall without affecting precision too much is not. In contrast to [213], we deal with real output of OCR software instead of a simulated one and we do consider all kinds of OCR faults instead of character rejections only.

In [166], it was shown that retrieval effectiveness (with regard to Boolean or relevance feedback queries) for complete large documents is not affected by recognition errors under certain assumptions. However, fuzzy or fault-tolerant retrieval mechanisms are necessary in certain situations, e. g. in case all locations of a specific character string are needed (like for hypertext conversion) or in case of single-term queries on short documents.

Fuzzy retrieval mechanisms for full-text databases have been developed before without focusing on the aspect of OCR databases in general. They have been developed with different aspects in mind: e. g. with regard to adapting to phonetic similarities of words, especially names, or to compensate misspellings of words that have occurred while typing in texts into the machine. Though the inclusion of errors during the manual transformation of texts appears to be similar to the inclusion of errors during the automatic conversion, there are differences:

- Types of errors. While errors during the manual conversion are mostly due to individual errors e. g. based on the position of keys on the keyboard, OCR errors are due to the appearances of patterns. Thus, in the first case, "v" and "b" can be intermixed during manual transformation, whereas such an error is unlikely to happen during automatic transformation. Another common human error is the transposition of characters.

- Frequency of errors. Normally, errors are more frequent in automatically transformed electronic texts than they are in manually transformed ones. Today, a recognition rate of 99.5 % is considered to be a very good result for OCR packages. That means on the average, one error may occur every 200 characters or every 25 words. In typewriter courses in German schools, your error rate has to be below one error every 400 characters in order to get a "B".

In the following, we will illustrate some of the methods that possibly can be applied in order to cope with OCR errors in full-text databases. Some of them concentrate on the special aspect of OCR errors, while others apply fuzziness in a more general way or even fuzziness primarily directed to other kinds of errors. By illustrating some of them, we concentrate on recall and precision. The speed of each method is not measured, but thoughts on complexity are given where appropriate. Finally, the results of each method's performance with regard to a restricted set of sample documents are given. This set contains documents from different sources and includes almost perfectly recognized as well as badly recognized ones.

## 11.2   Search mechanisms

### 11.2.1   Exact match

OCR full-text databases can be queried by means of exact terms or character sequences. Then, the recall

$$R = \frac{C}{S}$$

where C is the number of correctly retrieved documents parts (terms) and S is the number of document parts that should have been retrieved, is diminished according to the error rate of the used OCR software package. Recall can be improved by means of fuzzy queries as described in the following sections.

The precision

$$P = \frac{C}{D}$$

where C is the number of correctly retrieved document parts and D is the number of delivered document parts, of such exact queries' results, of course, cannot be improved by means of fuzzy operators. However, the precision of exact matching is not necessarily 100 %, because errors may turn some terms into other existing terms. This is especially true if the OCR software uses thesauri in order to improve its results.

In Information Retrieval, recall is defined as the proportion of relevant documents retrieved and precision as the proportion of retrieved documents which are relevant [227]. Thereby, relevancy is defined, to a certain extent, subjectively by users. We are using both terms with regard to full-text retrieval correctness: i. e. a document is considered relevant if it contains a specific string.

With regard to speed, exact matching is very efficient, because indexes to each database entry can be created. Therefore, each query evaluation is of complexity $O(log N)$, where $N$ is the number of different words within the document base.

## 11.2.2  Canonical forms

In this section, three methods are described that transform terms into their canonical form. The basic intention is to find a suitable function *canonic()* that maps different garbled forms of a single word $w$ to the same canonical form as the original word:

$$canonic(w) = canonic(garbled_i(w))$$

Thus, the original word and its derivatives are grouped together. If this grouping is successful, recall will increase. Furthermore, if the number of different garbled terms that belong to the same class is low, precision can be preserved. Finding a good function *canonic()* can be compared to finding a suitable hashing function with no or little collisions.

A big advantage of using canonical forms is the efficiency of such methods with regard to speed. The canonical form of each database entry may be computed at the time the database is filled. Then, at query time an exact term is mapped to its canonical form that is used for searching the database. By means of using indexes, the complexity of all these methods can be approximated by $O(logN)$.

### Soundex

A well-known algorithm that delivers a canonical form is the *Soundex* method by Odell and Russelli (see [137]). Soundex aims at phonetic similarities in order to enhance recall to a given query, especially with regard to names:

1. Retain the first letter of the word, and drop all occurrences of vowels, h, w, y in other positions.

2. Assign the following numbers to the remaining letters after the first:
   b, f, p, v → 1
   c, g, j, k, q, s, x, z → 2
   d, t → 3
   l → 4
   m, n → 5
   r → 6

3. If two or more letters with the same code were adjacent in the original word (before step 1), omit all but the first.

4. Convert to the form "letter, digit, digit, digit" by adding trailing zeros, or by dropping rightmost digits.

Step 4 was omitted in our tests in order to improve precision.

It may seem odd using an algorithm that aims at phonetic similarities in the context of OCR-garbled text. However, we wanted to know which effects such an algorithm has on recall and precision if it is not specifically dedicated to OCR errors.

| canonical element | elements | | | | |
|:---:|:---:|:---:|:---:|:---:|:---:|
| e | e | c | a | s | |
| 1 | 1 | l | I | i | r |
| O | O | o | 0 | D | C |
| f | f | t | | | |
| y | y | v | V | | |
| M | M | N | H | m | |
| S | S | 5 | | | |
| g | g | q | | | |
| h | h | b | | | |
| u | u | n | | | |
| F | F | E | | | |
| K | K | k | | | |

**Table 11.1** Possible equivalence classes for characters

### Character classes

In order to take into consideration OCR confusions of *single* characters, like e. g. '1' and 'I', character classes can be formed. Thereby, it is assumed that the relation *confuses_with(x,y)* for two characters $x$ and $y$ is *transitive*, *reflexive*, and *symmetric*. Thus, *confuses_with(x,y)* is an equivalence relation that groups characters into distinct classes (see table 11.1). For each class, a representative may be selected: the canonical element.

The *confuses_with()* relation may be defined in different ways. If the OCR database is filled by different OCR packages, then parts of a general confusion table should be used (e. g. as given in [190]). If the used OCR package is known, this confusion matrix may be tailored more precisely to the shortcomings of this given system. E. g. the table of most common confusions in [190] does not list the confusion of 'F' and 'E'. In our preliminary tests, however, this confusion was quite common: thus, adding it to the confusion table seemed to be appropriate.

The algorithm that makes use of the explained character classes may be quite simple:

1. For each word in the full-text database: replace all occurrences of characters that are listed in table 11.1 with their canonical element and store the transformed term into an additional attribute *cc_word*.

2. For each word in a given query: do the same transformation and try to locate the word(s) by means of searching in the attribute *cc_word*.

As a result of a query, each database entry is ranked either as a valid or an invalid answer. If an additional rank is desired, terms could be classified according to the three stages:

- valid according to exact matching,

- valid only according to character classes,

- not valid.

Additional ranks could be achieved if a hierarchy of character classes is given and evaluated. This is similar to the string correction method proposed for phoneme sequences in [222]: there, on each stage not necessarily exact matching has to take place but possibly selection by means of a term distance threshold.

### Similarex

In order to extend the possibilities of character classes, we have developed an algorithm called Similarex. Similarex has been implemented according to the principles of Soundex: on the one hand, try to get rid of unnecessary information (like vowels in Soundex). On the other hand, try to map those parts of the information most often confused to a common form:

1. Going through the character sequence from left to right, do the following mappings of sequences of length three:
   iii, iin, nii → M

2. Do the same for sequences of length two:
   in, iu, ri, rI, rn, ni, ui, tn → M
   ti → n

3. Do single character replacements:
   u, h, b → n
   m, N, H → M
   1, l, i, r → I
   o, 0, D, C → O
   v, V, y → Y
   t → f
   5 → S
   q → g
   E → F
   k → K

4. Drop all remaining occurrences of e, c, a, s.

In contrast to Soundex, Similarex is dedicated to the similar appearances of characters or character patterns. Therefore, also upper and lower cases of characters are distinguished and numbers are included. The advantage of Similarex over the usage of character classes is the integration of confusions with regard to character sequences instead of considering single characters only.

The same that is true for character classes is true for Similarex: the more information is known about the specific confusion characteristics of an OCR device, the more both methods can be tailored to a specific environment.

## 11.2.3   N-grams

In the context of correcting misspellings or searching in garbled text, n-grams are well-known. Thereby, for each term the set of contained character sequences (either with or without leading or trailing blanks) with length $n$ are computed. By means of comparing the n-gram sets of two terms or character sequences, the similarity of those terms can be evaluated: the higher the proportion of common n-grams is, the more similar both terms are. E. g. the term "empty" contains the digrams ($n = 2$): " e", "em", "mp", "pt", "ty", "y ".

According to [181], digrams with blanks perform very well with regard to searching in a database that contains errors. Therefore, we have chosen digrams as representatives for testing n-grams. The similarity value $S$ of a database entry $E$ and a query term $T$ is computed by

$$S = \frac{|digrams(T) \cap digrams(E)|}{|digrams(T)|}$$

By means of using this similarity value instead of

$$S = \frac{|digrams(T) \cap digrams(E)|}{|digrams(T) \cup digrams(E)|}$$

the omission of blanks can be overcome.

In contrast to the different methods that make use of canonical forms for fuzzy full-text searches (apart from the remarks made in section 11.2.2 with regard to hierarchical character classes), n-grams provide for a more elaborate ranking based on the different similarity values that are computed. Therefore, if only two ranks (qualified and non-qualified) are of interest, a fixed threshold has to be introduced in order to separate both groups. I. e. if the similarity is above the threshold, then the compared term qualifies as a research result, otherwise it is discarded.

With regard to complexity, n-grams can be handled efficiently: if $n$ is the number of n-grams in the database, the complexity of searching the most similar terms is $O(log\ n)$.

## 11.2.4   Linear scanning

The methods that were described in the previous sections all can make use of database structures in order to be executed efficiently. However, there are also methods that are based on linear scanning rather than database queries. Therefore, these methods, two of which are described in the following, cannot be used for on-line searches in large digital full-text libraries. However, their implementation can make sense in small libraries as well as in the context of incrementally processed large libraries.

### Levenshtein distance

The Levenshtein measure gives the distance between a term $X = x_1..x_m$ and a term $Y = y_1..y_n$ as the minimum number of insertions, deletions, and substitutions of single characters that are necessary in order to transform $X$ into

$Y$ [143, 178]. Thus, the Levenshtein distance $dist_{Lev}(X, Y)$ can be defined as $\delta(m, n)$:

$$\delta(0, 0) := 0$$

$$\delta(i, j) := min \begin{cases} \delta(i - 1, j) + 1 \\ \delta(i, j - 1) + 1 \\ \delta(i - 1, j - 1) + cost_{subst}(x_i, y_j) \end{cases}$$

where

$$cost_{subst}(x_i, y_j) := \begin{cases} 0, if \ x_i = y_j \\ 1, otherwise \end{cases}$$

The Levenshtein measure is used in any kind of string comparison and is therefore not specifically directed to OCR errors. By means of Seller's algorithm, this distance can also be computed for substrings [207]. Thus, omitted word delimiters can be taken into consideration.

Again, classifying database entries as valid or invalid search results has to be based on a specified threshold. This threshold may be either constant or depending on the length of the query term.

In order to compute the Levenshtein distance, efficient implementations exist (see [236]). Nevertheless its complexity is $O(N)$ due to the necessity of linear scanning.

### Modified Levenshtein distance

The basic Levenshtein distance can be further modified in order to take into consideration additional OCR errors as well as differences between specific errors (or types of errors) [166]. The merging of character sequences and the splitting of single characters are those error types that are taken into consideration by the modified Levenshtein distance additionally.

Differences between types of errors are taken into consideration by costs that are assigned to the different operations: $cost_{ins}$ (insertion), $cost_{del}$ (deletion), $cost_{subst}$ (substitution), $cost_{split}$ (splitting), and $cost_{merge}$ (merging). Therefore, the modified Levenshtein distance $dist_{ModLev}(X, Y)$ is defined as $\delta_M$:

$$\delta_M(0, 0) := 0$$

$$\delta_M(i, j) := min \begin{cases} \delta_M(i - 1, j) + cost_{del}(x_i) \\ \delta_M(i, j - 1) + cost_{ins}(y_j) \\ \delta_M(i - 1, j - 1) + cost_{subst}(x_i, y_j) \\ \delta_M(i - 1, j - 2) + cost_{split}(x_i, y_{j-1}y_j) \\ \delta_M(i - 2, j - 1) + cost_{merge}(x_{i-1}x_i, y_j) \end{cases}$$

### Confusion table

A linear scanning method that is specifically directed towards OCR errors can be implemented by means of the confusion table (see table 11.2). Thereby any kind of confusions as specified in this table can be taken into consideration. Thus, confusion of character sequences can be taken care of, as well as the insertion or deletion of word delimiters (such as blanks) or the insertion of "dirt" (such as

| char. | recogn. | char. | recogn. | char. | recogn. | char. | recogn. |
|-------|---------|-------|---------|-------|---------|-------|---------|
| 1 | 1 | O | 0 | e | c | m | rn |
| i | 1 | 0 | O | c | e | m | iii |
| 1 | I | 0 | o | nothing | , | m | tn |
| 1 | i | e | o | nothing | . | m | nii |
| i | t | o | c | nothing | ' | f | t |
| i | I | a | o | . | nothing | t | c |
| I | 1 | s | a | space | nothing | t | l |
| 1 | I | a | s | a | nothing | y | v |
| 1 | 1 | a | e | - | nothing | M | N |
| t | 1 | e | a | . | space | 5 | S |

**Table 11.2** Part of a confusion table

".,;'"). However, the complete rejection of characters, as signalled by means of '~' in Scanworx output, is not taken into account.

By means of the confusion table, a given query term is transformed into a regular expression. E. g. "empty" could be transformed into (in PERL syntax):

```
[ecao]?[ \.',]?(rn|iii|tn|nii|m)[ \.',]?p[ \.',]?[tcl][ \.',]?[yv]
```

Afterwards, the database is scanned by means of this regular expression. However, it is not advisable to accept each character sequence within the database that matches the regular expression. Instead, it is sensible to use an additional distance metric. To achieve this, e. g. the Levenshtein metric (described above) could be applied, but with some disadvantage: the Levenshtein metric basically reflects a different set of errors than the confusion table. Therefore, we have defined the distance operator $dist_{CT}(x, y)$ as the minimum number of errors that have to be made (according to the confusion table) in order to transform $x$ into $y$. If no such transformation is possible, $dist_{CT}()$ delivers -1. E. g.

$$dist_{CT}("empty", "empty") = 0$$
$$dist_{CT}("empty", "emptv") = 1$$
$$dist_{CT}("empty", "eiiiptv") = 2$$
$$dist_{CT}("empty", "digital") = -1$$

The threshold for accepting matching patterns can now be given either generally ($n$ errors) or as a function (e. g. $\lfloor string\_length(x)/m \rfloor$ for some constant $m$). The complexity of finding all matching patterns according to the confusion table is $O(N)$.

# 11.3    Experiments

## 11.3.1    Environment

For evaluating the described fuzzy methods' performances the following environment is used:

- The electronic sources of the analyzed documents are available. Thus, a completely correct full-text database can be used as a reference.

- The printed versions of these articles are processed by means of ScanWorX 2.1. In order to deal with varying types of OCR documents, training was used for some documents, while it was omitted for others.

- For efficient analyzing purposes, the database management system *Trans-Base* is used. There, the original text, the recognized text, the canonical forms of terms, and the n-grams are stored.

- For efficient analysis of the basic Levenshtein distance, *agrep* [236] is used. The programs for evaluating regular expressions based on confusion tables and for evaluating the modified Levenshtein distance are written in *perl* and *C*. *C* is also used for accessing the database.

For this chapter, a preliminary set of documents from four different sources (a mathematical journal, a journal of computer science, a news magazine, and a proceedings volume) has been used. This set contains almost perfectly recognized documents as well as documents with a recognition rate of approx. 50 percent (with regard to the recognition of words); see figure 11.3. In total, these documents contain 28600 terms including stop words and numbers.

## 11.3.2    Methodology

The evaluation of the methods is based on all *real* words occuring in the original text. Therefore, e. g. mathematical expressions are stripped from the original as well as the OCR text. This is done, because recognition of mathematical expressions cannot be handled by ScanWorX appropriately. However, stop words are not eliminated from the text bases. The original full-text is then used for querying the OCR database, i. e. the OCR data is searched by means of single-term queries using each word that is contained in the original text.

Then, recall is determined using the number of correctly retrieved positions of words. In order to compute the precision of a search method, the numbers of mistakes for each query are summed up. We have defined mistake as an incorrectly delivered word position. A word position is also regarded as being incorrect if e. g. inflected forms of a search term are located there. As an effect, the precision of those methods that also consider substrings (n-grams, Levenshtein, confusion table), is decreased due to the applied methodology of evaluation.

| str. len. $\geq$ | Exact Match | Sound. | Char. Classes | Simila-rex | Di-grams | Leven-shtein | Conf. Matrix | Mod. Leven. |
|---|---|---|---|---|---|---|---|---|
| 4 | 84.7 % | 85.5 % | 85.5 % | 86.7 % | 87.3 % | 89.6 % | 90.6 % | 90.7 % |
| 5 | 84.3 % | 85.3 % | 85.0 % | 86.0 % | 87.5 % | 88.4 % | 89.5 % | 91.9 % |
| 6 | 83.3 % | 84.3 % | 84.1 % | 85.0 % | 87.2 % | 87.5 % | 88.3 % | 92.3 % |
| 7 | 82.2 % | 83.4 % | 83.0 % | 84.0 % | 87.2 % | 86.0 % | 87.2 % | 92.1 % |
| 8 | 81.5 % | 83.0 % | 82.4 % | 83.3 % | 88.4 % | 85.4 % | 86.1 % | 91.9 % |
| 9 | 79.7 % | 81.1 % | 80.8 % | 81.4 % | 89.6 % | 83.9 % | 84.8 % | 91.8 % |
| 10 | 79.2 % | 80.4 % | 80.3 % | 80.6 % | 89.3 % | 83.2 % | 83.4 % | 91.2 % |

**Table 11.3** Comparison of recall values

| string length $\geq$ | Soundex | Char. Classes | Simila-rex | Di-grams | Leven-shtein | Conf. Matrix | Mod. Leven. |
|---|---|---|---|---|---|---|---|
| 4 | 54.3 % | 92.2 % | 54.2 % | 62.6 % | 5.1 % | 16.7 % | 16.5 % |
| 5 | 68.8 % | 93.9 % | 56.7 % | 59.8 % | 43.6 % | 34.1 % | 19.7 % |
| 6 | 80.0 % | 94.2 % | 67.1 % | 59.4 % | 50.8 % | 54.5 % | 20.4 % |
| 7 | 84.4 % | 93.9 % | 71.7 % | 59.1 % | 54.2 % | 64.6 % | 20.9 % |
| 8 | 88.6 % | 94.2 % | 75.2 % | 58.9 % | 57.3 % | 71.5 % | 21.3 % |
| 9 | 91.7 % | 93.5 % | 76.5 % | 56.3 % | 59.6 % | 74.1 % | 20.1 % |
| 10 | 93.3 % | 94.5 % | 78.9 % | 51.3 % | 63.8 % | 79.0 % | 21.9 % |

**Table 11.4** Comparison of precision values

Evaluating the usage of a *confusion table*, a single common confusion table is applied. It could be expected that better results for this method can be achieved if a adapted version of this matrix is stored with each document type (e.g. for each journal, document series etc.). The costs for adapting the matrix can be considered as low compared to the costs of manually correcting each OCR document.

For the modified Levenshtein distance, the following functions have been used: $cost_{ins}(x) = cost_{del}(x) := 0.8$, $cost_{subst}(x_i, y_j) := 0$ if $x_i = y_j$, else $cost_{subst}(x_i, y_j) := 0.5$, $cost_{split}(x_i, y_{j-1}y_j) = cost_{merge}(x_{i-1}x_i, y_j) := 1$.

Because most of the methods do not provide for an elaborate ranking of research results, we are concentrating on <recall, precision> pairs for each method depending on the length of the query terms. For the digram method, a threshold of 0.8 has been introduced for $S$ (see section 11.2.3) in order to separate between valid and invalid results. For the modfied Levenshtein distance, this threshold depends on the length of the original term $x$: $threshold = \lfloor stringlength(x)/5.5 \rfloor$.

### 11.3.3    Results

In tables 11.3 and 11.4 the performance of each method with regard to recall and precision is given in detail. Figure 11.1 shows which percentage of the recall gap between the recall of exact matching and 100 % could be closed by the tested methods (with regard to query terms of string length $\geq$ 6). Figure 11.2 shows the precision values of these methods again with regard to query terms of length $\geq$ 6.

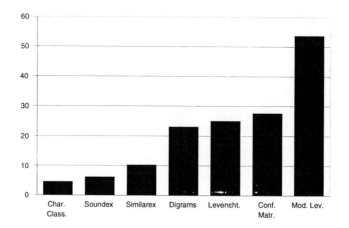

**Figure 11.1** Increase of recall (query terms of length $\geq 6$)

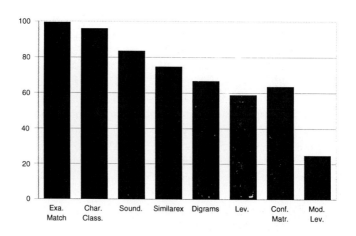

**Figure 11.2** Precision using terms of length $\geq 6$

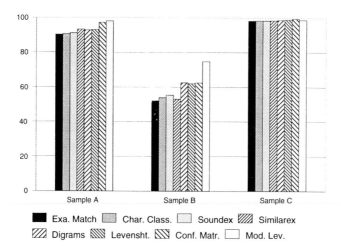

Figure 11.3: Variation of recall for different document samples (string length $\geq$ 6)

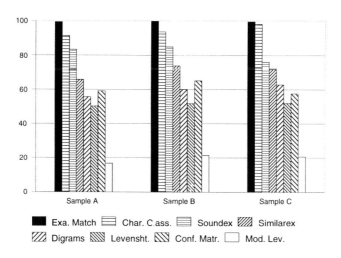

Figure 11.4: Variation of precision for different document samples (string length $\geq$ 6)

Looking at the figures 11.1 and 11.2 as well as at the figures 11.3 and 11.4, it can be seen that the intuitively correct statement seems to be true in almost all the cases: recall is inversely proportional to precision. One remarkable exception is the usage of a *confusion table*: it both provides for better recall values and precision values than the Levenshtein metric for query strings of length $\geq 6$. To a certain extent, this seems to be independent from the basic level of recall and precision (see figures 11.3 and 11.4).

The level of recall (and therefore also the level of precision) obviously can be varied based on a fine granularity of steps, in case the complexity of algorithms does not matter. However, in case of large document bases, only those methods that do use canonical forms or n-grams can be employed; thus, the range of varying recall is more restricted.

Figure 11.4 suggests that the variation of precision depends on the given algorithm but not (or to a very small extend) on the given sample. If this assumption holds, the algorithm for choosing an optimal fault-tolerant string searching algorithm could be based on the estimation of the desired precision value. By means of this precision value, this algorithm is chosen, that provides for this precision and best recall.

With regard to the test set, the following additional statements can be made:

- *Soundex* and *character classes* both slightly improve recall by means of introducing fuzziness. However in contrast to *Soundex*, *character classes* decrease precision only to a small extent. Therefore, they can be used if recall has to be increased at low risk. Whether better versions of some kind of *Similarex* algorithm exist, could not be tested by means of the restricted test set yet.

- By means of taking into consideration character sequences, *Similarex* has the highest recall value of all methods that use canonical forms (see table 11.3 and fig. 11.1). Whether a precision value of 60 % is acceptable, depends on the preferences of users.

- Using *digrams* with similarity threshold of 0.8 provides for the best recall values with regard to string lengths $\geq 7$ if the modified Levenshtein distance is neglected (see table 11.3). However, it may be possible to achieve better results by means of *Levenshtein* and especially by means of using a *confusion table* if the number of accepted mistakes for each query string is varied there.

- The performance of the *modified Levenshtein distance* has to be further tested by means of adjusted parameters, especially by means of an adjusted threshold parameter. However, it is obvious that a wide range of recall (and inversely precision) can be achieved by means of selecting algorithms and appropriate parameters.

- The use of regular expressions based on a *confusion table* has a good <recall, precision>-performance with regard to strings of length $\geq 6$ (see figures 11.3 and 11.4). However, testing of this method (as well as the Levenshtein distance method) is not complete, because the effects of modifying parameters, especially modifying of the matrix itself and modifying the threshold for the *dist*() metric as presented in section 11.2.4, could not be evaluated until now: for the presented evaluations here, a general threshold of one error has been used.

# 11.4  Summary and outlook

In this chapter, we have described several methods of fuzzy full-text searching that can be used in OCR databases. The preliminary results of our tests have shown that it is possible to increase recall to a certain extent without losing too much of precision. However, because almost each increase of recall has to be paid by a decrease of precision, the user or administrator, respectively, of an information retrieval system has to decide individually on the importance of each of these values: if the risk of decreasing precision should be minimized, a slight increase of recall can be achieved by means of using *character classes*. If the highest possible recall (together with a reasonable precision) is necessary, employment of a *confusion table* may be the appropriate choice. Of course, in case significant loss of precision is introduced into the system by means of a fault-tolerant string matching algorithm, additional tools have to be provided to ensure that a user is not flooded with unnecessary information, e. g. a KWIC index could be used in order to provide for a preliminary overview of results.

The tests as reported in this chapter are still extended at the moment. Extensions include the size of the analyzed full-text database as well as the addition of variations of some of the described methods, especially those based on linear scanning.

However, such a test can never be complete: different algorithms can be evaluated as well as variations and combinations of the ones described here. Furthermore, OCR errors are, to a certain extent, dependent from the OCR device. Therefore, different results could possibly be achieved by means of testing data from different OCR devices.

# Part III

# Network-Based Information and Resource Discovery

# Chapter 12

## Data Discovery in Large Scale Heterogeneous and Autonomous Databases

Athman Bouguettaya* and Stephen Milliner [†]

## 12.1 Background

With the exponential proliferation of databases that span countries and continents, and advances in wide area networking, interest in worldwide database interoperability has gained momentum. Scalability and language support for this new environment remain open questions which require solutions. In a large network of interoperable autonomous heterogeneous databases, the architecture should be flexible enough to allow negotiation to take place and establish a dynamic grouping of databases. This will provide extensibility and hence scalability to the network of interoperable databases. In such large environments, it is important that databases be made aware of other participating databases in an incremental fashion. Thus we propose an architecture aimed at the incremental data driven discovery and formation of dynamic inter–relationships between database nodes. We describe a language, called Tassili, that sits on top of a large network of databases and supports this new architecture termed FINDIT. Individual database nodes freely join, create, and leave a group of databases to which a meta–information object refers. This allows databases to retain a high degree of local autonomy and results in a high degree of system scalability.

### 12.1.1 Motivation

Sharing information among autonomous heterogeneous databases has been researched extensively. The major assumption for sharing to take place has been that component databases have *a–priori* knowledge about schemas of other databases. This assumption remains reasonable provided the number of participating databases and the amount of on–line information is small. In this chapter we describe the FINDIT system which aims to achieve database interoperability

---

*This research was partly supported by an Australian Research Council large grant ARC 95–7–191650010.

[†]Queensland University of Technology, 2 George Street, GPO Box 2434, Brisbane 4001, Australia, Email: {athman,steve}@icis.qut.edu.au

in the presence of large numbers of participating databases and large amounts of on–line information. Digital libraries are a typical application domain of our research. The fast proliferation of on-line digital libraries and the globalization of the *internet*, compound the long standing problem of interoperability. Important interoperability issues in large heterogeneous and autonomous databases are discussed in [40]. There has been a consensus that finding and interpreting remote information are major open problems that stand against solving interoperability among a large number of autonomous heterogeneous databases [103].

Heterogeneity spans several levels, the first of of which is the DBMS level. At this level transaction management systems are the hardest to interoperate. We include query optimization at this level although it is somewhat above it. The second level of heterogeneity concerns the integration of different schemas of the same or of different models. The third level of heterogeneity concerns the interoperation of different query languages. The fourth level of heterogeneity relates to the interaction of different database applications. Other lower levels involve operating system and networking issues that are considered outside the database research realm. This work is aimed at levels two and above. Our initial goal is to provide a system which both provides a platform for heterogeneity resolution, and facilitates the sharing and discovery of information in a potentially large network of heterogeneous databases.

System size and complexity precludes the *a–priori* explicit definition of inter–database relationships. Any viable system must, therefore, allow an incremental building up and sharing of inter–relationship meta–information. The proposed architecture provides participating databases with a flexible subdivision of the information space, and a means of sharing information. This is achieved through the use of meta–information types which provide a description of the structure and behavior of one or more database schemas. Meta–information types arise from the database relationships formed. Relationships are implemented using two basic organizational constructs: *coalitions* and *services*. Coalitions define a strong coupling of databases whereas a service defines a loose coupling of databases at a reduced cost. Information regarding coalitions and services is stored in *co–databases*. Each database has an associated co–database which is updated to reflect that databases' involvement in various coalitions and services. Coalitions and services thus provide a grouping of databases that share a common interest which equates to a single information meta type. This dynamic clustering makes information accessing more tractable by limiting the number of database nodes which must interact. That is, by first providing for *database discovery*, data discovery is facilitated. Databases dynamically join and leave coalition and service groupings based upon local decisions. Hence, inter–node relationships and the resulting meta–types are formed and dissolved as the system executes. At any given point in time a single database node may partake in several coalitions and services (see Figure 12.1).

FINDIT is independent of the underlying database organization. This is achieved by the separation of structural and information concerns, and by operating at a higher level of abstraction. In order to establish and maintain the organizational architecture, the Tassili language was developed. This language is also used for querying/exploring and extracting information from the system. Finally, FINDIT uses the notion of a *demonstration* to aid the understanding of remote database information and facilitate the interoperability process.

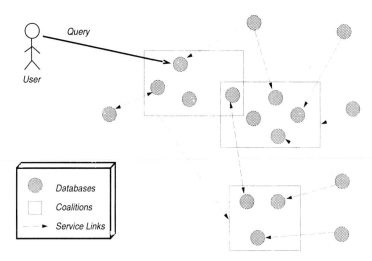

**Figure 12.1** Coalitions and Services

The chapter is divided as follows. In section 12.2, we present the related work. In section 12.3, we give an overview of the FINDIT database discovery system and present an example of its usage. A brief overview of implementation details is given in section 12.4. Some concluding remarks and a discussion of future work is provided in section 12.5.

## 12.2   Related Work

Related research has been performed in the areas of multidatabases, federated databases, information retrieval, and system naming. In multidatabase systems and federated databases, the focus has mainly been on sharing information, provided users know the information of interest and provided databases are willing to release a certain amount of their autonomy. In most multidatabase systems sharing is provided through partial or total integration [145]. Resource sharing through a global schema [212] requires integrating multiple schemas. The major problem associated with this technique is the manual, ad hoc translation of local languages and schemas into a global format. In addition, in most cases it is assumed that users have complete global knowledge. Because of the scale of systems being considered here, such global organization will lead to design bottlenecks.

An interesting commercial product that is somewhat more sophisticated is the French *Minitel* service [60]. This service is provided by the state run PTT.

Hundreds of databases are linked together to provide a wide range of information services. The main shortcoming of the service is its need of a uniform interface and access via specialized terminals. All databases linked to this service are text–based databases.

In federated databases, local integration is the means used for sharing information [120, 209]. This is achieved through *import* and *export* schemas, and a federal dictionary in which all databases are registered. The federated approach, as described in [120], does not address the issue of how the federal dictionary is to be designed in the presence of a large number of databases. In addition, the importing database has to understand the intrinsic organization of the imported schema. If there are tens (not even hundreds or thousands) of such schemas this method is at best inefficient and inadequate for locating information.

In most information retrieval systems, the emphasis is usually on how to build an indexing scheme to efficiently access information given some hints about the resource [200]. In [11] an approach is described that relies on *external indexing* for finding information in a network of information systems. However, this approach tends to centralize the search as a single index is used for the actual resource discovery. Potentially, if users make queries about all existing information space, all nodes would have the same index. It is not clear from the above references how the system behaves if several nodes can answer a given query. There is also no reference to how the actual node selection is performed. In [69] the *distributed indexing* approach is described. In this approach, however, registration of node *topics* and the proposed searching technique may result in performance bottlenecks.

Research in naming systems has mainly been geared towards finding a few simple information types, which carried little or no structure or behavior, in a network of computer systems [232]. Hence, little or no semantics are attached to the data. The search is usually instance based rather than type based. Most services use one single hierarchy to cope with extensibility [31].

A similar approach is taken in internet resource discovery. In [205], an interesting model for finding resources in a network of computer systems is presented. In this project, resources are typically unstructured text. As the research was conducted from a systems point of view, databases issues were simplified – no local structure of data resources is present to be understood, query materialization is based on contacting a single remote site, and no method is present for searching of any *clusters* of nodes which may be formed (i.e. subdivision of the universe of discourse). Other products such as Archie [85], WAIS [132], World Wide Web (or WWW) [24], and Gopher [159] use indices and browsing or a combination thereof to access freestyle documents. Once again, the basic assumption underlying most of these products is that the participating databases have little or no structure at all [205].

FINDIT can be differentiated from the above systems on several grounds. Firstly, FINDIT organizes database node interactions in a way that minimizes loss of local autonomy. Each individual database decides which coalitions/services should be entered into or left. As a result maximal local autonomy is maintained, inter–node organization remains distributed, and a high degree of system scalability is achieved. Maximal local autonomy is thus seen as an important precursor for scalability – as well as a method for restricting unlimited access to potentially sensitive information. Secondly, information sources in **FINDIT** are not plain text files. Thus local structures containing data must be understood and partial global structures constructed dynamically. Interaction with a database manager is required and a range of heterogeneity problems must be overcome. Finally, because of the potential size and complexity of the system, **FINDIT** does not attempt to statically define relationships between database node information components. Instead this data is constructed as the system executes. This allows for the incremental, data driven and dynamic construction of *clusters* of database nodes (via coalitions and services) formed in order to resolve a particular series of queries.

In all the systems considered above, except that of **WWW**, a static initial "global clustering" is performed. Any adjustment to this structure is then pursued solely from the local perspective of a static global organization (eg. via a user profile). In **FINDIT**, clustering is pursued by allowing database nodes to dynamically join and leave coalitions/services. The dynamic coalition and service schemas provide a means for *synchronizing* database node interactions. Thus, inter–database node organization and searching is pursued *actively* in both the global and local arenas.

By forming coalitions and service links, a subdivision of the network of databases is achieved. Interactions between database nodes proceed based upon this subdivision and performance scalability is partly achieved by this filtering out of superfluous communications. Scalability is aided by the physical restriction of coalition formation. That is, coalition formation must be "sanctioned" locally by the database administrator. In addition, coalitions only arise from the overlapping *areas of interest* between several database nodes.

## 12.3 The FINDIT Database Discovery System

In **FINDIT** the world of users is partitioned into privileged users and general users [‡] (Figure 12.2). Privileged users (eg. administrators) can issue both data definition and data manipulation operations. General users may issue read–only queries. The data definition section consists of two parts. The first part deals with coalitions and services formation. The second part deals with schema evolution. In that regard, a coalition is bootstrapped after formal negotiation between privileged users takes place using the Tassili query language. The coalition/service schema is stored and maintained in individual node co–databases. Schema updates are then propagated to the appropriate co–databases using a predefined set of protocols. This data is then accessed by the component database to provide users with information regarding the structure of the system and the nature of databases which constitute an information meta type.

---

[‡]When not qualified, the term "user" refers to general user status – privileged users are defined as having both privileged and general status

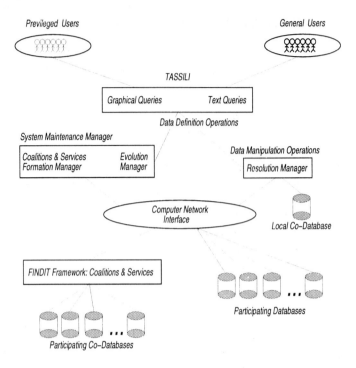

**Figure 12.2** FINDIT's Underlying System Architecture

FINDIT operates on several levels: an *architectural* level, an *interoperability* level, an *interaction/negotiation* level, and an *exploration* level. The architectural level provides a basis for clustering database nodes and provides a platform for proceeding with heterogeneity resolution in a scalable manner. Heterogeneity resolution is further aided by the incorporation of *documentation* into the interpretation level. Documentation comprises *demonstrations* which are provided by the remote database node. Documentation promotes the understanding of remote schemas and the correct interpretation of remote information. The interaction/negotiation level incorporates the Tassili language through which privileged users can form new node clusters or join existing ones. It also allows for the maintenance of the system organization via coalitions and services. Once this structural organization has been established, further heterogeneity resolution techniques can be employed on a relatively small set of database nodes. Finally, the exploration level allows users to explore the system and obtain required information. Once again the Tassili language primitives are used along with coalition and service information to educate users about database node inter–relationships.

## 12.3.1   The FINDIT Architecture Level

This level supplies an architecture for organizing/negotiating inter–node relationships. Coalitions and services provide the means for dynamically synchronizing database node interactions in a decentralized manner. By joining a coalition database nodes implicitly *agree* to work together, thereby sacrificing autonomy to some degree. However, database nodes retain control and join or leave coalitions/services based upon local considerations. Inter–node relationships are thus dynamic and formed in an incremental fashion.

Nodes within FINDIT are fully *logically* interconnected. This allows accessing of any information meta type defined by a particular clustering of database nodes. Interactions between nodes then proceed based upon the inter–node relationship groupings. If this subdivision is not performed, the search space is huge and the interoperability problem becomes intractable. Hence, information meta type formation and data sharing are also pursued in an incremental and dynamic manner.

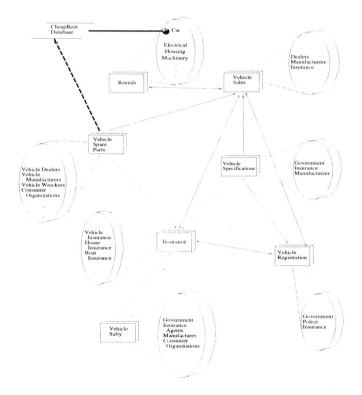

**Figure 12.3** Partial View of FINDIT Network

Consider the example of a car rental company *CheapRent*, which currently rents three types of vehicles : luxury, middle and economy. The company maintains two relational databases of its own : a stock database represented with one relation (attributes are: vehicle_registration, model, year, rental rate, booking, service_due, type, etc.) and a service database represented with one relation (attributes are: vehicle_registration, date_of_purchase, part_type, part_cost, times_replaced, etc.). The former relation is used to keep track of vehicle rentals and the latter is concerned with maintenance costs.

The CheapRent rental company is expanding and the managers decide to create a fourth car type "second–hand" which is targeted towards the lower end of the market. In addition, the company has decided to employ its own mechanics and set up workshops to maintain its expanding fleet. The question the managers are now faced with is which types of used cars should be purchased. After discussions, the following relevant categories were identified: fuel economy, popularity of the model, exhaust emission, usage of unleaded fuel, safety, parts, insurance, registration, resale value. How the relative weights will be attached to each of these characteristics will in part depend upon the number of responses.

Once CheapRent joins the FINDIT system, the environment it now has access to is presented in Figure 12.3. Here 7 coalitions are linked to each other through service links (full lines). For example, the following databases participate in the coalition with identifier *vehicle registration*: the government vehicle registration department, the police, and insurance agencies. The CheapRent database administrator joins the *rentals* coalition – this is depicted in Figure 12.3 by the solid bold line. The CheapRent administrator also enters into a service relationship with the *vehicle spare parts* coalition, as depicted in Figure 12.3 by the broken bold line.

Upon joining the FINDIT system, CheapRent users may attempt to resolve queries of the following type:

### Find Information With Attribute

$age \leq v$ *years*
$economy > w$ *km/liter*
*unleaded* $= TRUE/FALSE$
*emission levels* $\leq x$
$av\_cost\_of$ *parts* $< y$
$safety\_rating > z$

Where av_cost_of_parts is obtained by calculating the average cost of the twenty most replaced parts (derived from the company's maintenance database). Resale_value is the devaluation rate of a vehicle (calculated as initial sale price – current market value, divided by initial price and adjusted for inflation). Popularity has been defined as the number of new vehicles sold that year, divided by the total car sales for the year. The safety_rating attribute is calculated as an average of safety crashes indices of independent automobile safety authorities and manufacturer's crash tests indices. How the FINDIT organization is established and maintained is described in the following section.

## 12.3.2   The FINDIT Interaction/Negotiation Level

The forming, joining, and leaving of coalitions and services is controlled by privileged users. The primitives for these interactions are provided by the Tassili language, and result in the creation/maintenance of an object oriented coalition/service schema.

In some instances, users may ask about information that is not in the local database domain interest. If these requests are small, a mapping between a set of information meta types to a set of database (coalition) services is enough to resolve the query. If the number of requests remains high the database administrator may, for efficiency reasons, instigate the formation of a coalition with these remote "popular" databases or join a pre–existing coalition. Alternately, the database administrator may initiate a negotiation with other database members to establish a service with an existing coalition or database.

Currently the CheapRent co–database will contain no information regarding the *vehicle spare parts* coalition. However, this coalition can be accessed indirectly via the *vehicle sales* coalition which CheapRent's co–database does have knowledge of. A user can thus investigate the *vehicle spare parts* coalition in the hope of resolving the av_cost_of_parts aspect of the query. If this investigation proves fruitful a short term interaction with this coalition site will ensue. Because the rental company will be performing its own repairs, a continuous long term stream of queries will be sent regarding part prices, availability and so on. Thus, the rental database node administrator establishes a service link with that coalition (*vehicle spare parts*). In Tassili this negotiation process is performed using the following primitives:

**Inquire at** *GM_Spare_Parts* **With Message** "*Wish to establish a service link. What are the main attributes of your resource?*"

A message is sent along with the query to explain what is expected. If the query fails, a diagnostic is returned.

The query:

**Send to** *CheapRent* **Object** *GM_Spare_Parts.template*

is used by the target representative database to send information to the requesting database or coalition. If the specifications meets the servicing needs, no further action is taken. Otherwise, an *Inquire* query is sent back to the target entity for further refinement. This process of negotiation ends whenever the involved entities decide so. If the *Send* query is successful, nothing is returned. If the query fails, a diagnostic of the failure is returned. Other primitives exist to create data structures at local co–databases, to implement the service abstraction and to end the service.

When the car rental company joins the *rental* coalition a FINDIT schema update occurs. A class representing the rental company node is instantiated via an existing coalition member. The coalition member then propagates the change so that the other coalition members can update their local co–database. These changes are achieved using the primitive:

**Instantiate Class** *Rentals* **With Object** *Car* **With** *Name = CheapRent*

The rental database manager may then choose to allow remote access to certain local information. For example, the CheapRent database node may wish to allow access to the "rental_rate", "model" and "year" attributes in its stock database. This is achieved by adding methods to its class via the Tassili primitive:

**Add Method** *Rental_price* **With Body**

*if date.month $\geq$ Oct and date.month $\leq$ Jan then*
  *return(1.2 \* base_price)*
*else*
  *return(base_price)*

**To Class** *Rentals*.


Other Tassili primitives exist to remove methods and objects when a database node relinquishes access to local information or leaves a coalition. There are also more basic primitives which are used to establish/negotiate a coalition and propagate and validate changes. Each operation must be validated by all participating database administrators. The instantiation operation is an exception. In this case the database described by an object is the one that decides what the object state should be. If there is disagreement in the validation process, the administrator who instigated the operation will choose the course of action to be taken.

A joining database must provide some information about the data it would like to share as well as information about itself. The administrator of the coalition will then decide how the coalition schema is to be changed if the new database is accepted as a member. During this informal exchange, many parameters need to be set. For instance, a threshold for the minimum and maximum number of coalition members is negotiated and set. Likewise, a threshold on the minimum and maximum number of services with databases and coalitions is also set. Functional specifications may evolve during the implementation phase.

Initially, a database administrator is picked to create the root class of the coalition schema. Once this is done, the root of the schema is sent to every participating database for validation. If the operation is not validated, the rejecting database node sends an edited version of the object to the creator of the object. Based on this feedback, the creator will decide whether to change the object or not. This process will continue until there is a consensus. Changes are only made at a single site until consensus is achieved – at which time the change is made persistent and propagated to the appropriate nodes.

If existing classes/methods are to be updated responsibility lies with the database that "owns" it. Prior to any changes, the database owner tells every participating database to lock the object to be changed. After an acknowledgment from those databases, the local database administrator proceeds with implementing the changes. The update is then sent to all participating databases. In order to achieve consistency, control concurrency, and manage replication, use is made of the multigranularity protocol, two–phase locking, and the primary copy algorithm [29].

A coalition is dismantled by deleting the corresponding subschema in every participating database schema. This involves notifying all coalitions with which there is a service that the coalitions no longer exists. Local schemas are updated by their administrators. In addition, all objects that belong to the classes of that coalition are also deleted. The update of co–databases resulting from service changes is practically the same as defined for coalitions. The only difference being that changes in coalitions obey a stricter set of rules.

After CheapRent creates a service connection with the *vehicle spare parts* coalition, both it and the coalition members must update their co–database. Similarly, when CheapRent joins the *rentals* coalition co–databases must be updated to reflect the newly discovered inter–node structure. CheapRent thus builds up its local knowledge of remote sites and forms appropriate links with those containing applicable information. In this way FINDIT filters the amount of information which must be assimilated at the car rental node. Only databases which share common areas of interest with the rental database are considered in the interoperability phase. Further coalitions and services are contacted by CheapRent users as they attempt to access required information. The CheapRent database administrator may then choose to enter into/create further coalitions and services based upon users needs.

## 12.3.3 The FINDIT Interoperability Level

FINDIT documents information in a way that makes it understandable in the user's *own* environment. This is achieved through the introduction of *documentations*. These are sample behaviors or structures of certain classes of information. Documentation is attached to each information meta type shared with the outside world. Their aim is to explain/define that information meta type. Interactions are thus based upon the semantic information conveyed in documentations. Documentation is offered by the providing databases and is not an integral part of the FINDIT system.

In the example, documentation is required by CheapRent to make sense of remote database node methods *advertised* in the various coalitions it must interact with. Confusion may arise when interacting with databases in the *vehicle spare parts* coalition because of differences in price listings (eg. one database may include sales tax, others may not), differences in domains (eg. a database may only stock parts for one type of car), differences in the types of businesses (eg. a car wrecker may only display part availability, not price) and so on. Demonstrations may also provide details of information needed by the remote database node to access the required data. For example, a vehicle's year and make will be required to obtain a spare part's price.

Demonstrations thus provide a way of converting data (eg. price of parts versus price with sales tax), evaluating data (eg. the "best" insurance policy – cost benefit analysis), translating data (eg. demonstrations may be offered in several different languages), and interpreting data (eg. the definition of a "safe" car may be provided using a video of text demo – depending on local hardware).

### 12.3.4    The FINDIT Exploration Level

The first (architectural) level of FINDIT provides a logical interconnection of database nodes. The second level (interaction/negotiation) of FINDIT allows this architecture to be physically implemented (i.e. created and managed). Together these two layers allow us to organize interactions between the system's nodes. Once this high level organization/context has been established, lower level concerns may be addressed. Remote information must be understood and this is achieved in FINDIT's third (interoperability) level through the use of demonstrations. Lastly, the appropriate information must be physically accessed. This is achieved in FINDIT's fourth (exploration) level using the Tassili language, and the inter–node relationship information built up in a database's object–oriented co–database. The object–oriented paradigm was chosen because of its ability to easily model complex structures and behavior.

Querying in FINDIT is a task that is performed in two, not necessarily sequential, phases. The first phase consists of educating users about the information space and finding the target databases that are most likely to hold the required type of information. The second phase consists of dynamically specifying and querying the actual information. Due to the broad scope of the problem, we only focus on the first phase.

The syntax specifications of Tassili queries provide constructs to educate users about the available space of information as well as connecting databases and performing remote queries [39]. The information meta type name, structure, behavior, and graphical representation are used as a handle for identifying the appropriate information resources. Node co–databases maintain FINDIT schemas and it is to co–databases that all queries are directed.

A co–database schema consists of two subschemas as depicted in Figure 12.4. Each subschema consists of a lattice of classes that represents either a coalition or a service. Each class represents a set of databases that can answer queries about a specific type of information (eg. queries about *car parts*). A graphical interface has been implemented to help users navigate through the information space. The service subschema (left side of Figure 12.4) consists of two subschemas. The first subschema depicts services that coalitions it is a member of have with other databases and coalitions. The second subschema shows the services the database has with other databases and coalitions. Each of these subschemas, in turn, consists of two subclasses that describe services with databases and services with other coalitions respectively.

The coalition subschema (right side of Figure 12.4) consists of one or more subschemas, each of which represents a coalition. Coalition servicer descriptions include information about points of entry and contact with those coalitions.

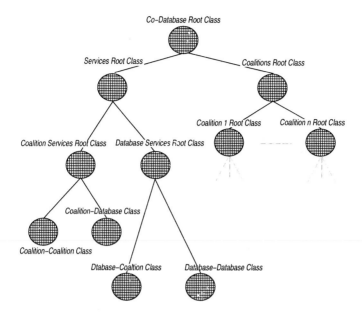

**Figure 12.4** Typical Co–database Schema Skeleton

Other descriptions provide information to local databases so the best point of contact can be chosen. It should be noted that the subschema representing the set of coalition servicers will be the same for all databases that are members of the servicing coalition.

The set of databases comprising a certain information meta type is represented by a class in the schema. Every class contains a description of the participating databases and the information meta types they contain. Some attributes describe the information meta type while the remaining attributes describe the databases that instantiate this information meta type. Database descriptions include information about the data model, operating system, query language, etc. A description of the information meta type includes its general structure and behavior. Since databases may have different views on the same information meta type, only the common parts of the view are represented in the class. These descriptions differ from demonstrations in that they only offer general structural information.

Using this structural information and various Tassili query primitives, a user at the CheapRent company can begin to resolve the query described previously. The CheapRent co–database is currently a member of the *rentals* coalition and has a service with the *vehicle spare parts* coalition. Because of these links Cheap-Rent has knowledge of the *vehicle sales* coalition stored in its co–database. This information may be accessed by a user through the Tassili primitives:

**Display Coalitions of** *CheapRent* – provides a list of coalitions CheapRent is a member of.

**Display Coalition Services** *Rentals* – provides a list of coalitions the CheapRent database and *rentals* coalition has a service with, *vehicle sales* and *vehicle spare parts* for example.

A similar query may be used to examine the services links of the *vehicle spare parts* and *vehicle sales* coalitions. In this way CheapRent users can discover the coalitions: *vehicle specifications, insurance* and *vehicle registration*. Lastly, by examining the service links to the *insurance* coalition, the *vehicle safety* coalition can be found.

Primitives also exist which display the classes of services and coalitions, and allow connections to remote coalition/database services. Users may utilize other primitives and stipulate an "information name" – for example "part prices" – which returns a list of possibly remote coalitions/services that have a corresponding class name. This process requires that nodes maintain an appropriate list of thesaurus terms. If no match is made a null list is returned. In this case a user may either submit another information name term or attempt to navigate through the system and discover the information incrementally.

In the car rental case, the service between the CheapRent database and the *vehicle spare parts* coalition is returned by stipulating the information name *spare parts* or simply by listing services. Once an appropriate coalition/service has been found, Tassili provides primitives for investigating its classes. For example:

**Display SubClasses** *vehicle_spare_parts* – displays all the subclasses of the *vehicle spare parts* coalition.

The query:

**Find Information** *part_prices* – displays information associated with the subclass *part prices* within the coalition *vehicle spare parts*.

Lastly, the query:

**Find Information With Attributes** *parts:"exhaust", model:"JaguarXJS", year:"1990"* – displays actual information.

Clearly these queries require increasingly greater knowledge of the coalition schema. Thus FINDIT caters for both expert and novice users. Further Tassili primitives are available for exploring objects more fully. For example, the "Display SubClass" query may return a list: cars, trucks, motor bikes and so on. A user can then use the query:

**Display Instances** < *blank* > **By Attribute Of Information** *Car*

By leaving the "instance" term blank all instances associated with the sub-class "Car" are displayed. Similarly, Tassili allows attributes of instances to be displayed. Finally, Tassili allows for further understanding of an information meta type using the primitive:

**Display Documentation of Instance** *Ford_spare_parts* **Of Information** *part_price.*

The query results in the running of a remote demonstration which can be in textual or graphical form. The query result requires a certain type of hardware and/or software to run. The user is thus prompted to provide some information about the local environment. If there is no behavioral capability or no suitable environment is present, the query fails. Otherwise the documentation is displayed.

## 12.4   Implementation Overview

This section discusses the important components of the FINDIT system which are described in more detail in [41]. The FINDIT architecture is divided into eight main modules as shown in Figure 12.5. Some of the modules use primitives defined in the data manipulation and definition primitives module.

User queries (textual or iconic) are first submitted to the Tassili interpreter. The interpreter calls the graphical toolkit display routines corresponding to Tassili display instructions. Display class windows show users the various attributes of a class and allows further investigation of information meta types. Display class also displays subclasses for that class. The display coalitions lists all coalitions that a database is a member of or has a service with, and allows users to choose a coalition and view it. This is similar to displaying services. The documentation windows offer a choice of displaying information textually, visually, audibly, or any combination thereof. The graphical interface is designed to run on workstations using the X windows protocol. The interactive part consists of a series of windows providing the following functions:

1. Control the use of iconic queries.

2. Choose an object to display (be it a class or instance).

3. Display an object.

4. Operate a command line query.

5. Create and store a script corresponding to an icon.

6. Display on-line help

7. Display the current or history of, query execution.

As an example, Figure 12.6 shows a documentation query about the instance *lotus_123* of information type *spreadsheet*. This instance represents a database

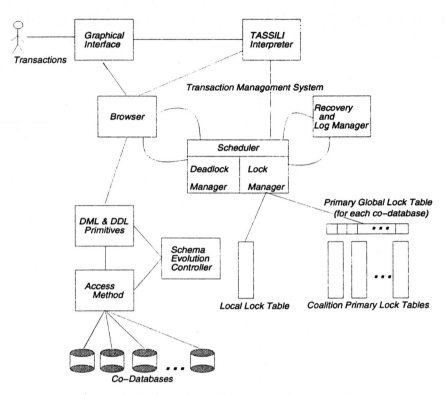

**Figure 12.5** Overview of the FINDIT Architecture

that stores information about the spreadsheet lotus_123. The documentation is meant to give an idea to users what this software is all about – only a sample documentation is displayed.

The browser takes a query and passes it to the transaction management system to get all locks necessary. It may have to submit the query to a remote database. This remote database may in turn submit the same query to other remote databases until all the appropriate information has been identified. The browser follows an algorithm that determines the steps to follow for educating users about information and locating databases.

**Write** transactions are performed by privileged users, i.e, the system administrators. There will thus be many more **Read** than **Write** transactions in FINDIT. Concurrency control is achieved using a locking mechanism instead of a timestamping algorithm. This is done for two main reasons: simplicity (allowable because the number of **Read** operations heavily outweigh **Writes**); and because the overhead in keeping track of timestamps and synchronizing clocks across sites becomes a factor in decreasing efficiency and hence concurrency.

We distinguish two kinds of situations for managing FINDIT transactions. The first case is when a coalition is being formed. In this instance, no problem arises as **Write** transactions are only performed one at a time by the admin-

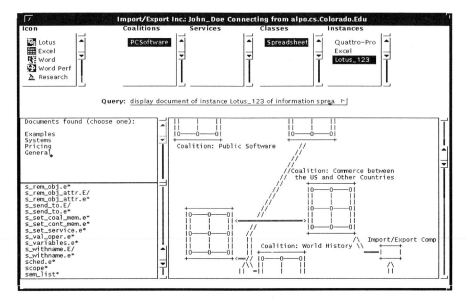

**Figure 12.6** Example of a Documentation Request

istrator initiating the coalition. After each round of negotiation one **Write** is performed. The second case is when a schema is being updated by a privileged user while being read by one or more users. Here a two-phase locking algorithm is adopted with the requested object being locked in all participating co–databases. Changes are introduced and then propagated to all participating co–databases.

In order for a transaction to get a lock on an object, it first has to get a lock on the copy located in the primary site. Once it is granted this lock then no other transaction can get it until it is relinquished by the current owner. This approach was chosen because of its simplicity and the low number of messages needed to get a lock. This basic method makes no provisions for site crashes. Thus, the primary site of an object is migrated from time to time ensuring only temporary unavailability of sites. This extension only incurs extra overheads when lock tables are updated during the migration of lock responsibility.

The deadlock manager uses time-outs to detect possible deadlocks. Each transaction is given a timestamp when it starts being processed. While waiting for its lock request, a transaction checks whether the time–out has been exceeded. For the sake of simplicity, the current transaction is aborted. The deadlock manager undoes everything that may have been updated and unlocks every object locked by that transaction.

## 12.5    Discussion and Future Directions

One of the most important features of FINDIT is the flexibility and ease with which databases join and leave the system and organize themselves within the system. An interesting aspect of the system lies in the fact it is designed to learn from query failures. The system reacts to failures by extending the scope of structural information.

By incrementally deriving structural knowledge and exploring the information sources available via demonstrations, FINDIT enables the user to navigate through the information search space. The highly interactive form of FINDIT warrants the use of interpreted queries. Hence Tassili also accepts graphical queries [41] which are currently iconic in nature. A user thus forms text queries to find a certain piece of information and then maps this to a graphical representation. Any subsequent query to this information can then be made graphically. The space of information is dynamic, thus users are notified about the possibility of an outdated script. Certain updates on the script could be performed without any notification such as name or attribute changes. Other changes are hard to perform automatically because of their semantics. Future work will include a study to determine what other types of graphical queries might be useful.

Implicit in this chapter has been the existence of a *relationship space*, in addition to the *information space*. In future work we will be exploring how the inter–relationship space may be defined, subdivided, and explored. This will be based on the architecture proposed in [165] and combined with the existing FINDIT architecture to provide a more complete method of resource discovery and data sharing in large scale systems.

# Chapter 13

## An Intelligent Agent for the K-12 Educational Community

Dr. Mark E Rorvig[*], Mark W. Hutchison[†]. Dr. Robert O. Shelton[‡], Stephanie L. Smith[§], Marwan E. Yazbeck[¶] [‖]

## 13.1 Introduction

In order to be considered an intelligent agent, it is proposed that such a device must possess at least two characteristics. First, it must be selective, that is, capable of discriminating knowledge sources, and evaluating them according to the wishes of its owners. Second, it must be resource efficient, that is, act in a manner which does not jeopardize the functions of its host. In this last case, the host environment, or body in which the agent resides, is the Internet. Such a device has been constructed for use by primary and secondary educators and it has been deployed through the Texas Education Agency's Texas Education Network (TENET) facilities at the University of Texas at Austin beginning in December, 1994 [231].

Though the technology of intelligent agents is in its infancy, a number of such tools now exist on the Internet. Others have been commercially announced. Existing, non-commercial agents on the Internet as of January, 1995 numbered about ten [64]. Variously referred to as robots, web wanderers, and spiders, these devices perform a wide range of functions: counting server sites; retrieving documents on specific subjects; and gathering and reorganizing server site listings for better retrieval. At least one of these, called InfoSeek [63] by its authors,

[*]Software Technology Branch, Lyndon B. Johnson Space Center, National Aeronautics and Space Administration, Houston, TX 77058

[†]Science Applications International Corporation, 17049 El Camino Real, Suite 202, Houston, TX 77058

[‡]Software Technology Branch, Lyndon B. Johnson Space Center, National Aeronautics and Space Administration, Houston, TX 77058

[§]Hernandez Engineering, Inc., 17625 El Camino Real, Suite 200, Houston, TX, 77058

[¶]LinCom Corporation, 1020 Bay Area Blvd., Suite 200, Houston, TX 77058

[‖]* This paper describes a NASA owned invention, Case No. MSC-22551-1. Inquiries for use may be made to Mr. Hardie Barr, Patent Counsel, Lyndon B. Johnson Space Center, NASA, Houston, TX 77058, telephone 713/483-1003. This work was funded under WBS 509-40 as part of the Information Infrastructure Technology Applications program of the High Performance Computing and Communications Divison, Code RC, of the National Aeronautics and Space Administration.

has evolved to search a compiled catalog [151] of the net with a complex query.

Commercial knowledge robots are mostly in the prototype stage of development. Entries to the marketplace include AT&T's Personalink–a product designed to assist users in shopping and organizing electronic mail. Another firm, General Magic has announced a product called Telescript. The structure of the networks which support these agents and a description of many agent functions has appeared in the formal literature within the last year [?] [?].

The general approach to our agent, referred to as ILIAD (Internet Library Information Assembly Database), consists of five steps: First, conversion of a user's natural language query into the structured terms of the Dewey Decimal Classification (DDC); second, generation of a server list previously mapped to the DDC by either automated or manual methods; third, retrieval of the documents from the individual servers by passing the query to the server and obtaining the results; fourth, linguistic filtering of the retrieved documents using a partial match vector formula [?] [104] ; fifth, a neural net preference filter operating on style and readability characteristics of the retrieved documents [193] [?] [211] [186] [208]. Retrieved documents which survive the linguistic and preference filters are simply mailed back by electronic mail to the person who originally submitted the query. A chart displaying the overall system design is presented in Figure 1.

## 13.2   The Agent

The agent which we have constructed, though generalizable to many domains, has been oriented toward elementary and secondary education [111] [168]. In this regard, we attempted to take advantage of the large scale electronic library infrastructure created by government (Federal, State, and local) during the preceding several years [149].

Specifically we concentrated on the more than 500 WAIS servers on the Internet, since (a little over a year ago) these servers represented almost all areas of knowledge and permitted ranking by relevance to the query of their content objects. The distribution of these servers among the schedules of the Dewey Decimal Classification (DDC) (the classification system used in most K-12 American educational institutions) is shown in Figure 2.

We do not hesitate to note that the simple growth of the Internet has made this approach insufficient to service many of the requests which have been put to the agent, and our initial reliance on WAIS has been expanded to include use of the catalog of Uniform Resource Locators as collected by the Lycos application at Carnegie Mellon University [157].

The specifications for our agent were drawn from conversations with the managers and participants in the Texas Education Network. The agent was to address text data alone. Above all, educators stressed the need for the agent to be highly selective, noting that an abundance of poor material was already easily available to teaching communities. Finally, the interface to the agent was to be entirely comprised by email, since network resources for graphical interfaces

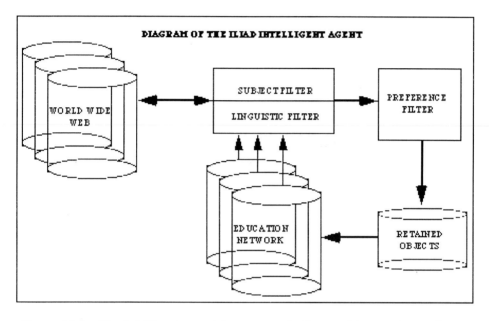

Figure 13.1: The intelligent agent is composed of several interacting software components: A subject filter which converts a natural language user query into the controlled vocabulary of the Dewey Decimal System; a linguistic filter which qualifies retrieved documents; and a neural net preference filter, trained to reflect style charcteristics of preferred documents. The subject filter receives requests from networks, identifies the Internet resources which could meet the request, and sends requests and receives material from these sources. The linguistic filter uses a partial match formula to eliminate unnecessary material and then passes its received source material to the preference filter, which decomposes the received objects into signature patterns. These patterns are then matched against the preferred patterns for a user or class of users, and the resulting material returned over networks to the requestor.

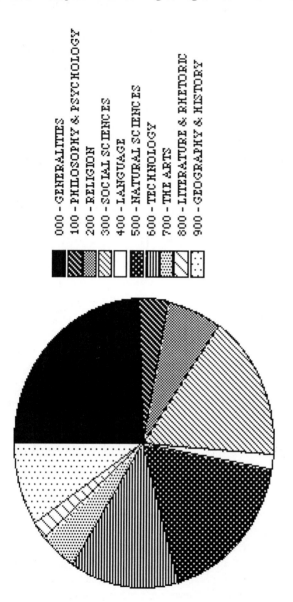

Figure 13.2: The relative subject distribution of 905 servers (some are duplicated among subject categories) which follow the Wide Area Information Server (WAIS) index structure and communication protocol is displayed as a pie graph. The large number of servers (222) listed under the subject heading "Generalities", reflects the origins and development of the Internet, since the 004-007 classes contain the headings for computer science, software and methods. The Dewey Decimal System, first devised by Melvil Dewey in 1894 is now in its 20th edition and is thought to be the most widely used classification schedule in the world.

could not be assumed to be available at the vast majority of Texas schools.

The specificity of the educators' remarks give rise to difficulty in assessing the system, since traditional measures for assessments of information retrieval systems, i.e., precision and recall, do not actually fit this situation. The potential recall of the system may be estimated from multiplying the number of servers contacted for any query by ten, since only the top ten scoring items were retrieved from each WAIS server. However, since we were unable through our charter to be sufficiently intrusive with the client population to obtain human judgments of the relevance of the final documents, precision cannot effectively be estimated.

Although operational data for the agent are limited, it is clear that WAIS sources alone are insufficient to meet many queries. Indeed, out of 160 queries processed in 45 days, more than one in five were returned with no relevant documents selected. Gopher sources and http sites are required to service educator needs for learning resources from the Internet environment in the future. Figure 3 and Figure 4 below summarize the existing data on the agent performance in its first weeks of operation.

More seriously, after January, a large number of WAIS sources discontinued responses at their former logical port server addresses. It is thus speculated that many servers are now accessible only through the logical port addresses formerly associated with uniform resource locators, or URL's. The agent response was discontinued in late February until new server resources from the Lycos data file could be used in place of the former WAIS associated structure. The new system returned to service in mid-April.

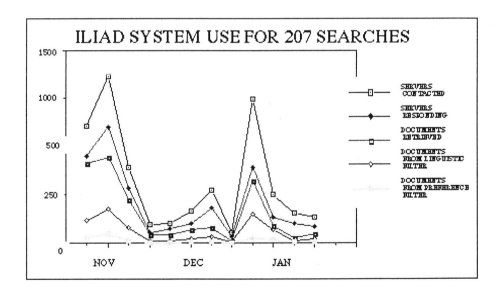

Figure 13.3: Operational data for the agent during its first 90 day of operation. beluse

| | (1) SERVERS CONTACTED | (2) SERVERS RESPONDING | (3) DOCUMENTS RETRIEVED | (4) DOCUMENTS SURVIVING THE LINGUISTIC FILTER | (5) DOCUMENTS SURVIVING THE PREFERENCE FILTER |
|---|---|---|---|---|---|
| WEEK 1 | 909 | 677 | 617 | 175 | 43 |
| | 1290 | 903 | 668 | 262 | 71 |
| | 583 | 426 | 338 | 122 | 17 |
| | 147 | 84 | 65 | 15 | 4 |
| | 155 | 112 | 61 | 13 | 1 |
| | 252 | 150 | 104 | 31 | 8 |
| | 406 | 270 | 120 | 49 | 9 |
| | 82 | 47 | 19 | 9 | 2 |
| | 1117 | 587 | 480 | 222 | 44 |
| | 381 | 201 | 134 | 104 | 23 |
| | 235 | 149 | 43 | 17 | 8 |
| WEEK 12 | 200 | 127 | 76 | 29 | 8 |

Figure 13.4: Operations of the agent during its test and open periods in the Fall and early Winter of 1994. The table reflects the happenstance nature of the Internet, in that, at any given moment in time, a large number of servers do not respond. The actions of the linguistic and preference filters tend to screen out these descrepancies, however, with the average ratio of documents surviving to servers contacted at 30 to 1. Although recall and precision figures could be calculated for the agent, it is not clear that such figures would reflect its performance, since the server response rate tends strongly to condition the subsequent processes.

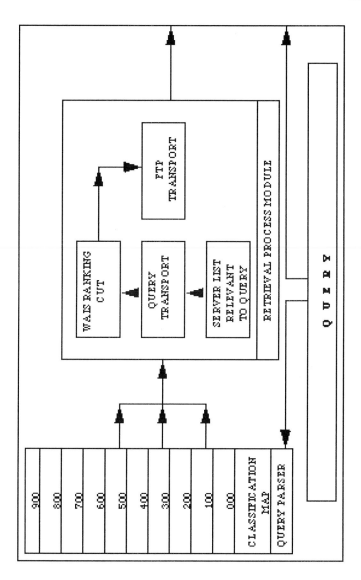

Figure 13.5: The information flow and component layout of the subject filter is diagrammed. Queries, i.e., user requests for information, are received and parsed into search strings. These strings in turn are matched against the classification descriptions of the Dewey Decimal System, 20th Edition by means of the Salton cosine-vector formula. Assuming an appropriate matching threshold, the original query is forwarded to the topically relevant server sources. The top ten objects are then requested by means of the file transport protocol (FTP) and passed, together with the original user request, to the linguistic and preference filters.

The subject filter was created by searching the catalogs of WAIS servers with queries composed of the words associated with each decal division of the DDC. Manual methods of classification are very difficult to perform and it should be noted that the assignment of WAIS sources to decal divisions of the DDC required a trained librarian more than three months effort. Future work will employ automatic methods of classification using techniques originally evaluated with respect to online public access library catalogs [139].

Returned responses from WAIS sites were limited to only the top scoring objects. The performance of the agent is thus constrained by the quality of linguistic descriptions at the server sites and the effectiveness of the ranking algorithms at each site. During the first year of operation of ILIAD within the TENET system, only text files will be retrieved on an operational basis. On a selective basis, a small number of institutions may be permitted multimedia access in the specialized area of earth observing images. A diagram of the subject filter components are shown in Figure 5.

The most complex component of ILIAD is its preference filter. To begin with, such preferences must be recorded by non-verbal means, since it is usually quite difficult for individuals to explicate preferences for specific information content styles and formats. Further, though the operation of the subject and linguistic filters ensure, through matching formulas and cutoff thresholds, that received objects will be at least topically relevant to a query, topical relevance alone is insufficient. The preference filter must thus ensure that retrieved objects,meet the indirectly expressed preference responses of its users.

These objectives are accomplished with a series of operations. First, the preference profile is contructed for a randomized sample of materials retrieved from each DDC schedule division where the schedule description itself is used as a query. A Thurstonian scaling technique is used (a description of this method is available in [193] to elicit preference judgments on pairs of text stimuli, (but which could also include mixed pairs of images and text, text and text, and sound and text, or any pair combination.) The result is an ordering of objects according to the probability that each would be chosen over the others in the choice set [?]. This ordering may be rendered by representative groups (as performed in this application by stratified samples of K-12 educators), or by an individual. Those objects with the highest probability of choice are then analyzed to obtain a series of feature "signature" scores. These scores are then normalized by converting the various measures to common unit normal deviates of the normal curve, according to procedures developed earlier for NASA [194] [?]. The overall structure of the preference filter is displayed in the diagram of Figure 6.

Once the object feature signature scores of preferred objects have been obtained and stored by DDC class, they may be invoked whenever a new query is serviced. As new objects are received by DDC class from the subject filter in response to a query, they are decomposed by the same object features used to establish the signatures of the preferred objects, normalized, and matched, class by class, against the stored object feature signatures of preferred objects. Those

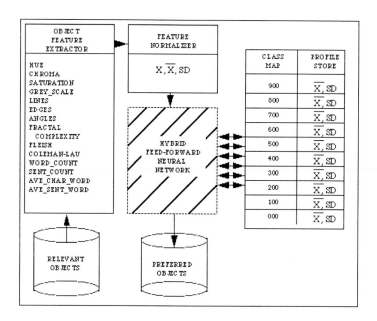

Figure 13.6: The information flow and component layout of the preference filter is diagrammed. Objects are passed to the preference filter by the linguistic filte r for decomposition into feature signatures or patterns. Some of the features present ly used by theintelligent agent are listed. The measures hue, chroma, saturation, g rey scale, lines edges, angles and fractal complexity refer to image processing measures which were used experimentally. The production measures used in the text only system were the Fleish, Coleman-Lau, and various word frequency counts for text preference detection. The measures as a whole reflect the multimedia capabilities of the system of software components. Since features are quite dissimilar, they are normalized as standard units under the normal probability curve for all items received. These patterns are in turn matched by a neural network to the preferred signatures stored for a user or user class. Those objects meeting the preference standards are retained and mailed to the requestor's point of origin. The precision, or ratio of preferred items to less preferred items correctly matched during testing, appears to lie in the 55-70group of practicing teachers. There is some evidence that preference signatures for engineers would be easier to match.

new objects failing to fall within the boundaries of the signature of preferred objects as determined by a new form of neural net [208], are deleted from the retrieved set. Those objects within the boundaries are retained and forwarded to the requesting educator or educational institution.

The feed-forward neural net was invented [208] to perform electrical signal matching from Space Shuttle telemetry. As electrical devices are used, their identification is required in order to monitor total power consumption during spaceflight. Automation of this function by the new hybrid feed-forward neural net is expected to lead to reduced ground crew expenses during Space Shuttle missions.

The agent, ILIAD, and other similar devices represent an important addition to Internet searching technology. However, this advance also raises a number of unique social issues over the availability and cost of information. Although a good deal of government information is available presently on Internet at no cost, such information is neither as uniformly described nor quality controlled as those from commercial sources. The technology of intelligent agents may put the equivalent of a personal library clerk at the disposal of many persons, but its performance will be only as refined as the information sources from which it draws.

## 13.3  Acknowledgements

The authors gratefully acknowledge the contributions of the following persons: Mr. Robert T. Savely, Chief Scientist for Software Technology (of NASA); Dr. Timothy Cleghorn (of NASA) for his advice on the application of fractels to image understanding; and Ms. Linda Blount, Executive Director of the Partnership Center for Education Enhancement for her organization's assistance in locating educators for construction of our test and validation data sets.

## 13.4  Appendix A - Example of Question and Answer Responses from November and April

1. NOVEMBER FIRST QUESTION AS OF 11-4-94:
   Documentation ¡/h1¿ ?*Q1 : How far is the earth from the sun and the moon from the earth? I would l ike to know the distances between planets in the Solar system and the distances between galaxies and our own galaxy.
   Research and Visiting Appointment - MAX-PLANCK-INSTITUT FUER ASTROPHYSIK
   AUSTRALIAN NATIONAL UNIVERSITY - DOCTORAL, MASTER'S & BACHELOR'S THESES ABSTRACTS
   :source :version 3 :ip-name "Hypatia.gsfc.nasa.gov" :tcp-port 210 :database-name "HST_data"
   HTML Version of AstroWeb Database

Subject: Re: ASTRONOMERS DISCOVER NEARBY SPIRAL GALAXY HIDDEN BEHIND THE MILKY WAY

2. APRIL LATEST QUESTION AS OF 4-10-95:

?Q1: Tell me about the Hubble Space Telescope?

TALE OF TWO CLUSTERS YIELDS SECRETS OF STAR BIRTH IN THE EARLY UNIVERSE

¡H1¿¡IMG ALIGN=bottom SRC="../STScI.xbm" ALT="STScI"¿ NASA Hubble Space Telescope¡/H1¿

¡title¿STScI Documentation ¡/title¿ ¡h1¿STScI On-line Documentation ¡/h1¿

¡Title¿HST Data Handbook¡/Title¿ ¡HR¿ ¡H1¿HST Data Handbook¡/H1¿

SEARCH FOR RED DWARF STARS IN GLOBULAR CLUSTER NGC 6397

GALAXY M100 RESOLUTION COMPARISON

Frequently Asked Questions about the Collision of Comet Shoemaker-Levy 9 with Jupiter

¡Title¿STScI/HST Pictures¡/Title¿ ¡H1¿Hubble Space Telescope Public Pictures¡/H1¿ ¡IMG ALIGN=bottom SRC="PicsBanner.gif" ALT="Pictures"¿

¡H1¿¡b¿The HST Archive¡/b¿¡/H1¿

HST OBSERVES THE SUPERNOVA IN THE WHIRLPOOL GALAXY

# Chapter 14

## Interface Issues for Interactive Multimedia Documents

Robert B. Allen[*],[†]

## 14.1  INTRODUCTION

### 14.1.1  Multimedia Documents

Documents may be distinguished from collections of loosely-linked information objects in having a high-level organization. A logical high-level document structure offers many cognitive advantages for the reader as compared to presentation of disjoint information objects. Ideas organized by an author's understanding may be easy for a reader to comprehend. In addition, the author's conceptual structure may be acquired by the reader and may provide a framework for that reader to organize additional information.

Recorded lectures are particularly good examples of multimedia documents because they are lengthy, coherent, and may incorporate a wide variety of media. Moreover, lectures may be enhanced with other materials such as student notes, simulations, associated texts, and problem sets. Indeed, the lecture itself might be enhanced, for instance, by providing multilingual versions. Because these enhancements provide many advantages over live or even videotaped presentations, online multimedia lectures and textbooks may greatly improve the quality of education.

Other examples of complex multimedia documents are radio and television news programs and documentaries. For instance, an electronic newspaper could contain a wide variety of material such as images, video, maps, and historical texts. While there has been much discussion of personalized news media, (e.g., [1]) a strong case can be made that it is too difficult to anticipate users' interests and that a consistent document structure (like a traditional newspaper) and powerful document browsing tools will be more effective in giving the user access to relevant material.

---

[*]Bellcore, MRE 2A367, 445 South Street, Morristown, NJ 07960, Email: rba@bellcore.com

[†]

## 14.1.2   Multimedia Browsers

Current multimedia viewers take little advantage of high-level structure for presenting information objects. Many of these systems simply display the objects retrieved from a database. Even among those systems that present connected material, there is little structuring by semantic content. For instance, one common interface style for presenting the content of a video simply tiles a screen with frames. A second common type of interface uses variants of the video streamer [83] that presents overlapping edges of video frames. Only minimal semantics of the content are used in organizing the material. Timelines (e.g., [66, 72]) have also been widely employed to allow users to browse multimedia presentations but, again, they generally incorporate only minimal semantics.

Streams [66] is a multimedia viewer which presents thumbnail views of several concurrent media channels and lets the user focus on one of them. Thus, a lecture recorded with Streams might include a video of the lecturer, a video of the audience, and a channel showing the lecture's view-graphs. The implementation of Streams provides timelines and a video streamer for indicating position. However, Streams was designed so that no human analysis of the video was necessary; thus, there is no semantic searching capability, no high-level semantic organization such as a table of contents (TOC), and no linking across time between objects.

## 14.1.3   Internal Representations

In much of the previous work on multimedia documents, the emphasis has been on the representation of the structure of the documents rather than on the accessibility of the information. Hypertext interchange models such as Dexter [118] deal primarily with simple information objects. HyTime [170], an extension of the Standard Generalized Markup Language (SGML) for linking hypermedia objects, and MHEG [184] allow very general representations of multimedia, but they do not prescribe how these objects may best be arranged for user access. While internal document representation is important in providing efficiency, the emphasis in this work is on the design of usable interfaces.

# 14.2   PRESENTATION   ISSUES   FOR MULTIMEDIA DOCUMENTS

Capabilities such as linking, searching, and TOCs have proven important for presentation of text documents. For instance, the SuperBook$^{TM}$ document browser [?] uses these features to allow readers to move around the high-level structure. However, the SuperBook browser does not manage multimedia as effectively as it manages text. When it launches a multimedia diversion, the user cannot return from the multimedia diversions to other parts of the text nor does it synchronize several concurrent channels of multimedia events as Streams does.

## 14.2.1   Tables of Contents (TOCs)

A TOC is a composite set of links that provides pointers into a corpus. Unlike the timeline, which provides only limited linking, the TOC has a rich semantics. In addition to helping a user navigate a document, the TOC provides context for understanding the structure of a document. The TOC is probably especially important if there is no semantic searching capability. While fisheye TOCs are fairly common for text-based documents, they have not previously been applied to image and video collections.

As illustrated by the interfaces developed in Section 3, the TOC can be applied to multimedia documents. Indeed, as shown below (in Figure 14.4), the TOC itself need not be purely text. Even, an audio menu could be considered to be a TOC for an all-audio document. User-placed book-marks can also be organized as a type of TOC. Not only do these allow the user to note and later access sections of a document, but a collection of them can also provide a personalized high-level view of the structure of a document.

## 14.2.2   Linking

One interface principle for links is that they should indicate as clearly as possible where they lead. A second principle is that there should be an easy way to undo the link transition. For linking in multimedia documents, there are two additional issues: Linking across spatial and temporal extent. First, for complex graphical material, such as the view-graphs, it is difficult to determine what aspect of the graphic is the link anchor. This may be resolved by hot-spot graphics in which moving the mouse in different parts of the graphic allows relevant links to be highlighted. However, some links may be anchored by several different points on a single graphic. Second, for temporal media (e.g., audio and video) links may be dynamic and may appear and disappear as the material is presented. Moreover, these solutions are not general because a user may wish to get a broader view of the links such as those links that are active in surrounding material when viewing a presentation.

When linking between complex multimedia documents, it may be necessary to provide some of the context for the link anchors. This might be done with a TOC-like link anchor (it is also similar to the graphical link viewer of [95]).

There are similar link problems for accessing user annotations when they are linked to a document. However, because annotations may themselves be multimedia documents there also involve the larger problems for managing links between two multimedia documents.

## 14.2.3   Searching

When a user wants to explore a new topic for which a TOC or links are not readily available, a search may be used to identify relevant documents or parts of a document. A few interfaces allow database-style searching across collections of multimedia materials [144, 155]; however, in almost all cases, the queries are stated textually rather than in some other medium. Of course, if available, the full-text transcript of a lecture would greatly improve search quality. Relartively little is known about handling non-textual queries, but it is possible to imagine queries to the audio track or to the visual material. Indeed, complex queries involving several media would be possible, although quantitative comparisons of the similarity of search hits across media would not be trivial. Searching across multiple media introduces difficulties for rank ordering search hits because weights for the contributions of different modalities are unknown.

A useful feature of the SuperBook browser is the display of search hits on the dynamic TOC. In a multimedia document interface, there are a variety of possibilities for how to post search hits on multiple TOCs and how to coordinate browsing of search hits across several media. Yet another challenging problem is how the best "focus of attention" (see Section 2.5) might be selected for presenting the results of a search. For instance, if search hits were clustered primarily in a video, it would make sense to highlight that material.

## 14.2.4   Supporting Partially Guided Tours

Guided tours have been widely discussed (e.g., [219, 241]) for controlling the presentation of collections of hypertext objects. Like guided tours, computer based training (CBT) [221] imposes a structure on a user for browsing an information space, although transitions may be a complex function of previous responses.

Rather than strictly guided tours, the approach proposed here may be termed *partially guided tours*. Instead of being read straight through, a textbook is probably more frequently accessed as a reference document in a semi-random order. Replaying a part of a lecture rather than the whole thing, is a simple example of a partially-guided tour. To make multimedia documents effective electronic textbooks, it seems necessary to find ways to support these partially guided tours. Thus, if a user is following a course outline and decides to interrupt the course to browse other material, it should be possible for the user to resume the course at the point he/she interrupted it. In a related vein, the document should support multiple levels of tours. for instance, there could be a quick overview and other, successively more complex views.

## 14.2.5   Locking Concurrent Multimedia Streams

Multimedia document interface management gets more complex when a user is able to detach one media stream from other streams. For instance, a user might want to browse view-graphs while listening to the audio track of the lecture. Indeed, there is ambiguity even for the relatively simple interfaces described earlier in this chapter about the interactions of the visual and auditory media. A similar problem occurs if the media streams are related, but do not cover identical material. For instance, a lecture may not exactly follow a textbook. The notion of detaching media suggests that the streams are not "locked" together. An issue is whether TOCs should automatically expand if the audio is in auto-play mode.

When a document interface allows the user to detach and browse different streams, the media may be said to be unlocked. In addition, the diversions in the SuperBook text browser are essentially 'unlocked' from the text. A view-graph launched from the SuperBook browser remains open until the user closes it. This is fairly straightforward for single images, but it may be much more confusing when there are multiple diversions in complex documents. The CD-ROM encyclopedia *Encarta* has a simple locking mechanism; it allows images to be either locked or unlocked from the text.

A user who is following a guided tour and may want to browse other material or to explore linked documents. The simplest solution would be to be suspend the guided tour while the user browses other material and then have the tour reinstated when the user finishes browsing. Indeed, the suspension point could be much like a bookmark and if there were several of them, they could be stored in a list. This bookmark style would be the easiest to implement. However, it does not handle complex, but probably common, cases in which the user wants to do concurrent actions such as browsing view-graphs while listening to an on-going audio presentation.

If media in a document are not locked together, or if several loosely-coupled documents are being browsed, then the user needs to be aware of which streams are being coordinated in actions such as searching. A "focus of attention" could indicate which of the several groups of media is active. It is analogous to the focus window for a window manager. Perhaps, spatial grouping or the coloration of widgets could indicate which streams are locked together.

# 14.3 TOC INTERFACE IMPLEMENTATIONS

Four interface implementations, programmed with Motif widgets under the X Window System, are described below.

## 14.3.1 Corpora

Two related sets of multimedia materials were obtained. 98 view-graphs for a Bellcore Training and Education Center (TEC) course on Asynchronous Transfer Mode (ATM) and were arranged into modules that formed a simple hierarchy. In addition, a one-hour videotape of a lecture on ATM was MPEG1 encoded and stored. This video was the first part of a three-hour course that roughly paralleled the view-graph course. The images used in the course video that were not available as view-graphs were digitized from the screen images. The audio track of a lecture was $\mu$law encoded and stored separately. The times at which the view-graphs appeared in the audio (and hence also in the video) presentations were noted and stored.

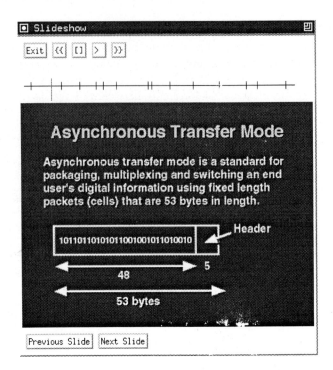

**Figure 14.1** Timeline Slideshow Interface for View-Graphs and Audio.

## 14.3.2   Timeline-based Audio-Slideshow Browser

Figure 14.1 shows an interface for presentation of the lecture audio and view-graphs. The audio of the lecture can be played from any point with the view-graphs presented at appropriate points. Alternatively, the view-graphs can be browsed without accompanying audio. A timeline of the lecture is presented with view-graph transitions marked along it. The user can skip to the points in the lecture by clicking on the timeline. The view-graph associated with that interval is then displayed. This interface is similar to Streams [06] in that the audio and associated view-graphs are always locked together. Cassette-like audio controls are shown at the top of the widget. In this case, { means jumps back, [] means stop, > means play, and }} is jump forward. The view-graphs are controlled by the buttons at the bottom.

Several modifications to the basic interface would be possible. For instance, some of the structure of the document could be displayed by marking the timeline with different colors. In the implementation shown in the figure, the audio and view-graphs were locked so that changes to audio position updated the view-graphs and vice-versa. However, users might want to clone the view-graph display so that they could browse the view-graphs while not interrupting the ongoing audio presentation.

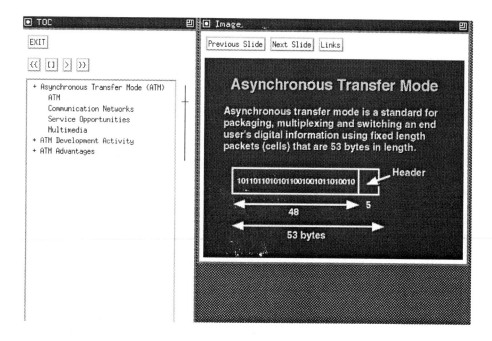

**Figure 14.2** Dynamic TOC for Controlling Audio and View-graphs.

### 14.3.3   TOC-based View-graph and Audio Browser

The timeline in the audio/view-graph interface presented minimal semantic information about the content of the view-graphs. A text TOC may have semantic labels that can help the user navigate the lecture. Figure 14.2 shows a hierarchical TOC for controlling audio and view-graphs. The text part of the TOC widget resembles the TOC used in the SuperBook document browser. Entries that have subnodes and can be expanded are marked with a "+". A single click on a TOC node opens the subnodes and displays the associated view-graph. A second click closes the subnodes.

In addition to the audio being coordinated with the view-graphs (and hence the TOC), the audio can also be controlled with the modified VCR-buttons at the top of the TOC. To the right of the TOC, a hash mark indicates the position of the audio being played. It may be noted that is not an interval representation of the positions of the view-graphs and that its length changes as the TOC changes.

### 14.3.4   TOC-based Video Browser

As shown in Figure 14.3, a hierarchical TOC widget, similar to the one used in the previous interface, was developed to control a video player. The video

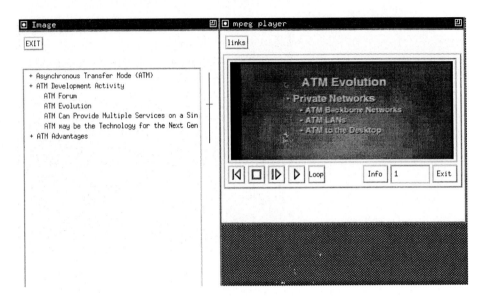

**Figure 14.3** Dynamic TOC for Controlling Video.

player was adapted from the freeware UCB MPEG1 player. This interface could subsume the functionality of the view-graph TOC browser by presenting still video frames of the view-graphs. However, some of the video view-graphs were not static and could not easily be displayed in a system that presented still frames.

Video allows advantages that audio does not. It is probably easier to search for events in fast-forward video than in sped-up audio. On the other hand, the lecturer is shown during long periods of the video. Thus, side-by-side displays of both the video and the view-graphs might be useful.

Browsing and searching could be greatly improved by effective automatic semantic processing of multimedia material. For audio, audio processing might improve search, word spotting, and speed play back. The structure of videos can also be analyzed automatically (e.g.,[78]). Sometimes, as in a entertainment video, there is not a clear hierarchical structure in a multimedia stream. Thus, videos may be processed automatically to extract hierarchical or other more complex structures such as grammars (e.g., [196]).

## 14.3.5   Visual TOC Browser

For materials, such as the view-graphs, which have rich semantic and visual structures, a graphical browser may supplement the purely word-based TOC

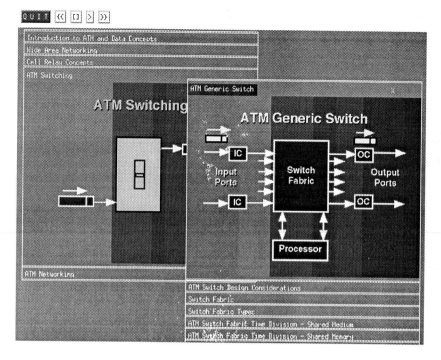

**Figure 14.4** Visual TOC Browser.

used in the other interfaces. A prototype interface that merges graphics into the TOC is presented in Figure 14.4. View-graphs displaying top-level nodes are shown down the left side of the screen. The stack of view-graphs is controlled by a type of "notebook interface" such that clicking on one of the titles raises that view to the top of the stack and displays it. In the figure, the "ATM Switching" view-graph has been opened and the user has asked to see subnodes under it. The "ATM Generic Switch" view-graph is the top of the stack of subnode view-graphs.

# 14.4 DISCUSSION

## 14.4.1 Other Media, Other Structures, and Other Widgets

The lectures for which these interfaces were developed were relatively simple multimedia documents. Moreover, the view-graph collection used here was able to be hierarchically decomposed easily. Not all multimedia documents will be partitioned as cleanly.

This work has emphasized developing interfaces to enhance the presentation of existing lectures. Of course, these are common and their format is familiar and has a long tradition. Authoring lectures explicitly for hypermedia distribution is probably tricky; but if they were to be widely distributed, it might be worth the effort. For lectures which consist of logical modules, whether explicitly authored that way or not, paths through the course at several different levels could be developed. Alternative views of modular lectures could also be developed. Alternate hierarchies or, possibly, alternate structures such as timelines [?] might be used to organize the material.

An archive of several multimedia courses itself may be considered a large document and individual courses and lectures within those course may be considered to be subdocuments. Indeed, courses themselves may be aggregated and the whole collection may be organized hierarchically in much the way that [10] extended the hierarchical SuperBook interface to the management of libraries.

## 14.4.2   Possible Social Impact of Multimedia Lectures

With some planning, videotapes of lecturers can be delivered at almost any time and place. The lectures supplement and sometimes replace live lectures. Moreover, they allow VCR capabilities such as pausing, reviewing, and fast-forwarding. However, digitized multimedia lectures presented across a network with viewers such as those described here can provide substantial enhancements over videotapes. As discussed in this paper, even more can be done if a full range of multimedia document tools are included. Digitized lectures presented via a sophisticated video-on-demand service. For instance, they allow high-level information-access tools such as TOCs, content searches, and hypertext links. A digitized lecture can, of course, also be readily merged with other computer-based training aids such as simulations.

This technology can, potentially, have a positive impact of making exceptional lectures widely available with powerful tools. An open question is whether this will have an effect on live university lecturers. Even if they do reduce the need for some live university lectures, digitized multimedia lectures are unlikely to eliminate the need for the rich interactions among students and professors such as in small group classes or tutorial settings. It also seems likely that universities will continue to be centers for high-end computing and communication equipment which will be necessary for the most effective teaching.

## 14.4.3   Envoi

It is hoped that the interfaces described here will enhance the student's understanding of the structure of a document and enhance the ability to access information by providing a coherent framework for that information. Although there are many other aspects of multimedia documents interfaces that remain to be explored, multimedia documents seem likely to be an important framework for information delivery.

# 14.5   ACKNOWLEDGEMENTS

I thank Janet Allen, Mike Bianchi, Gil Cruz, Paul England, Selma Kaufman, Dan Ketchum, and Deborah Schmitt for helping to collect and prepare the lecture materials.

# Chapter 15

## Searching and Discovery of Resources in Digital Libraries

Nahum Gershon[*], William Ruh[†], small Joshua LeVasseur[‡], small Joel Winstead[§], small Adrienne Kleiboemer[¶],

## 15.1 Introduction

We live in an exciting time. Connecting numerous information-stuffed computers dispersed around the world has created an exciting universe of information. This information revolution has enabled us to explore this universe of digital libraries from our desktop computers. Setting up these digital libraries resources will enable us to

- Find and obtain useful information from distributed information resources (libraries) as cheaply and as efficiently as possible, and

- Enhance the creative thinking of the user to better solve his/her current problems.

Users would like to interact with digital libraries and other distributed resources to find out:

- What they are looking for (it is not always clear to the user in the beginning of a search);

- Where the interesting information is located (e.g., in which documents);

- Where the relevant pieces of information reside in the documents. This step involves extracting and assimilating interesting pieces of information; quite often, it is not a simple process.

[*]The MITRE Corp., 7525 Closhire Drive, McLean, VA 22102-3481, Email: gershon@mitre.org

[†]The MITRE Corp., 7525 Closhire Drive, McLean, VA 22102-3481, Email: war@mitre.org

[‡]The MITRE Corp., 7525 Closhire Drive, McLean, VA 22102-3481, Email: jlevasseu@mitre.org

[§]The MITRE Corp., 7525 Closhire Drive, McLean, VA 22102-3481, Email: jwinstea]@mitre.org

[¶]The MITRE Corp., 7525 Closhire Drive, McLean, VA 22102-3481, Email: akleiboe]@mitre.org

However captivating, we still have a long way to go before the use of this information universe is easy and intuitive.

Information is dispersed across many sources over the Internet; at times users feel lost, confused, and overwhelmed (justifiably so). To find required information or to browse through information, users need nowadays to conduct frustrating searches through arrays of (at times) debilitating menus and "belligerent" computer systems. Some of the remote sources are massive and once the user has the information, he or she needs to browse through large amounts of text, tables, and images. How should the user know where the sources of the relevant information reside, how to get them, and, once the sources are accessed, how to get the relevant information from them?

The World Wide Web (WWW), or simply the Web, developed at CERN, Switzerland [?] and Hyper-G, developed at Graz University of Technology [14], allow the user to roam via menus and embedded links through information spaces of documents or images. Captivating browsers, such as the National Center for Supercomputing Applications (NCSA) Mosaic (for the WWW) [204] and also Harmony (for Hyper-G) have transformed the process of getting information from Internet servers. However, some major difficulties still remain.

If we do not involve the users in designing digital libraries and its interfaces, we will create useless information systems. As long as there is a human being sitting in the front of the screen, the interface to the digital libraries needs to be user-oriented (UO) or user-centric, taking the user needs into account. Users would like to interact with the information preferably forgetting that there is a computer separating them from the information. A good human-computer interaction (HCI) is a must, but it is not enough.

Advances in interactive computer graphics methods, hardware, and software and mass storage have created new possibilities for information navigation, access, and retrieval in which visualization and user interface (UI) could play a central role. The question is how to exploit the advances in graphics technology and experience while understanding how the human mind works in order to reduce the frustration, time, and cost of using information dispersed over the Internet.

The work described in this chapter is concerned with improving the way users interact with information embedded in digital libraries and other distributed resources. The process of interaction with the information starts with browsing, continues with digesting and assimilating pieces of information, terminates with generation of new information, and begins anew with analysis of pre-existing and new information. The methods developed are for browsing through hyperspace without becoming lost, overcoming the rigidity of the WWW, aggregating and classifying relevant information, and classifying information and extraction of metadata.

# 15.2 Browsing Through Hyperspace Without Being Lost

While "surfing" over the Internet with current browsers, users often traverse a multitude of documents via hyperlinks. After opening a number of linked documents, users often do not know where they are in the information space and do not remember how they got there. In short, users feel lost or become disoriented. This is a major problem. One solution is to provide users with both a local and a global view of the information space. These views should be represented visually to promote quick perception and understanding of the hierarchical structure of the hyperspace and to help the users quickly locate where they are in hyperspace, i.e., to re-orient themselves.

We developed an enhancement of NCSA Mosaic that allows the user to view the hyperspace depicted as a tree structure (see Figure 1). The user can "jump" from one document to another by pointing and clicking the mouse without having to go back resource by resource or "page by page." Recently, two additional approaches for visualizing hyperspace structures were independently proposed [167]. These approaches focus on how to make complicated tree structures more comprehensible.

Often, users would like to view the names of documents and how they are linked to each other without actually opening and reading each document. Our enhancement allows the user to let the tree grow automatically up to a specified number of levels. After observing the tree structure and contents, the user could decide to open and read none, some, or all the documents represented on the tree or to save them in his/her own personal space. In cases where changes to the content of a document is an important piece of information, saving Web documents allows the user to compare old and new versions.

# 15.3 Overcoming the Rigidity of the WWW– Building One Owns Information Hyperspace

Another current problem with information distributed over the World-Wide Web is the rigid organization of the information. Creators of documents placed on the Web link them to other documents. Quite often, these hyperlinks reflect the document creator's own point of view and current interests, or some arbitrary considerations. Thus, pieces of information are linked together in a rigid structure where no changes are allowed.

However, these pieces of information could be related to each other in various ways depending on the application problem, personal way of thinking and perception, experience, or culture. For digital libraries to be effective and to enhance problem solving and analysis, they should allow each user to construct his or her own information space with links and associations (among pieces of information and whole documents and images) that fit the personal problem, application, or ways of thinking and perception.

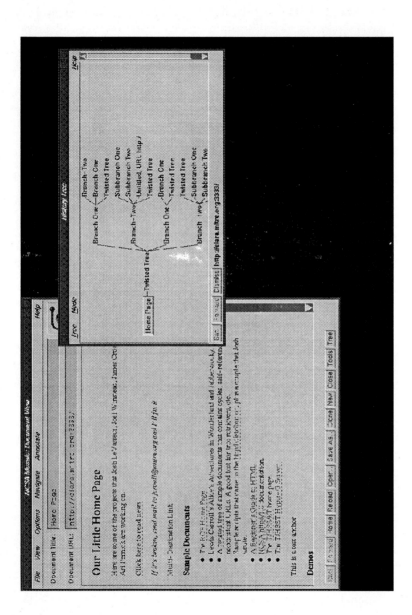

Figure 15.1: A graphical view of the hyperspace of a document depicted as a tree structure. The user can "jump" from one document to another by pointing and clicking the mouse button without the necessity to go back resource by resource. This eliminates the necessity to go back "page by page".

Another of our enhancements to NCSA Mosaic enables the user to modify interactively the links among the documents and images using a point-click-and-drag operation on the display of the hyperlink hierarchical structure. This enhancement allows the user to effectively generate new, personalized links and to (visually) view the new and "old" information space globally and locally (see Figure 2). The new hyperlinks are stored at the end of the documents and could be saved for future viewing and sharing with other users. The user can add annotations accompanying the new links.

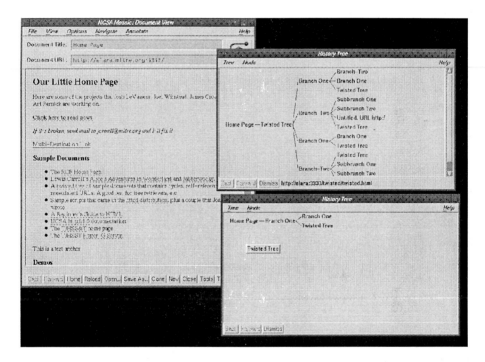

Figure 15.2: The MITRE enhancement to NCSA Mosaic enables the user to modify interactively the links among the documents and images using a point-click-and-drag operation on the visual display of the hyperlink hierarchical structure. The user can generate new, personalized links and to (visually) view the new and "old" information space globally and locally. The new hyperlinks are stored at the end of the documents and could be saved for future viewing and sharing with other users.

Another problematic aspect of current distributed information systems such as the World-Wide Web is that the smallest unit of information is a document (or HTML "page"). Users often find that a paragraph, a sentence, a word, or even a part of an image is a piece of information relevant to their problem. Our enhanced version of NCSA Mosaic allows the user to define new documents that contain fragments of existing documents and link them to other documents as he or she wishes. With these enhancements, the user could create his or her own version of the information space, thus reflecting the current problem or his or her own interests and view of the information.

## 15.4  Finding New Information in Retrieved Documents– Aggregating Relevant Information

Once the user has retrieved the documents that are related to his or her problem, he or she often needs to analyze the different pieces of information and find out new information by doing so. We have developed a method and tool that could assist the user to do just this, based on the concept of aggregating relevant information.

One example where digesting and assimilating existing information could create new information is word correlation. Documents are automatically analyzed and the proximity of any pair of words is calculated. Words that are contained within one sentence, or if they are separated by no more than a given number of other words (the number is pre-defined by the user) are considered to be correlated.

|           | fatigue | aches | ailments | nausea |
|-----------|---------|-------|----------|--------|
| fat       | 22      | 10    | 2        | 15     |
| smoking   | 3       | 3     | 4        | 5      |
| snacks    | 47      | 11    | 4        | 33     |
| sedentary | 2       | 4     | 3        | 1      |

Table 1: Correlations of 4 words to 4 other words in a document.

The correlations among words in a document could be represented by a table where the rows and the columns are the list of words and each cell of the table contains the number of positive correlations in the document between two words in a pair. Such a table could be very large and the high correlations are generally scattered throughout all over the table.

Users find it very difficult to locate the highest correlations across a large table and to integrate and make sense of them. For example, the correlations of 4 words to 4 other words in a document (a subset of the full correlation table) could be represented by Table 1.

The information analyst wishing to identify the high hits of incidence needs to "fish" them individually from the various table cells. This is a slow process and could require the user to be very meticulous when the tables are large.

In scientific data, where the rows and columns are numerical coordinates, they are naturally ordered by increasing values of the coordinates. With words rather than numbers representing the rows and columns in tables of information, the order of the entities is arbitrary and thus one could permute them to yield the following representation depicted in Table 2.

|           | fatigue | aches | ailments | nausea |
|-----------|---------|-------|----------|--------|
| fat       | 22      | 10    | 2        | 15     |
| snacks    | 47      | 11    | 4        | 33     |
| smoking   | 3       | 3     | 4        | 5      |
| sedentary | 2       | 4     | 3        | 1      |

Table 2. Correlations of 4 words to 4 other words in a document after aggregation (the high incidences are aggregated in the upper left corner).

In this representation, the highest correlations are aggregated and it is easy to see which pairs of words are highly correlated. The analyst can then investigate why particular words are correlated and whether there is any significance in real life.

In small tables it is almost straightforward to permute the rows and columns and aggregate the high hits. However, in a large table of a few thousand rows and columns it is hard to do it manually. We have implemented a fast algorithm that could aggregate information in large tables of n dimensions and the results are represented graphically on the computer display for visual inspection and analysis (humans still tend to perform pattern recognition faster and better than any existing computer). The user can then zoom on the interesting part of the aggregated table and observe the words that are highly correlated. The development of the visualization tools for representing unaggregated and aggregated correlation information was based on extensions of AVS (Advanced Visualization System). This tool is invoked from our enhanced Mosaic interface.
‖

## 15.5 Classification of Information and Metadata Extraction

An additional tool for analysis of information contained in retrieved documents is analyzing the information by its type. We found that classification of information embedded in text according to people, geographic locations, organizations, major topics, and chronological events is helpful. For text data, this classification was done by an automatic tagging process using a linguistics-based algorithm and requiring only a small amount of domain knowledge. We are investigating and developing various approaches for generating different types of (metadata) tags. Examples include statistical approaches for part-of-speech tagging, and linguistics-based heuristics for generating semantic content tags.

We use the Standard Generalized Markup Language (SGML) to represent the automatically generated metadata as SGML tags, so that they can be processed by tools from various developers or vendors. SGML is rapidly becoming an international standard of choice in the electronic publishing community and has been adopted by several U.S. Government agencies. One of our system's underlying tenets is the automatic enrichment of raw information with metadata

---

‖The algorithm has been developed by Brian Dickens and further refined by Joel Winstead.

(such as results of the classification process) that is efficiently managed and exploited to facilitate interactive assimilation of otherwise overwhelming volumes of information.

Our experience points out that the complexity of information should be embedded in the tagging (generation of metadata) rather than surfacing in the query process. Tagging is generally performed when adding new information to a collection. However, in libraries containing untagged data, the tagging could be done after retrieval to facilitate further searching and information discovery.

Tagging should not be limited to text data but could be extended for image and video data. However, video tagging is a complicated process that could possibly be done during editing. In addition, standards and accepted methods for video tagging still need to be developed. We have developed a tool to assist in annotating or tagging images and to facilitate their subsequent retrieval. **

Tagging is not an ideal solution for representing metadata. Not all metadata could be practically embedded in the resulting tags. And, the process is tedious especially when done manually. For the time being, tagging should be investigated and pursued, while still searching for a better solution.

## 15.6   In Conclusion

The digital library is a new concept involving new enabling technologies and user interface. The situation has similarities with the one prevailing when the movie camera was invented. At that time, people tried to imitate theater via a stationary camera. They later discovered that these two media have different characteristics and were able then to better use the advantages of the new medium. Learning the new medium of the digital library and further understanding how humans process and interact with information will enable us to provide new methods for discovery and searching of resources, enhancing creativity and thinking. In this sense, the term 'digital library' might be misleading; it might be beneficial to explore metaphors beyond the traditional library.

The developments reported in this chapter make use of advances in interactive computer graphics and visualization technologies as well as the understanding of how human beings search and process information. They could make the information that is distributed in digital libraries more intuitively searchable, accessible, and easier to use by people from all walks of life and interests. This will enable full use of the Internet's information universe from our desktops.

## 15.7   Acknowledgments

The authors would like to express their appreciation to the many exciting discussions with Brian Dickens and for his work on the information aggregation algorithm. We would also like to acknowledge the efficient and innovative help

---

**Developed by Tom Polger, Dolly Greenwood, and Clem McGowan.

of Ari Pernick and James Croall in developing the capability of manipulating excerpts of documents and for teaching us Hyper-G.

# Part IV

# Design Issues and Prototyping

# Chapter 16

## The Almaden Distributed Digital Library System

David M. Choy*, Richard Dievendorff, Cynthia Dwork, Jeffrey B. Lotspiech, Robert
J. T. Morris, Norman J. Pass, Laura C. Anderson, Alan E. Bell, Stephen K. Boyer,
Thomas D. Griffin, Bruce A. Hoenig, James M. McCrossin, Alex M. Miller, Florian
Pestoni, and Deidra S. Picciano

In this chapter we describe the architecture for the Almaden Distributed
Digital Library System, which is intended to support an emerging "information marketplace". Using a distributed server approach and accommo-
dating heterogeneous environments, the system is designed to meet the
diverse needs of the publishers, distributors, and users of scientific journal information at low cost, while protecting the information assets of the
publishers and the privacy of the users. A prototype is currently being
implemented in a joint effort by IBM Almaden Research Center and the
Institute for Scientific Information. A pilot is planned to test the system
and to explore new economic models.

## 16.1   Introduction

Traditionally, people access information from books and journals which are
stored in local or departmental libraries. However, as computing technology
evolved during the 60's and 70's, other sources of information access became
available. These included on-line services where people could access large databases
housed on mainframes. This led to the emergence of numerous on-line information services based on metered access to the data (e.g., [76]).

These on-line services, an example of which is depicted in Figure 16.1, have
several limitations in function and convenience. Typically, an on-line service
maintains databases which contain textual descriptions of documents (e.g., authors, titles, abstracts) but not the documents themselves. These services have
traditionally been accessed through low speed dial-in connections, and have provided rudimentary interfaces that include mainly a simple text search capability.

---

*Contact author: David M. Choy (dmc@almaden.ibm.com)

# Database Vendor

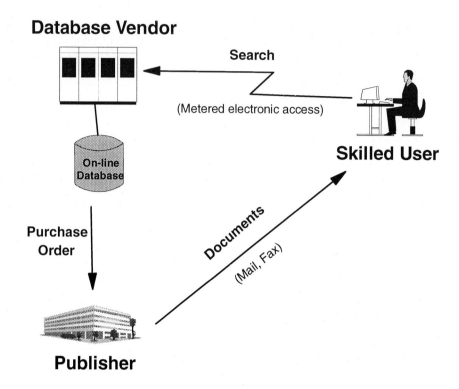

**Figure 16.1** Traditional On-Line Service

The query interface has been command-based and required training on the part of the user [6], and thus access has frequently been limited to information specialists. The use of these services is costly to a user, who typically has to pay a charge based on connection time and activity, in addition to the communication cost. Some on-line services do offer a document ordering service. However, in that case, the orders are usually filled by the respective publisher or an authorized distributor, and the documents are delivered via a separate channel such as postal mail or fax. The turn-around is slow and a user often does not know whether the documents he/she ordered are actually useful to him/her until the documents arrive.

In recent years, however, the cost of electronic storage has decreased to a point that is comparable with the cost of paper and film for storing documents. Thus, keeping documents on-line in large volumes has become practical. With the emergence of powerful low-cost servers, high-bandwidth networks, and user-friendly multimedia browsers, attractive alternatives to these traditional dial-in services are becoming feasible. Main-frame servers have been replaced by PC-based or workstation-based servers with large amounts of secondary or automated tertiary storage, and access costs have been reduced by use of packet-switched wide-area network (WAN) technology. New data mod-

| Decade | 60's | 70's | 80's | 90's | 00's |
|--------|------|------|------|------|------|
| Era | Batch | Timeshare | Desktop | Networked | **Information Marketplace** |
| User | Expert | Specialist | Individual | Group | **Anybody** |
| Location | Glass House | Terminal | Desktop | Mobile | **Anywhere** |
| Data | Numeric | Text | Graphics | Multimedia | **Anydata** |
| Objective | Calculate | Access | Present | Communicate | **Exploit** |

**Table 16.1** The changing paradigm of computing

els and user interfaces have also emerged, of which the best known example is World-Wide Web (WWW) and Mosaic [13]. These technological advances have lowered costs (sometimes appearing to be "free" to the users) and eased access to large amounts of information. The challenges have now shifted to become those of (1) searching and navigating among vast amounts of distributed data, (2) providing reasonable performance, especially in accessing large objects such as images, and (3) overcoming real and perceived security threats.

Such a revolution in information access signals the beginning of a shift in the computing paradigm, taking us beyond an advancing set of paradigms that has been proposed by several authors [206]. These paradigms progress from batch computing by the specialist through today's networked computing, which has become a social vehicle for the sharing of information (particularly through e-mail). But we believe that the next era in this progression will not be a technical step, so much as a change in the way people use and view these networks, see Table 16.1. As suggested in the last column of this table, we predict that information will be ubiquitous and easily accessible, that any data type will be supported, and that emphasis will be on data exploitation rather than on simply access or communication.

A central entity in this new paradigm of computing is the digital library [108, 100, 115, 234, 55, 201, 99, 88] serving as the repository for all data, whether it be archival, news, opinion, creative works, or others. A more descriptive label for this era is perhaps "Information Marketplace". It conveys a more symmetric model in which anyone can be both a provider and a consumer of information. More importantly, it reflects a shift from a technology-centered model to a usage-centered model.

While the recent advances in the storage, server, network, and user interface technologies are a prerequisite for an Information Marketplace, serious problems remain. For example, users wish to see quality images and multimedia clips quickly and free-of-charge, but the existing communications infrastructure does not support the data volume at the speed desired by users, and certainly the supplier of quality information will expect some form of payment for his intellectual property. For the information marketplace paradigm to prosper, new services will be needed, including the following:

- Data overload will continue to increase. Services that reduce, summarize, organize, index, and relate data to produce easily accessible and consumable information will become ever more in demand and will be expected to have higher filtering and semantic capability.

- Consumers will demand one-stop shopping (as opposed to separate sources for searching and acquiring information) and rapid response to highly interactive accesses, such as on-line browsing of a multi-page image document. This requires a system with integrated functions, an architecture and infrastructure that enables fast delivery of information to the users, and a friendly graphical user interface (GUI).

- There will continue to be a demand for quality, branded sources, which filter and check their material for validity, accuracy, quality of expression, and value, and which also assure consumers of the authenticity of the distributed material. We believe editorial service will continue to exist regardless of media change in information storage and delivery. In fact, its role will become increasingly important in an age of information explosion.

- Information collection, refinement, organization, extraction and distribution services will be developed only if the providers of these services are remunerated. This in turn poses the need for accounting capabilities to support a fine-grain, consumption-based model of information vending, such as pay-to-read, pay-to-print, pay-to-search and pay-to-mine, as well as a subscription-based model. Information tracking, copyright protection, usage metering, and electronic money or credit services are needed to enable these controls.

- With usage metering and behavior monitoring, user privacy and confidentiality, such as data reflecting "who is interested in what information", will become an issue. Adequate protection of such data will be a necessity.

Our objective is to develop a system that address these and other issues, and to provide a testbed for exploring suitable economic models to bring us closer to an Information Marketplace. In this chapter, we describe the architecture of a distributed digital library developed at the IBM Almaden Research Center. A prototype system is currently being implemented jointly by IBM and the Institute for Scientific Information (ISI), a large secondary publisher of academic and scientific literature such as Current Contents[†] and Science Citation Index[‡]. The system will support a pilot to investigate new models for information vending, distribution, and access, as well as to study the feasibility and acceptance of the new library concept and to explore techniques for managing distributed library servers.

In Section 16.2 we define our goals more precisely by describing the library principals and their individual needs. In Section 16.3 we describe the architecture of the Almaden Distributed Digital Library System. Section 16.4 discusses

---

[†] Current Contents is a registered trademark of the Institute for Scientific Information, Inc.

[‡] Science Citation Index is a registered trademark of the Institute for Scientific Information, Inc.

security-related issues, such as protection of information as it passes from a source server to a customer server and from there to individual client, information authentication, watermarking, and user privacy. Section 16.5 describes the status of the prototype system at time of writing and discusses further work.

# 16.2 The Library Principals and their Needs

A digital library for published information must address the diverse and sometimes conflicting needs of its principals, which include the information consumers (users), the information custodians (librarians, secondary publishers, distributors), and the information suppliers and copyright holders (primary publishers). A perspective on their needs is given below. The Almaden Distributed Digital Library System attempts to address each of these needs in a balanced manner. For our planned pilot, our focus is to support scientific periodicals. Although our system is not the first attempt to provide electronic access to scientific journals [217, 121, 158, 52, 161, 162, 199, 86], we believe it is the first to support the requirements of the information suppliers, the custodians, as well as the consumers.

## 16.2.1 The consumer

Typical consumers for our pilot will be research and development professionals and public library patrons. A primary concern for the consumer is ease of use, which includes, broadly, functions, convenience, performance, and transparency (such as a single "place" to access all information). User's expectations of ease of information access (search, acquisition, retrieval, browsing, printing, etc.) is high. Another concern is availability of quality information (to assure an acceptable level of value), and the integrity and authenticity of retrieved information. Authenticity is of particular concern, because tampering is less evident for digital documents than for traditional printed documents. For example, the malicious tampering with chemical formulae or medical dosage information contained in an article could lead to dangerous results. Still another concern is the privacy regarding the user's access to information. Cost can also be an issue since consumers traditionally do not pay for individual rights-of-access to a library. Many users, especially those in an institutional setting, favor the existing subscription model of unlimited usage for periodicals in which they have a prolonged interest.

## 16.2.2 The librarian

Librarians are the information professionals who aid users by ordering publications and subscribing to periodicals that are of interest to their clientele (consumers), performing specialized searches, teaching consumers how to use information retrieval tools, and handling copyright-related matters. Libraries must balance service objectives with budgetary pressures. The librarian needs to know which periodicals are actually being used by the customers as a group, often down to the department level, but does not need to know for each individual what he or she is reading. To reduce cost uncertainty, librarians have generally expressed a preference for subscription arrangements with unlimited user access and printing, as opposed to "pay-per-view" arrangements and controlled printing.

## 16.2.3   The primary publisher

The primary publisher obtains articles selected for publication by its editorial staff, composes periodical issues, and markets print and electronic products to consumers and libraries. The publisher thus needs to manage a large volume of source information, to continually capture new information and produce new products, and to distribute the products to the consumers. For marketing reasons, publishers are very interested in gross statistics about the readership of their products, such as the percentage breakdown of academic versus industrial readers, total number of readers, etc.

The publisher must safeguard its intellectual property in order to protect its investment and its ability to continue to do business. A publisher often permits fair-use copying of its products in limited quantities, but significant revenue is lost due to unauthorized photocopying. Publishers have expressed great concern that digital copies of their copyrighted products may be exposed to mass unauthorized replication and redistribution, all with no loss in the quality of presentation. This concern is balanced by the increased market opportunities available in an easy-to-use digital library, by the opportunities in new products enabled by computer (such as hypertext, multimedia, active and adaptive documents), by the diminishing subscriptions to scientific journals due to increasing cost of print products, by budget cuts at many libraries in recent years, and by the risk of quickly losing market share due to competition's electronic publishing capability [174, 233]. Furthermore, since publishers add their value by filtering and organizing information, it is important to them that the integrity (and thus the value) of their products can be assured. On the other hand, to allow themselves a chance to adapt to the transition to electronic distribution of publications, many publishers are reluctant to forego the traditional subscription-based model that has provided them a predictable revenue stream, at least not until a pay-to-use economic model is proven. Thus, inevitably, each publisher will take a different stance in how their products should be protected and priced. Protecting the integrity of information, managing rights, metering and pricing the usage of information, as well as the flexibility to accommodate non-uniform publisher needs, are keys to electronic information publishing and vending.

## 16.2.4   The secondary publisher

Secondary publishers produce tools to aid information search such as indices, inverse references (citations), classification, and linking of articles that span publishers. Additionally, secondary publishers provide alerting or awareness extracting services, and reprint services when authorized by the respective primary

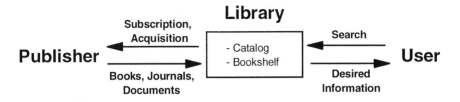

**Figure 16.2** Traditional Library

publishers. Like primary publishers, they need to manage a large amount of information, to capture new information, and to distribute information. They have to work with multiple primary publishers and to enforce their respective copyright control and pricing terms. Electronic tools can greatly enhance secondary publishers' products and services, in terms of new products and functions, higher availability and accessibility of information, broader publication coverage, and faster information delivery.

## 16.3 Architecture of the Almaden Distributed Digital Library System

From one angle, our architecture can be thought of in analogy to a conventional library, which is depicted in Figure 16.2. A librarian orders books and articles and subscribes to periodicals that are of interest to the local clientele from the publishers. The client in turn finds the material he/she is interested in and reads it at, or borrows it from, the (local) library. The Almaden Distributed Digital Library System is arranged in a Client/Server/Server configuration as depicted in Figure 16.3, featuring a two-tier library server: a Source Server to support an information supplier (e.g., information owner, publisher, broker, or authorized distributor) and a Customer Server to support a local community of users (local library).

It has been argued that in an electronic publishing world, there is no place for a traditional library which pre-selects material for a local community of users [234]. While this debate will certainly continue for some time, the Customer Server in our architecture is intended to serve important system functions, as we shall see, rather than being the result of an attempt to mimic the conventional paradigm. Our approach does not intrinsically depend on, or require, the existence of a local organizational entity that pre-selects a static holding of information for users, although this traditional model can easily be accommodated.

In our approach, a Source Server, typically located at an information supplier's site, serves as a "warehouse" of information and as a "factory" for producing information products. It "pushes" information in an anticipatory and customer-specific manner (such as by subscription or by customer profile) to the individual Customer Servers over high-speed links such as Integrated Services

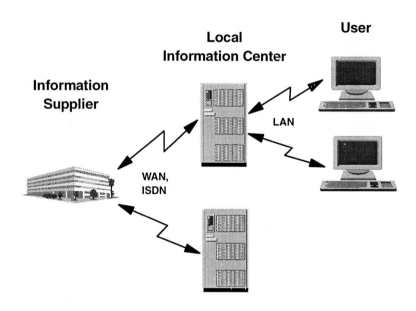

**Figure 16.3** Distributed Digital Library

Digital Network (ISDN) lines. A Customer Server, typically located at an institutional customer's site, maintains a subset of suppliers' information that is of interest to the particular user community at the respective site. A user, from his or her desktop system which is connected to a Customer Server by a local-area network (LAN), may search on and view the material stored on the Customer Server. For information that is not available from the Customer Server, a request may be sent to the respective Source Server to "pull" the needed information. In addition to the push and the pull models, this configuration also supports a "consignment" model, whereby a publisher may pre-distribute certain information to a Customer Server before any information transaction (subscription or acquisition) takes place. This leads to opportunities for a publisher to exploit low-cost methods of bulk distribution of information, to negotiate package or volume deals, and to generate additional business in a proactive manner (e.g., running promotions).

This arrangement is well-suited to addressing the performance, asset protection, accounting, privacy, cost, and local infrastructure issues mentioned above:

- LAN speeds, which typically exceed wide-area communication speeds, provide excellent service to users, even for challenging image and multimedia material.

- The Customer Server provides a cache for information, which via a combination of anticipatory prefetching and demand-fetching of information develops a working set that is appropriate for the local clientele, without the need for a local library to physically acquire, store, and retain all the information that the clientele may potentially need.

- The Customer Server, which contains a trusted base, protects the integrity of publications, manages publisher's rights, and meters information usage (such as pay-to-read, pay-to-print), thereby serving as an agent for each information supplier.

- As a server on a customer's LAN, the Customer Server can accommodate and exploit any tools and services that are provided by the local computing infrastructure. It can handle user registration, authorization, and accounting in accordance with the local institution's policy. Local registration and accounting also helps a relatively small supplier by avoiding the potentially prohibitive cost of maintaining a large volume of user registrations and accounts at its Source Server and the cost of separate billing for each individual user. The architecture, however, does not prevent a supplier from doing so.

- The Customer Server can serve as the place for a user to access published information and to conduct "one-stop shopping". It guarantees the integrity of the information that it delivers to a user. Furthermore, it provides a first line of defense to protect the privacy of users by safeguarding user identity as well as information access and behavioral statistics (unless a user conducts transactions with a supplier directly). In these manners, the Customer Server acts as an agent for the individual users.

Our prototype will initially support a single Source Server, capable of distributing a large repertoire of scientific periodicals and related bibliographic information.

### 16.3.1   The Source Server

The Source Server is a home base for the distributed digital library, running on one or several LAN-connected server machines at an information supplier's premises. For the prototype, each server machine is an **IBM RS/6000** running the **AIX** operating system. The Source Server contains:

- A relational database to store structured data and relationships and to support attribute search,

- An object repository to store objects such as images and text files, to manage object retention, and to backup and archive data,

- Index manager(s) to support content search for specific type(s) of objects (such as text),

- A hierarchy manager that supports tertiary storage (such as optical disk) and automated libraries ("jukeboxes") so as to be able to accommodate a large amount of data,

- A document server that manages information delivery to the individual Customer Servers,

- A "fire-wall" to prevent unauthorized accesses from Customer Server connections,

- A collection of applications that handles information capture, processing, and extraction, and

- A graphical user interface for system and library administrators.

The relational database contains the descriptive as well as the actual information available for feeding the individual Customer Servers. Examples are bibliographic information, titles, authors, abstracts, tables of contents, publication dates, citations, reviews, book series, and relationships among them. Since much of the design of this database depends on the specific application and on the nature of the information to be stored, the full Structured Query Language (SQL) Application Programming Interface (API) is directly accessible by the applications. Direct access to the SQL API is also necessary in order to support a high-volume workload. In the prototype, this relational database is managed by **IBM DATABASE 2 for AIX** [128]

Furthermore, the database also contains the metadata for objects stored in the object repository, such as object names, types, sizes, dates, versions, descriptions, and linkages. In the prototype, this repository is managed by IBM's ADSM (ADSTAR Distributed Storage Manager) [127], which supports automated libraries and manages a large storage hierarchy. ADSM supports an API that is the base for the X/Open[§] backup services standard [237]. IBM Search-Manager/6000 [130] will be used to provide text search. To facilitate application development, an object API and an object access toolkit is available, which coordinates object accesses so as to provide a level of data consistency between the objects and their metadata stored in the relational database, without paying a large penalty on performance. This API and toolkit also shields the underlying implementation to facilitate the exploitation of emerging database technologies to support objects, and also to facilitate the integration with application-specific databases.

In addition, the database also supports institutional customers as well as individual users who conduct transactions directly with the information supplier, and tracks the individual Customer Servers. Included in the database are contractual agreements, periodical subscriptions, server configurations, encryption keys, information distribution log, caching strategy, and cache states, as well as information access and usage data metered by the Customer Servers. The metered data may be used for accounting and billing, marketing analysis (e.g., for product planning, packaging, pricing, and promotion), and system tuning (e.g., cache management, communications requirement). Collected solely for these purposes, such data are handled carefully so that user privacy and institutional confidentiality ("who is interested in what information") are assured.

The information stored at the Source Server may be in a source format (e.g., LaTex, scanned image, OCR text) and/or in a delivery format (e.g., compressed image with boiler-plates and hidden watermarks, PostScript[¶]). A continual or periodically scheduled process loads newly published or captured information into the database and the object repository. Other processes operate on these data for cleansing, filtering, classification, generating derived information, and indexing. At regular intervals and also on demand, extraction processes select relevant data and package them in a generic format for delivery to the individual Customer Servers in accordance with their respective subscriptions and caching schemes.

## 16.3.2   The Customer Server

Located at a customer site in a protected area and connected to the Source Server via a high-speed link (e.g., an ISDN line), a Customer Server is an outpost of the digital library, maintaining a subset of the information stored at the Source Server. From a systems perspective, this subset is managed as a cache for the Source Server. The data stored at a Customer Server are protected by

---

[§]X/Open is a trademark of X/Open Company Limited.
[¶]PostScript is a registered trademark of Adobe Systems, Inc.

encryption, by an audit mechanism, and by contractual responsibility of the customer's system administrator or librarian to safeguard the Server and to deter unauthorized use, replication, and redistribution of copyrighted information. On the other hand, being connected to the customer's LAN, the Customer Server appears as an on-line local library to the users, who access information from heterogeneous client machines. The information collection that is physically maintained on the Customer Server, however, is determined by the caching scheme (which considers many factors, including publication subscriptions and available storage) and by user demand rather than determined statically and explicitly by a librarian. For the prototype, the Customer Server runs on an IBM PS/2 Model 95 server under the OS/2 operating system. To fit into different customer environments, as well as to support different applications, the Customer Server is designed to use with a variety of groupware, including Lotus Notes∥, VisualInfo [129], and HTML/HTTP [233] servers.

Information is distributed from the Source Server to a Customer Server periodically as well as on demand, as determined by the customer's business arrangement (e.g., customer profile, subscription, acquisition, promotion by supplier). The physical delivery of information depends on the caching scheme. For example, individual deliveries may be prioritized according to their urgency and to the type of data to be delivered (e.g., table-of-contents, abstracts, page images of an article). A similar prioritization may be used to cast out less important data from the cache when the cache is full, whereas certain essential information may be "pinned" in the cache.

A Customer Server also contains a shared database, an object repository, and indices. The Server supports interactive users, so content search (e.g., for text) and navigation capabilities are very important. When new data are received from the Source Server, they are loaded into the database and/or the object repository. All applicable indices are updated accordingly.

In addition to managing data and supporting interactive access to information, the Customer Server also handles user registration and authentication, access control, information-usage metering, local accounting, statistics recording, and copyright protection tasks such as watermarking documents, data encryption, and controlled printing. The Server has a "fire-wall" to prevent unauthorized accesses to the customer's computing systems from outside through its connection with the Source Server.

As an option, a Customer Server may also provide a "pass-through" service to allow users to conduct transactions directly with an information supplier, such as ordering an article that is to be faxed to an individual's home and charged to the individual's credit card. For this pass-through service, the Customer Server merely provides a communication path for submitting requests and delivering requested information, but does not participate in the transaction.

---

∥Lotus Notes is a registered trademark of Lotus Development Corporation.

### 16.3.3 The Client

Client machines are connected to a Customer Server via a LAN and are usually a part of an institutional customer's existing computing infrastructure. Therefore, they often are heterogeneous machines running in an uncontrolled environment. Our client code provides a graphical user interface for a user to search, retrieve, and browse information that the customer subscribes to. It also allows a user to print a document on a convenience printer when such printing is authorized (according to the applicable licensing terms). A small cache may be maintained at the client, which may prefetch information from the Customer Server to support fast browsing. For information that is not currently stored on the Customer Server, a request is generated to fetch the information from the Source Server. If the information is not covered by the customer's current subscriptions, an acquisition transaction is conducted according to the terms set by the respective publisher.

To browse the page images of a document, a special browser is used, which authenticates the images by checking their digital signatures and decrypts images on-the-fly without leaving clear data in non-volatile storage. The browser has the ability to convert images from any one of the popular formats to another. For the prototype, it also has the ability to capture a variety of behavioral events, and passes the statistics to the Customer Server. These statistics, accumulated and summarized, are eventually forwarded to the Source Server for analysis and system enhancement. The collection of frequency statistics on how articles are browsed, and conditional statistics such as what determines whether a reader will purchase a copy of the article, are believed to be of great value to the publisher and indeed the scientific community. The potential of using this data to further help in curbing the information overload problem that is engendered by the enabling technology can be explored.

## 16.4 Security and Rights Management

In a conventional information system, the term "security" usually applies to access control [73], that is, making sure that only authorized users are allowed into the system, and, once in, that they only have access to the data to which they are entitled. In the information marketplace paradigm, where it is desirable that published information be widely distributed, this conventional view of security no longer applies. Instead, we have a system where the security is applied to the individual transactions, to ensure that the users do not get more (or less) than they pay for [202, 152, 22, 125, 106], that their privacy is maintained, and that the information they receive is genuine, and is not (excessively) redistributed without authorization.

In our pilot we have the distinct advantage that the value of each individual document (measured by the cost of obtaining a legitimate copy) is low, relative to the value to the user of their ongoing access to the system. We are not distributing highly sensitive material (e.g , classified documents), highly priced information (e.g., investment tips), or products with a mass market (e.g., the latest rock video). Thus, as long as the system retains the capability to lock out a user (or an institution) who is flagrantly violating the copyrights of the information owners, that user (or institution) risks far more than he or she stands to gain by abusing the system. This non-technical fact drives the design of our security architecture.

Each document sent from the Source Server to the Customer Server is encrypted with an individual document key. This is a symmetric key [210], initially known only to the Source Server. The Source Server further encrypts the document keys for each Customer Server with a server-specific public key [77]. Thus, when the documents and the document keys are sent to the Customer Server, the information assets of the Source Server and the privacy of the Customer Server are protected. In addition, a cryptographic hash (or "fingerprint") of each document is signed [192, 164, 229] by the Source Server and sent, encrypted, along with the document, so that authenticity of the document can be verified.

Keeping the documents encrypted allows us a great deal of flexibility in system design. We can stage the documents from one platform to another without worrying about whether the document has been purchased for viewing. For example, while a user is reading an abstract to decide whether or not to view the document, we can transmit the document from the Source Server to the hard disk on the Customer Server. If the user later decides not to view it, nothing has been given away except the minimal bandwidth required to send it there. It is the delivery of the respective, relatively short, document key that confers the right to view the document, and this can be delivered very quickly once the user decided to purchase the document.

Intuitively, data stored at the Customer Server is held by the librarian. As in a conventional library, the librarian is viewed as a trusted party. Document keys are protected at the Customer Server, and documents are never kept unencrypted in non-volatile storage. However, the system is not resistant to reverse engineering of, and tampering with, the code running on the Customer Server. The Server should therefore be protected with conventional physical and system security, such as being kept in a locked room to which only the library staff has access. This raises the problem of rebooting the system if it should crash in the middle of the night or on the weekend when the library staff is unavailable. Our system automatically reboots after power failure. Steps are taken to prevent anyone from connecting to the Source Server and impersonating an authorized Customer Server at power-on.

Communication between an individual user and the Customer Server is encrypted under a session key. This, combined with the fact that each individual document is encrypted under a document key, helps protect the user against eavesdroppers on the LAN. There is a small privacy exposure here: if a user $U$ legitimately receives a specific document $D$, then an eavesdropper who also legitimately receives $D$ can recognize that $U$ is receiving $D$. This could be avoided if the Customer Server were to decrypt and re-encrypt $D$ under a fresh key each time it was requested, but we judged this to be an excessive overhead for the

Customer Server. Nevertheless, no record is kept of the fact that the individual user $U$ received document $D$, although in some cases it may be recorded that $U$'s department (or a budgetary unit of interest to the librarian) accessed the periodical in which $D$ appears. As noted above, by conducting transactions with the Source Server directly, an individual can avoid the recording of even this statistical information at the Customer Server.

Copyright holders are concerned about the ability of users, having legitimately obtained a copy of a particular document electronically, to then widely redistribute it (in its original quality) in violation of the copyright. On the other hand, the copyright holders see new revenue opportunities: a user may be willing to pay for the convenience of having material delivered to his or her desktop, whereas conventionally it would be necessary for the user to physically go to the library and possibly to wait for days to obtain the material if it is not available in the library. The easier and more pleasant it is to use the system, the more additional revenue generated. In contrast, the revenue lost to illegal copying (sometimes called "downstreaming") seems to be a relatively small amount that will vary according to the strength of the system protection (assuming the value of the information is relatively low as noted above). This observation has led us to conclude that the best system design for this type of applications is one which implements as much protection as possible while maximizing ease of use and system performance. We therefore settled on the following moderate measures to protect copyrighted information against unauthorized redistribution.

When the document image is decrypted and decompressed, we mark the document as belonging to that user. This is sometimes called "watermarking" [42, 158, 12]. We employ watermarking on both the electronic and physical images. If illicit copies of the document are detected somewhere in the world, it might be possible to trace the leak back to the original user who legitimately obtained the document. Another scenario is that the unauthorized redistributor destroys his watermark, say, with an image editor, and releases a copy with a missing or "smeared" (syntactically incorrect) watermark. Anyone holding a document with a missing or smeared watermark is holding an unauthorized copy (electronic or physical). Moreover, this extra step required to damage a watermark is another, though small, disincentive to illegal redistribution. It requires an overt action by the perpetrator, making it hard to argue that the violation was unintentional. This approach does not inconvenience the legitimate user. We note that it is possible to mark the documents in such a way that by visual inspection one cannot determine the legitimate owner, but by using additional information stored in the Customer Server the ownership can be determined from the mark.

Users have a real concern that digital library technology enables data to be recorded about their reading habits and personal interest, which can be very sensitive. As mentioned above, we do not retain records of who reads what. Moreover, we make that information very hard to gather via eavesdropping. This slightly complicates billing and watermarking. However, with digital signatures and one-way functions [192], these complications can be overcome. Since our protection schemes are not completely foolproof, we rely on the honesty and good will of our users. We believe this is a two-way street, and that we must protect information about the users (their reading habits and interest) as well.

## 16.5   Summary and Future Work

In this chapter, we proposed a distributed-server approach to digital library, and described the architecture of the Almaden Distributed Digital Library System which allows efficient usage of electronic libraries from the desktop. A prototype is currently under development jointly with ISI to handle scientific publications. Unlike other prototype systems that provide access to scientific publications, our system is designed to meet the needs of the publishers, distributors, and interactive users at low cost and good performance while protecting the information assets of the publishers in customizable terms as well as protecting the privacy of the users.

A pilot is planned at selected beta sites, which include university, industrial laboratory, and public libraries, to test the distributed server approach, information protection schemes, economic models for electronic information vending, as well as system usability and administration. A large collection of scientific journals from a number of participating primary publishers will be offered. The pilot will also give us an opportunity to investigate communications requirements, suitable cache sizes, caching and prefetching schemes, and many other systems issues.

Besides scientific publications, we are also building a digital library of US patents, which will soon be made available to IBM laboratories. To test the generality of our approach, we are working with another company on a patent system.

Our prototype system may be extended in several ways. The two-tier library server may be extended to a multi-tier one. For example, an "intermediate server" may be used to support an information distributor while the Source Server supports a publisher and the Customer Servers support local libraries. (See Figure 16.4). Similarly, a multi-site enterprise may use an intermediate server to feed information received from a Source Server to its local Customer Servers. A multi-tier server structure may be created by cascading two-tier structures so that the Customer Server of one stage feeds information into the Source Server of the next stage. The inter-stage interface must consider performance issues as well as the role-shift in information control and client support.

Another extension to the prototype is to support multiple Source Servers, each of which may distribute information to any Customer Servers. (See Figure 16.5) Multiple Source Servers are needed to support multiple information suppliers. The cascaded approach is well-suited to supporting multiple Source Servers as well, by making the inter-stage interface recognize multiple information sources.

Still another extension, further towards the information marketplace paradigm, is to support information creation. Authoring, manuscript submission, review,

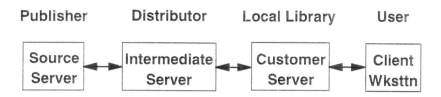

**Figure 16.4** Example of a Multi-Tiered Library Server

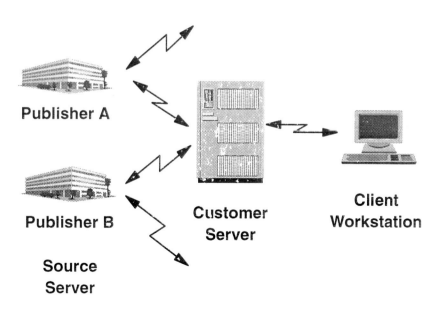

**Figure 16.5** Multiple Source Servers

and revision directly by users can eliminate many slow and expensive publication processing steps that are required today, and thus can significantly reduce costs, improve publication turn-around time, and enhance information presentation. It also enables the creation of non-linear and/or active information (e.g., hypermedia) and third-party authoring (e.g., annotation, linking, indexing). Since an information producer (author) is also an information consumer, this requires an efficient two-way information flow between a Source Server (publisher) and a Client (user) as opposed to a predominantly one-way flow in the case of publication distribution. This in turn requires interface extensions, performance considerations, and a more sophisticated rights and royalty management. We believe in this paradigm the publisher will continue to provide an important function by filtering, authenticating, classifying, organizing, and indexing information for users as noted in the Introduction.

In parallel with our work on the Almaden Distributed Digital Library System for scientific publications, at IBM Research we have been investigating other classes of digital library applications. Not surprisingly, we find that digital libraries designed with different bases of requirements and economic dynamics pose different challenges, with correspondingly different solutions. For example, in the area of cultural and heritage libraries one major problem seems to be the ability of the archive to ensure that data will not be lost over very long periods of time – even if the media survive, there may be no working device, software, or system environment required by that software to read the data [195]. To date there is no satisfactory solution to this problem. As another example, the use of digital library technology by government bodies for distribution of public information will pose yet a different set of challenges. There is evidence that public access libraries of such information will constitute one of the most widespread applications of this technology used by the public at large. While copyright protection is not an issue for such information, a major challenge is how to maintain universal access by all members of society. The challenges include universally available access means (such as telephone and fax) as well as new standards of ease of use.

### Acknowledgments

We would like to thank Henry M. Gladney for his contribution to IBM's digital library strategy, and to thank Ted C. Loewenberg for his contribution in handling the business matters for our project. We are also grateful to our joint study partner, an ISI technology team under the leadership of F. Licata, which included S. Adibi, M. Fishkow, B. Johnston, B. Williams and others, for their leadership in organizing the pilot, their contribution to requirements specification, and their active participation in the prototype development.

# Chapter 17

## Alexandria Digital Library: Rapid Prototype and Metadata Schema[*]

Christoph Fischer[†], James Frew[‡], Mary Larsgaard[§] and Terence R. Smith[¶] Qi Zheng[‖]

## 17.1   Introduction

The Alexandria Project is focused on the design, implementation, and deployment of a digital library for spatially-indexed information [93]. The Alexandria Digital Library (ADL) will eventually comprise a set of nodes distributed over the Internet, with each node supporting a variety of library components that include interfaces, catalogs, databases, and ingest facilities [**]. Two major classes of user activity supported by ADL are access to many classes of spatially-indexed materials and the application of procedures that extract useful information from accessed items. The collections of the library currently involve geographically-referenced materials, such as maps, satellite images, digitized aerial photographs, and associated metadata. These collections are being extended to include graphical materials involving more general forms of spatial indexing and referencing, such as astronomical images, digitized plans, digitized images of artwork, multimedia, and remote services (e.g. WWW sites). The library will also contain

---

[*]Work reported in this paper is supported by funding from NSF, ARPA, and NASA under NSF IRI94-11330 and by product contributions from the Digital Equipment Corporation and the Environmental Systems Research Institute, Inc.

[†]Alexandria Digital Library, UCSB, Santa Barbara, CA 93106, Email: fischer@alexandria.sdc.ucsb.edu

[‡]Alexandria Digital Library, UCSB, Santa Barbara, CA 93106, Email: frew@crseo.ucsb.edu

[§]Map and Imagery Laboratory, UCSB, Santa Barbara, CA 93106, Email: mary@alexandria.sdc.ucsb.edu

[¶]Department of Computer Science, UCSB, Santa Barbara, CA 93106, Email:smithtr@cs.ucsb.edu

[‖]Department of Computer Science, UCSB, Santa Barbara, CA 93106, Email:zheng@cs.ucsb.edu

[**]The Alexandria Digital Library Project is a consortium of universities, public institutions, and private corporations headed by the University of California at Santa Barbara. Alexandria is one of six digital projects jointly sponsored under the Digital Libraries Initiative of the National Science Foundation, the National Aeronautics and Space Administration, and the Department of Defense.

textual materials, such as gazetteers, containing geographic and spatial references to many classes of objects that possess spatial "footprints".

The need for a digital library supporting such materials arises because spatially-indexed information is currently a largely inaccessible intellectual resource. Many important collections of such information are currently stored in non-digital form (e.g., paper maps, photographs, atlases, gazetteers), and collections of considerable size and diversity are found only in the largest research libraries. While a growing amount of such information is available in digital form, it is still inaccessible to most individuals. A major goal of the Alexandria Project, therefore, is to make such resources available to a broad community of users ranging from school children to academic researchers and to help attain the social and economic benefits accruing from easy access to these classes of materials.

The present chapter is intended to serve three purposes. The first is to describe the goals and strategy of the Alexandria Project and the general architecture of ADL. The second purpose is to describe the architecture, implementation, and functioning of a rapid prototype system of ADL that is now complete. We structure this description in terms of the major components of the rapid prototype, including its interface, catalog, storage, and ingest components. Since meta-information and indexes for a library's collections are critical components for the efficient functioning of the library, a third purpose of the chapter is to provide detailed insight into our approach to designing and implementing a metadata repository for the rapid prototype system.

## 17.2   Goals, Strategy, and General Architecture of ADL

The fundamental goal of the Alexandria Project is to permit users who are distributed over the Internet to access broad classes of spatially-indexed materials that may themselves be distributed over the Internet and to derive useful information from such materials. Access may, for example, take the form of browsing, viewing, or downloading data and metadata, while useful information may be derived by the application of various procedures. The achievement of this goal will be determined by the degree to which ADL is eventually able to answer a broad array of queries. Examples of such queries include:

1. requests from a business person concerning the availability of map-based information and associated textual materials about the numbers and incomes of customers at various potential business locations. The person may wish to browse a subset of this information, and to download a subset of the browsed information. The user may request information about procedures that may be applied to the information to help determine an optimal location.

2. A family planning a vacation may request information about the route to follow during a car-trip taking them past points of interest, as well as

locations of hotels and restaurants that might be used. The search may involve viewing browse files and requesting materials about the history of various areas to be traversed, followed by a request to download a map marked with an "optimal" route and points of interest.

3. A research hydrologist may request information about the latest satellite images of a specific region from which soil moisture determinations may be made at a specific level of accuracy. After having browsed and downloaded various files, the user may request the application of procedures for registering the images to a given collection of digital elevation models in a personal library of maps.

4. A school child may ask the library to locate a book with a photograph of Amelia Earhart in Australia and a map of her last flight, and then to download digitized versions of both the photograph and map for inclusion in an essay.

While queries of such complexity are not answerable in current versions of ADL, they are clearly supportable with current technology.

## 17.2.1   The Strategy and General Architecture of ADL

The strategy adopted by Project Alexandria to achieve the goal of being able to respond to such queries involves the conceptual modeling of analog and digital library enterprises; an evolutionary approach to the development of a digital library based both on these conceptual models and on use of the Internet; and an initial focus on accessing and processing geographically referenced materials, with phased extensions to more general classes of spatially-indexed and textual materials.

We have developed a conceptual model of current "analog" libraries as well as a conceptual model of "digital" extensions to such libraries that are supportable with current technology. Our conceptual model of an analog library involves obvious major components: *catalogs* of meta-information and *stores* of collection items. The catalog component of the digital library may be viewed as both a database of metadata that is analogous to the catalog system in an analog library as well as an engine for searching the catalog and store. The catalogue system contains metadata and indices about the items stored in the main datastore of the library, and includes textual descriptions of the data and reduced datasets. The catalog component provides responses to user queries, and particularly to queries involving content-based search. The storage component of the digital library holds the main collection of digitized library items, although reduced versions of some large items are stored in the catalog, providing high-speed access to large collections of spatially-indexed items.

The conceptual model of the analog library also involves representations of classes of *users* and classes of *librarians*, as well as various interfaces between these classes of individuals and the catalog and storage components of the library. The user interface of a digital library may be viewed, for example, as a

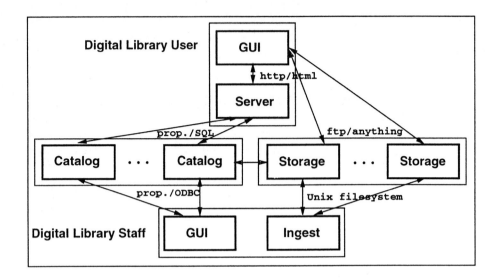

**Figure 17.1** General Architecture of the Alexandria Digital Library

representation of the current state of a user's search of the catalog and holdings, a user's interaction with librarians, and a user's processing of accessed items. The librarian interface component of the digital library may viewed, in part, as a librarian's interaction with the catalog and storage components of the library in relation to the extraction and cataloging of information about new items and the placing of these items into the library store.

Examples of extensions that we have incorporated into our digital model are: generalizations of the concept of catalog information to include large amounts of meta- and browse information about collection items, as well as a blurring of the distinction between store and catalog items; library "assistants" tailored to every user; workspaces for processing retrieved materials that are tailored for different classes of users; collections that may be "restacked" in arbitrary orders to increase the benefits to browsing; and "private" collections of items that may be assembled by users from existing library materials.

An architecture for ADL reflecting the most basic components of our conceptual model, as well as the relevant communication links, is shown in Figure 1, in which the catalog and storage components are represented as collections of distributed catalogs and stores. The user interface is represented in terms of a graphical user interface and an associated server supporting access to the various library components and librarian services in both graphic and textual terms. The librarian interface may be viewed as a set of mechanisms permitting librarians and systems managers to add new items to the store, to extract relevant metadata from the items, and to add this metadata to the catalog component. The communications links between components indicate how the system is integrated into the Internet.

# 17.3 The Rapid Prototype System for the ADL

The Alexandria Library is being developed in an evolutionary and incremental process during which the functionality, accessibility, collections, and distribution are continually augmented. The first stage, which is now complete, involved the construction of a "stand-alone" rapid prototype system (RPS). The RPS is the focus of the current chapter. The second stage involves the migration of an augmented version of the functionality of the RPS to the Internet, and the establishment of Web sites.

The basic reason for constructing the RPS was to have online, as soon as possible, a primitive digital library focused on digitized maps, images, text, video, and remote Web sites. Specific reasons for constructing the RPS include;

1. the completion of a working system that could be used to evaluate and refine specifications for system components, such as the user interface and the catalog;

2. the assessment of the applicability of current spatial data handling technology in general and geographical information systems (GIS) technology in particular, as a basis for supporting digital libraries of spatially-indexed information; the evaluation of an RPS based on such technology provides a useful benchmark against which the performance of later versions of ADL may be measured;

3. the provision of a limited facility providing local users with access to collections of digitized maps, images, airphotos, and other graphical information relating to Santa Barbara, Ventura and Los Angeles Counties in California.

One of the most important of the reasons for developing the RPS was to provide a facility permitting the development of catalog information that could be used for spatially-indexed items.

The requirement to design and develop the RPS quickly [††] was achieved by placing significant constraints on the RPS. First, the RPS software consists entirely of either commercial "off-the-shelf" products, or scripts written in high-level interpreted languages. Second, we took advantage of substantial existing hardware and data resources to assemble and load the RPS. Third, we limited RPS to a single installation in order to manage the development effort [‡‡].

---

[††]The system was designed and implemented in less than four months.

[‡‡]It is possible to access the system remotely as an X11 client.

## 17.3.1   Classes of Queries and the Functional Architecture of the RPS

The set of queries supported by the RPS is a subset of the large set of queries exemplified above. In particular, the RPS is focused largely on queries relating to the access of individual items in a relatively restricted set of digitized maps, aerial photographs, and satellite images and in the associated set of metadata. Based on both empirical and theoretical considerations, it is possible to distinguish two major classes of queries relating to the access of spatially-indexed information. Based on the experience of the UCSB Map and Imagery Laboratory (MIL) in serving analog spatial data to many diverse users (over 30,000 users annually from the general public and from university, government, and industrial organizations) the set of user requests is dominated by queries in which users wish to discover phenomena that occur at specified locations or locations at which specified phenomena exist. We may term the former a "what's here?" query and the latter a "where's this?" query. A simple example of a "what's here?" query is: *What phenomena occur on the Channel Islands off the Santa Barbara County coast?* A simple example of a "where's this?" query is: *Where are the rivers in Santa Barbara County?* From a more theoretical point of view, if one views entities in the real world as possessing an essential "spatial projection" (or footprint) which is captured to some degree in *spatially-indexed representations*, one may, in the simplest cases, query the non-spatial properties associated with a given spatial projection (what's here) or one may query the spatial projections associated with a given set of non-spatial properties (where's this) [214], [215].

In order to answer such queries, it is critical that ADL possess sufficiently powerful facilities for representing, manipulating, and displaying the footprints of entities. A system supporting "what's here" queries, for example, must be able to "understand", represent, and manipulate the user's representation of a footprint in determining the "here" aspect of the query, while a system supporting "where's this" queries must be able to represent the "where" part of the query in a manner that is easily interpretable by the user. Users employ a variety of means for referring to the footprint of some entity possessing spatial extent. There are, for example, that involve explicit reference to a footprint in terms of concrete representations of points and boundaries using some coordinate system. A user may, for example, refer to the footprint of point object in terms of a latitude and a longitude (e.g. "latitude 34 degrees 25 minutes north, longitude 120 degrees 54 minutes west" Other approaches involve implicit references to footprints associated with various symbolic representations of entities. A user may, for example, refer to a footprint of a building by giving a "name" of the building, as in the example "Campbell Hall, UCSB" More generally, users typically employ a mix of means when referring to footprints of entities.

A minimal requirement for the RPS, therefore, is that the system contain useful representations of footprints for any items in its collections that possess a footprint and that are referenceable in terms of such footprints. The entities of greatest interest in the RPS are digitized maps, digitized aerial photographs, and satellite images. Since such entities typically possess a well-defined footprint, the

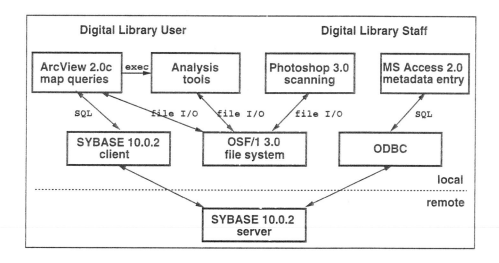

**Figure 17.2** Architecture of the ADL Rapid Prototype System

preceding requirement implies that the system contain representations of these footprints in its catalog (as "metadata") and that it be able to display them at its interface. In general, this requirement was satisfied in the RPS with representations of footprints consisting of bounding rectangles.

The functional architecture of the RPS was designed to support the two classes of queries indicated in the previous section, as well as the ingest of new items. The architecture of the RPS is a special case of the architecture illustrated in Figure 1. It is not a distributed system, having only one catalog component and one storage component. These components are represented by the enclosing lighter boxes in the figure. A representation of the RPS architecture is shown in Figure 2. We now describe the system components and their implementation.

# 17.4  The Interfaces to the ADL Rapid Prototype

The interface to the RPS comprises two components. The first is a user interface supporting graphical and textual input of user queries and displays of accessed information and meta-information. The second is an interface that librarians may employ during the task of loading data and entering metadata into the system. We now describe the first component of the interface and consider the ingest interface in a later section.

## 17.4.1   The User Interface to the RPS

In Figure 3 we show a screen dump of the user interface as it existed at some point during an actual query session. The items displayed in the figure include:

1. a "zoomable" background map that provides a basis for spatial queries. In Figure 3, the user has zoomed in from maps of the world, the U.S., and California, to a map of parts of Southern California showing county boundaries.

2. A query form allowing the entry of a thematic keyword, the type of dataset, bounding coordinates, and time (not shown in Figure 3).

3. A table showing summary metadata about items in the collection that satisfy specific criteria. This is the middle lower window in Figure 3. Selection by the user of any item in this window is displayed on the base map by highlighting the associated footprint.

4. A window showing detailed metadata about a specific item, which is displayed to the user as soon as an item is selected from the previous table. This window is illustrated in the lower left of Figure 3 and shows 29 fields from the metadata.

5. A set of "thumbnail" sketches or icons of items held in the collection, shown in the lower right of Figure 3.

6. A set of footprints displayed on the base map, showing the search area and items found.

7. Displays of specific *raster* items held in the RPS store. In Figure 3, the user has selected an aerial photograph of the west end of Santa Cruz Island.

8. Displays of specific *vector* items held in the RPS store. In Figure 3, this is a TIGER file containing line features (transportation and rivers) in Santa Barbara County.

9. Displays of video and remote Web sites. In Figure 3, for example, icons for a remote Web site (#14) and for an MPEG video (#15).

10. Hypertext document retrieval using a Web browser, including hyperlinks to other objects in the library, shown in the upper right of the figure. The footprint for this text is shown over the Channel Islands in the base map.

Additional functionality that is currently supported at the user interface includes: ArcView GIS capabilities; the retrieval and application of procedures, such as overlay, to retrieved datasets; image processing (using KHOROS, for example); and export, or "checkout", facilities.

We briefly consider how these interface tools are employed in answering the two major classes of retrieval queries supported by the RPS. For "where's this?" queries, the basic query interface provided by the RPS is a form into which the

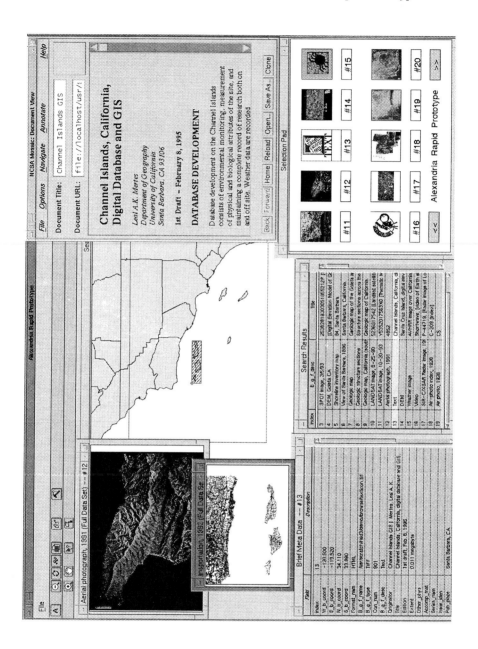

**Figure 17.3** Screen Snapshot of the Alexandria RPS

user types metadata values describing the desired data attributes (media type, means of acquisition, date acquired, etc.). This is the only interface provided for "where's this?" queries, since the phenomenological attributes being entered by the user may not have an unambiguous or easily-manipulated graphical representation. The query form provides significant error checking. In many cases, the possible values for a particular field are sufficiently few to allow simple selection from a menu. A "where's this?" query returns all the metadata for any data in the RPS whose metadata match the (range of) values specified in the query form.

For "what's here?" queries, the RPS provides an additional, graphical interface comprising a hierarchy of base maps. These maps are displayed starting at the lowest resolution (the entire Earth); the user then draws a rectangular region of interest with the workstation's pointing device. The selected region is then enlarged to fill the query window. This sequence may be repeated; as the resolution increases, additional details (e.g., state and county boundaries, rivers, etc.) are added to the current base map to keep the user oriented. Once the user is satisfied with the region of interest, its coordinates are copied to the query form, where they may be manually edited if necessary. A "what's here?" query returns all the metadata for any data in the RPS whose footprints overlap the region of interest. We note that in general a single query usually includes both "where's this?" and "what's here?" components, since all graphical input is ultimately reflected to, and the query issued from, the form interface.

If any granules are located whose metadata satisfy a query, then the metadata are displayed as a table, or as footprints drawn on the base map, or both, according to the user's preference. Individual footprints are linked to individual rows in the table, so that selecting/deselecting one may highlight/hide the other. This is useful both for verifying a granule's location, and for disambiguating overlapping footprints. In addition to, or in place of, the granule table, the user may request that a data type table be displayed. This table has a single row for each data type retrieved. For example, if a query finds 10 Landsat Thematic Mapper images, then the granule table contains a row for each image, whereas the type table contains a single row for all 10 images. This helps the user to both un-clutter the display, and to refine a subsequent query.

The user will typically wish to examine specific data granules. These can be retrieved by selecting the appropriate footprints, or rows in the granule table. The default retrieval action is to display a browse image of the granule. Browse images are optimized for rapid retrieval, rapid display, and visual information content; this optimization is generally achieved by sacrificing spatial (and, for imagery, radiometric) information content believed to have minimal visual impact. A typical browse image is a small TIFF [75] or JPEG [114] file. After viewing a browse image, the user may request the system to retrieve the original granule. If no browse image exists, as for example with tabular data, then this is the default retrieval action. The granule is displayed if the metadata indicate this to be possible. The user is prompted for the granule's disposition (e.g., save to a local file, send to a printer or tape drive, ship over a network connection to a remote system.)

# 17.5 The Catalog and Metadata for the ADL Rapid Prototype

The catalog is a central component of the RPS and contains meta-information about the collections held in the library. In particular, metadata in the RPS is stored in a relational database management system (RDBMS) constructed and maintained by "ingest" library staff. The design and implementation of such a component involves both a variety of issues concerning content and exchange standards, the design of a database schema, and various implementation issues.

## 17.5.1 A Comparison of the USMARC and FGDC Metadata standards

In order that metadata be easily exchangeable between different organizations, including libraries, it is essential that either national or preferably international standards (ISO) be followed. There are currently two standards of some importance in the U.S. for representing spatial metadata. The first is the USMARC, which has been a national standard in the library world since the 1960s, and has been the basis for an international standard (UNIMARC) and for various other national standards, such as UKMARC. USMARC is a format for ingesting descriptions of items into an automated database. Its content and structure are based directly on the AACR2R (Anglo-American Cataloging Rules), which provides the body of rules that USMARC implements in the machine environment, and which is thus more closely the analog of the FGDC Standard than is USMARC.

The second standard is the Federal Geographic Data Committee (FGDC) Standard which was mandated for use by U.S. Federal agencies in 1995 [59]. The FGDC was established to promote the coordinated development, use, sharing, and dissemination of surveying, mapping, and related spatial data [2] and in particular to formulate a metadata standard for geospatial data in digital form. The FGDC standard is important because most map collections in the U.S. are heavily populated with spatial data (both analog and digital) received through the U.S. depository system. In Table 1, we illustrate some of the basic properties of, and differences between, the two standards.

Table 1. Nature of USMARC and FGDC Standards

|  | FGDC | USMARC |
|---|---|---|
| *Nature* | Content standard | Database standard |
| *Introduced* | 1994 | 1969 |
| *Creator* | Federal Geographic Data Committee | Library of Congress (de facto national library of U.S.) |
| *Basis* | 1992 conference; meetings, users | Anglo-American cataloging rules |
| *Purpose* | Federally produced geospatial data; consistent documentation | Libraries could automate cataloging operations; speed up cataloging operations; allow sharing of catalog records |
| *Audience* | Federal geospatial data producers | Libraries in the U.S. |
| *Implementations* | no | yes (UNIMARC, CANMARC) |
| *Structure* | directed graph | hierarchical (two levels) |
| *Number of fields* | ca. 300 | ca. 3,000 |
| *Field labels* | no coded field labels; no unique labels; | fields are integer- and letter-coded |
| *Coded fields* | no | yes |
| *Data to which it may be applied* | spatial data in digital form, | information to which library provides access |
| *Associated standards* | yes, e.g., SDTS, ASTM, Z39.50 | yes; e.g., LC subject headings, Z39.50 |
| *Prescribed formatting* | no | yes |
| *Number of items to which applied* | 1,000,000 | 60,000,000 |

It is clear from Table 1 that many differences exist between the two standards. We present a representative example of specific differences. USMARC has several instances in which information appears in two places, once in the area that the public-catalog users see and once in the computer-searchable fields. The latter tend to be coded or abbreviated fields. A good example involves data for bounding-coordinates. For the U.S. Geological Survey 7.5-minute topographic quadrangle of Goleta, California, the USMARC values are:

```
034 $d W1195230 $e W1194500 $f N343000 $g N342230
255 $c (W 119 52'30"--W 119 45'00"/N 34 30'30"--N 34 22'30")
```

In comparison, the FGDC data elements from Section 1.5.1 for the same information are:

```
West-bounding coordinates    -119.875
East-bounding coordinates    -119.75
North-bounding coordinates    34.508
South-bounding coordinates    34.375
```

FGDC expresses coordinates in decimal degrees only using negative values for longitudes in the Western Hemisphere and for latitudes in the Southern Hemisphere. USMARC expresses coordinate values in degrees, minutes, and seconds using "W", "E" for longitude values and "N", "S" for latitude values. It also uses one field for computer search (034) and another for user display (255).

Finally, we note an important relationship between USMARC and FGDC that is of value in solving the metadata issue for digital libraries of spatially-indexed information. An important property of the FGDC Standard is the creation of USMARC fields for any FGDC Standard fields for which USMARC fields do not already exist. A first version of a "crosswalk" between the FGDC Standard and USMARC was drawn up in 1994 [154], with the goal of determining which USMARC fields or subfields would need to be created in FGDC [154]. Agreement was reached by MARBI (MAchine-Readable Bibliographic Information), the decision-making body for the USMARC format in 1994, prior to the adoption of the FGDC standard by government agencies. This property permits us to combine, in a rational manner, the two standards in the catalog of a digital library.

## 17.5.2   General Issues in Implementing USMARC and FGDC Standards

The metadata implementation must be driven by user needs and not by the implementation of a specific standard. The main implementational issue, besides the provision of sufficient information to locate DL objects of interest, is performance of the user interface (i.e., response time for read transactions). Another interface that also relates to performance is metadata ingest (i.e., response time for read/write transactions). Even though the read transactions from the DL user interface will outnumber the read/write transactions from the metadata ingest interface, it cannot be neglected since metadata ingest is crucial to the quantity and quality of metadata available in a DL. Even though all fields in the RDBMS are searchable, there are trade-offs in expediting searches on certain fields.

In USMARC all metadata regarding a library object are assumed to be stored in a single record composed of four components: Leader, Record Directory, Control Fields, Variable Fields. These components are defined in detail in [176]. This assumption favors the implementation of a flat-file structure by requiring all metadata for a library object to be stored in a single record. The advantage of this construction of a metadata record is that no prior structures (e.g., tables, objects) need to be defined, and all information (field identification and field content) is stored within the record. There is a tradeoff between the overhead of prior structure and the overhead of storing the field identification in each record. The disadvantage is that search operations on fields that do not have a predefined location in the record are inefficient.

The FGDC Standard is new and little can be said about its usage and acceptance, although the number and diversity of implementations are steadily growing (e.g., document.aml, which originated from USGS's Water Resources Division and is now marketed by ESRI Inc.; Geolineus marketed by Geographic Design Inc.). The diversity of implementations derives from the fact that the FGDC Standard does not define physical details of a metadata record; it only defines and describes the fields and their logical relation in a hierarchical structure over several levels.

The physical implementation of a metadata repository can be completely independent of any metadata standard as long as the repository provides an import/export function. In the case of USMARC, this function would read or write USMARC records according to the standard's specifications. Our interpretation of the USMARC record definition is that it provides a means of exchanging metadata records between different DLs. The FGDC Standard does not define the physical structure of a metadata record, therefore no generic import/export function for the FGDC Standard exists. The ASTM version of the FGDC standard, however, may provide a mechanism through SGML. In order to import/export metadata, it is necessary to have an extended data dictionary that maps the field names used in the metadata repository into the field names defined in a metadata standard. This approach reduces the restrictions on the implementation of metadata standards and also allows the incorporation of several metadata standards into one DL, which greatly increases the capability of automatically ingesting metadata.

The separation of metadata standards from the physical implementation of metadata repository leads to the question of the best data model for a metadata repository having several thousand fields although single metadata records are typically composed of far fewer fields (approximately 80 fields for the FGDC Standard and USMARC). The metadata repository must handle metadata for several million DL objects. It must also provide the capability of storing browse graphics, abstracts, or any other representation of a DL object.

## 17.5.3    Combining the FGDC and USMARC Standards in the RPS

A central decision in the design of the RPS is the choice of standards for content and exchange of metadata. An obvious resolution of this issue is to base a representation of metadata on either USMARC of FGDC. The FGDC standard is appropriate for organizations dealing only with *digital* spatial data, while USMARC is appropriate for organizations having both analog and digital materials and who are willing to tolerate the lag-time between FGDC definitions of new fields and the incorporation of those fields into USMARC. Hence neither USMARC nor FGDC alone is completely appropriate for ADL.

Furthermore, neither is currently accepted as a general standard by all organizations, although most organizations employ one or the other. Hence we felt that a combination of the two was essential for the Alexandria Project. When ADL began the process of metadata ingest, the FGDC standard possessed a good definition of the fields necessary for cataloging digital geospatial data. The corresponding USMARC fields were in the process of being finalized at that time. In addition, the FGDC Standard had a relatively small number of fields, an important consideration in the implementation of a rapid prototype system. It was necessary, however, to add USMARC fields for analog spatial data which the FGDC standard, by definition, does not handle. USMARC also allowed us, through its local-use fields, to create additional fields for analog spatial data that were absent from both standards. USMARC, unlike FGDC, already possesses thesauri (e.g. for subject headings).

Using the FGDC Standard and USMARC together has enabled Project Alexandria to catalog all forms of spatial data thus far encountered, including remote-sensing imagery, digitized maps, digital raster and vector datasets, text, videos, and remote Web servers. The metadata scheme for the RPS has evolved into an implementation of approximately 350 fields, including all FGDC fields and selected USMARC fields. Of the 350 fields, 29 are visible to the user and 8 may be used for search by the user.

A DL metadata repository based on the *relational data model* requires the mapping of metadata standards into Entity-Relationship (ER) models (logical schemas), and the merging of the ER models into one model which needs to be transformed into at least third normal form (3NF). Once the normalized model (physical schema) is translated into SQL (Structured Query Language), it can be implemented in any commercial RDBMS which provides SQL. There are, however, two major drawbacks. First, SQL is set-oriented, which means that a query result can only be handled in an all-or-nothing manner; it does not allow parts of the query result to be displayed before the query is finished. Therefore the response time increases as the query-result quantity increases. Second, given the fact that many metadata fields are independently repeatable, the metadata information for one DL object is scattered over many tables. In order to retrieve all metadata for a specific DL object, multiple join operations are necessary, which also increases the response time.

The FGDC Standard production rules have been converted into an E-R model using an E-R modeling tool. The model contains 288 attributes and 245 entities, and parts of it have been normalized as the metadata scheme evolved. The additional USMARC fields have been directly included into the physical schema. We used an E-R modeling tool to generate the necessary SQL statements in order to create the metadata scheme in the RDBMS employed as the metadata repository. In addition, an extended data dictionary was created with the E-R modeling tool. This extended data dictionary contains the following elements: schema field name; datatype; schema table name; domain; default value; FDGC Standard data element name; FDGC Standard data element description; FGDC Standard data element tag name; FGDC Standard data element section number; USMARC field name; USMARC description; and USMARC field number.

## Problems in Applying the FGDC and USMARC Standards in ADL

We encountered several problems while implementing the FGDC Standard and USMARC. We discuss here only those problems that are common to both FGDC and USMARC. USMARC-specific problems are too detailed in nature to be addressed in this chapter. With respect to the FGDC Standard, we note the following problems:

1. Map Projection (4.1.2.1.2): twenty-one are listed with the corresponding set of parameters, and a twenty-second, Other Projection's Definition (4.1.2.1.3). While Other Projection's Definition is necessary, the way the standard (production rules) is set up (storing each projection along with its parameters in a separate entity; not allowing parameters for certainly Other Projection's Definition) does not work out well in application. The same problems are with Grid Coordinate System (4.1.2.2).

2. Entity and Attribute Information (5): The following circular relation of compounds is defined: Attribute (5.1.2) consists of Attribute Domain Values (5.1.2.4) which consists of Enumerated Domain (5.1.2.4.1), RangeDomain (5.1.2.4.2), or Code Set Domain (5.1.2.4.3). Enumerated Domain and Range Domain consist, if applicable, of one or more Attribute (5.1.2) compounds. The FGDC Standard does not provide any information about the Attribute compound used Enumerated Domain and Range Domain.

3. The production rules lack a number of intermediate compounds in order to be consistent.

With respect to problems common to applying the FGDC Standard and US-MARC, we note that approximately 80% of all spatial data is composed of map series, air-photo flights, and satellite-image projects. This means that parent-child relationships and the ability to express these in metadata are extremely important, since users request spatial data at the sheet or the frame level. This means metadata has to be provided on different levels (e.g., series level, sheet level). In order to avoid repeating metadata information it is essential that the information stored with a given child item is unique to that item. While AACR2R allows for different levels of description, USMARC did not until the introduction of linking fields. Since the vast majority of all cataloging is done through the use of automated systems, standard library cataloging does not deal well with the non-repetition of information common to every child. It does have the capability of tying children to each other and to their parent. Further, when one moves into digital data, especially GIS datasets, the parent-child analogy does not sufficiently express all of the relationships. Superset-set-subset comes closer to the situation of a GIS dataset with many layers (and also with tiles), and each layer (or tile) having component parts.

# 17.6   The Ingest and Storage Components of the Rapid Prototype

The ingest component of the RPS is primarily used to create library objects from existing digital files, which are then placed in the storage component. Some of these objects are used as background maps to support search at the user interface and to serve as sample data sources described by meta records. A flatbed scanner is employed for the ingest of aerial photographs, maps, and limited text files. As described above, metadata meeting FGDC and USMARC standards is created for each of these files. We are also importing existing metadata files from, for example, a NASA/Ames database of remotely-sensed images. The import of meta data already existing in digital form requires the conversion of source fields into target fields. Datatype conversion and units of measurement conversion are typically involved in such a process. If the minimal requirements for a metadata record are not fulfilled, additional metadata must be added manually.

Since the storage component of the RPS was constructed from standard equipment, we focus attention on the collections supported in the RPS. Our goals in selecting items to be loaded into the RPS were to achieve both breadth, in terms of the number of data types supported, and depth, in terms of the availability of multiple data types, as well as multiple instances of a single type, for a particular location. We illustrate the collections loaded in Table 2. To meet the depth requirement, we selected a subset of California (specifically, Santa Barbara, Ventura, and Los Angeles Counties), for which the MIL has an especially rich set of holdings. All data classes loaded into the RPS included at least one item overlapping this region. In addition to thematic depth, we were able to achieve some striking multitemporal layerings, including coincident aerial photography from the 1920s and satellite imagery from the 1980s. We selected datasets from a variety of data types to satisfy the breadth requirement (see [9], [177], [226].)

| Table 2. Collections in Rapid Prototype System | | |
|---|---|---|
| *Raster:* | *Scanned analog items* | air photos, air-photo index, geologic maps<br>views of Santa Barbara, geologic sections<br>shoreline inventory map, USGS topographic sheet |
| | *Digital items* | Landsat satellite images, Landsat composite (CA)<br>SPOT satellite image, DEM (USGS) |
| *Vector:* | | TIGER (U.S. Census Bureau boundary, line files)<br>- layers: transportation, monuments, Census zones<br>DLG (USGS)<br>- layers: hydrography, railroads, roads, airports |
| *Text:* | | Channel Islands accompanying text |
| *Remote services:* | | AVHRR image of western U.S. |
| *Multimedia:* | | MPEG video of Earth showing ocean radiation |

## 17.7    Software and Hardware Components of the ADL Rapid Prototype

The RPS was built primarily from three large software packages: the Sybase RDBMS; the Tcl/Tk scripting language and user interface toolkit; and the ArcView GIS. We use a Sybase server, running on a remote host, to store and manage the RPS's metadata, using our previously described hybrid spatial metadata schema. The modeling tool with which we developed the schema automatically generate Structured Query Language (SQL) statements necessary to instantiate the schema in Sybase. Tcl/Tk [179] is a "freeware" package with two components. The "Tcl" component is a high-level interpreted language, which we use as the master control language for the RPS (everything is ultimately invoked from a Tcl script.) The "Tk" component is a set of extension to Tcl that correspond directly to X11 "widgets" (user interface elements). We use Tk to write the "where's this?" query form and miscellaneous other user interface components. ArcView [126] is a GIS for PCs and workstations. Its principal advantage in our application is that it incorporates a scripting language, "Avenue", that allow us to modify its user interface. We use ArcView to implement the "what's here?" query, and for all non-text data display (base maps, data footprints, retrieved maps and images.) We also take advantage of ArcView's ability to query the Sybase server.

The RPS runs almost entirely on a single Digital Equipment Corporation

(DEC) Alpha workstation in the MIL. In addition to a color X11 display, the RPS workstation hosts a 50 GB disk array and a 105 GB optical disk jukebox, so all RPS data are stored locally. Additional workstations and X terminals are available on the MIL's local Ethernet and have been used for software development and metadata entry, but are not required to run the RPS. Also on the Ethernet is a PC system with a high-resolution flatbed scanner; this system is the primary means by which we ingest aerial photographs into the RPS. The only remote component of the RPS is the Sybase metadata server, which runs on an IBM RS/6000 workstation and is accessed over an Ethernet.

## 17.8 Unique Features of the RPS, Lessons Learned, and Next Steps

The Alexandria RPS has several unique features. Traditional library catalogs, and most of their current online equivalents, are for the most part text-oriented. The RPS is unique in its ability to search library holdings geographically and to employ footprints for representing the spatial relationships between retrieved items. The thumbnails returned with each retrieval allow the user to browse and select library holdings based on purely visual attributes, as well as on more traditional metadata. Finally, unlike many existing spatial data libraries, which are effectively "closed stack" the RPS allows the user to completely control the search and retrieval procedure, down to the level of the individual holding.

Several lessons were learned from the construction of the RPS that are influencing our current design and development. First, current GIS architectures are too monolithic and inflexible for building systems required to support large digital libraries. Large software packages containing built-in extension languages are much easier to deal with than those that do not. The programmability of ArcView, via its Avenue language, was critical to the success of the RPS. Second, high-level extensible scripting languages, such as Tcl/Tk, are excellent tools for building integrated systems from otherwise isolated software packages. Coding at this "module coordination" level is far more productive than having to implement individual modules. Third, we found metadata to be the most problematic issue. The rich history of structured metadata management for traditional library holdings does not exist for digital spatial data and the RPS schema is one of the first of its kind. We spent significant amounts of time constructing a coherent metadata schema from the current array of standards. Once the model was constructed, we spent additional time building interfaces for ingesting and validating metadata, and inserting it into the DBMS. Finally, we encountered significant limitations from both the lack of a spatial query language and from the use of rectangular footprints.

### 17.8.1 The Next Stage in constructing ADL

The RPS is essentially a monolithic system with only the connection between the catalog and user interface components being potentially scalable into a distributed system. The Alexandria Project is now focusing on the construction of a system comprising multiple, geographically distributed instances of the ingest, storage, catalog, and user interface components. Allowing multiple libraries to enter their holdings into Alexandria will require a robust, portable metadata ingest facility. Metadata in the RPS system were laboriously processed by hand from free-text entries into SQL INSERTs and UPDATEs. We are re-developing the metadata ingest procedure based on a microcomputer RDBMS with a visual form-builder interface. Once the metadata schema is loaded into the microcomputer RDBMS, we allow the metadata entry personnel to design entry forms that best accommodate the particular datasets they are working on. Using the form-builder, they implement the forms themselves. Metadata collected through these forms are periodically transferred to the catalog RDBMS via a network ODBC gateway. Such a system can be easily and cheaply implemented at any participating library with a PC.

In order to expose ADL to a broad user community, we are connecting the RPS to the World Wide Web (WWW). This involves replacing the ArcView-based user interface with a Hypertext Transfer Protocol (HTTP) server, a collection of Hypertext Markup Language (HTML) scripts, and a Common Gateway Interface (CGI) connection to the Sybase metadata catalog. The user interface will be created on-the-fly in the user's WWW browser (e.g. Mosaic) by transferring the appropriate HTML scripts. ArcView map queries will be replaced by HTML "imagemaps" while the Tcl/Tk and ArcView forms will be replaced by HTML forms. Thumbnail images will be loaded directly into the user's browser, while full data files will be obtained via browser-initiated FTP transfers. Although WWW browsers are far more ubiquitous that ArcView or other GIS packages, HTML has far fewer capabilities than a GIS. It will be a challenge both to construct a GIS-like user interface in HTML, and to support complex, hierarchical queries in a stateless medium like HTTP.

We plan to migrate from the relational model for the metadatabase to an object-oriented model. This will facilitate the representation of complex objects in the catalog. Such objects will arise, for example, from the use that we plan to make of generalized and fuzzy footprints and from the need to incorporate information concerning complex spatial entities from gazetteers. The distribution and replication of metadata must be independent of the data model used for implementation of a DL metadata repository. This will improve performance, reliability, availability, expandability, and sharability to the DL, but it will also add additional complexity, cost, and security problems [175]. The holdings of metadata records will be increased to over 2.5 million metadata records. In addition metadata distribution and replication will be explored.

## 17.9   Summary

The rapid prototype system for Alexandria Digital Library has proven of great value in clarifying the issues that we will have to resolve in the next stages of development of a digital library for geo-spatial information. In particular, we resolved several important issues concerning both the user interface and the catalog. In relation to the catalog, metadata standards arose as a key issue for the exchange of metadata between different digital libraries. Unfortunately, the number of metadata standards is growing and an international metadata standard for DLs appears unlikely to appear soon. In consequence, we need to be able to import and export different existing metadata standards.

A metadata scheme for a DL must handle all possible cases of DL objects. Owing to the limited focus of different metadata standards, it is likely that more than one will need to be implemented. The larger number of fields available does not mean that each metadata record will use all of them. Query response time is the crucial element for metadata scheme implementation. Metadata ingest in manual or automated form determines the quantity and quality of data stored in the metadata repository. The Alexandria Project will continue to evaluate and develop prototype metadata repositories. It is likely that a data model suitable for all DL requirements may be composed of multiple paradigms such as Relational-Object-Oriented or other combinations.

## ACKNOWLEDGEMENTS

The authors wish to acknowledge Michele Aurand, Barbara Buttenfield, Larry Carver, Meg Gardner, Michael Goodchild, Greg Hajic, Keith Park and Mark Probert for their important contributions to the design and construction of the Alexandria Rapid Prototype. The Alexandria Project would like to thank Kelly Chan, Jack Dangermond, and Clem Hendriksen of ESRI Inc., Rob Crombie of DEC Inc., Arlene Allen, Glenn Davis, and Sue Woodill of the UCSB Computer Center, and Debbie Donahue of the UCSB Institute for Computational Earth Systems Science, for their support of the Alexandria Digital Library Project.

## FURTHER INFORMATION

Further information about the Alexandria Digital Library is available on the Web at URL
http://alexandria.sdc.ucsb.edu/ or from the Project Director, Terence R. Smith (smithtr@cs.ucsb.edu).

# Chapter 18

## The ELINOR Electronic Library

Dian G Zhao* and Anne Ramsden

## 18.1   Introduction

There are three fundamental changes when moving from a traditional library to an electronic library environment and the potential advantages resulting from the changes are: 1) Books and journals are no longer stored in printed form but in electronic forms, which are theoretically always available for viewing. No book shelves or store rooms are needed for physically holding printed documents. A range of problems related to physically handing printed books in the traditional library, such as shelving and checking in and out of books, disappear. 2). The "reading space" in an electronic library environment is no longer restricted to the physical reading rooms. Computer networks can bring a vast amount of information resources on the network to the users at home or at work and allow many electronic libraries to be accessed at the same time. 3) Users, instead of reading printed documents, will be reading electronic documents on computer screens. With searching and browsing software getting more powerful and easier to use, reading on screen can be a quicker and more accurate way of getting information.

However, an electronic library is not merely about storing electronic data and connecting everyone and everything together. There are a number of technical and socio-economic challenges in developing the electronic library. The ELINOR electronic library project, now in its third year of research and development, has investigated several aspects of the electronic library. The user aspect concerning the user interface, user studies and user modelling, has been recognised as an important research area. The second area is the system aspect concerning how to capture, organise and store the electronic data economically, so that searching, browsing, filtering and sharing can be efficiently supported. This determines the file formats, document models, document organisation and the system architecture of the electronic library. The third area is access control and management. Data in the electronic library may include intellectual properties which are protected by law, but data in electronic forms in the networked

---
*Information Centre, De Montfort University, Milton Keynes MK7 6HP, UK, Email: dz@dmu.ac.uk

244 Chapter 18 The ELINOR Electronic Library

environment can be copied, changed and distributed easily. Proper mechanisms for protecting copyright materials must be enforced.

Existing electronic libraries can be classified according to their document models. A document model concerns the storage, composition and handling of the documents in the electronic library. Three basic document models, the free text model, the document image processing (DIP) model, and the hypermedia model are often employed by existing electronic libraries. In the free text model, a document is a piece of text which can be identified, indexed, and presented. WAIS [133] falls into this category. In the DIP model, a document is a sequence of pages with each page represented as a bit mapped image file. Text can also be attached to some or all image pages for indexing and searching purposes. MERCURY [225], ELINOR and several other electronic library systems fit into this document model. The third document model is the hypermedia model. All WWW virtual libraries [92] fit into this model. New document models, such as the HyTime [198] document model, are also being developed. The ELINOR project has been influenced and inspired by several of the existing research projects notably the CORE [142] project for its user interface study and the MERCURY project for its system architecture. Standards and other research and developments [105] [97], such as WWW [92], WAIS [133], GOPHER [160], the Z39.50 information retrieval protocol [148], the Dexter hypertext model [116], and user modelling [163] have also influenced the project.

The ELINOR (Electronic Library INformation Online Retrieval) electronic library project, jointly funded by De Montfort University, the British Library and IBM UK, started in March 1992[90][91]. One of the important objectives of the project is to build an electronic library (or digital library, or virtual library) system containing a large collection of the full contents of high use materials including books, journals, course materials, and multimedia learning packages, which can be directly accessed by students and staff via Windows-based PCs and workstations. A pilot system was implemented at De MOntfort University in 1993 to experiment with the various aspects of the electronic library. PixTex/EFS from Excalibur Technologies, a free text retrieval system with integrated imaging functions, was chosen as the core software for the pilot [89]. The pilot database, with some 35 000 pages of teaching materials, has since been used to assist in the teaching and learning of one undergraduate course.

The project has focused on several research areas, including copyright management, the user aspect and the modelling aspect of the electronic library. A small scale user study with the objective of establishing a formal user study method was carried out in the autumn term of 1993. A prototype gateway allowing the WWW browsers to access the pilot database was also implemented. A copyright management system, including usage statistics collection and management and printing control, was implemented in-house [242]. The pilot system is now being extended both in terms of the subject coverage and network access. This chapter covers the user aspect and the system aspect of the ELINOR electronic library. Theoretical work focusing on building an adaptive user model and a suitable data model for the electronic library has also commenced.

# 18.2   Using ELINOR

## 18.2.1   The Database

The ELINOR electronic library follows the DIP document model – stores a document as a sequence of pages. Each page is represented as a TIFF G4 image. Some or all pages of a document can have corresponding free text for indexing purposes. A document can be searched by the free-text associated with its pages, can be browsed page by page or randomly accessed. Documents are filed into the database hierarchically by subject. The ELINOR electronic library system uses the metaphor of "fileroom", "cabinet", "drawer", and "folder" to organise documents into hierarchies. The organisation is similar to that of the subject indexing scheme used in traditional libraries. Figure 18.1 shows a portion of the information hierarchy of the pilot database. The advantage of such an hierarchical organisation of documents is that it supports effective browsing.

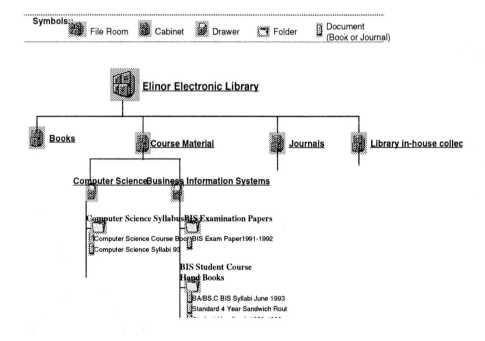

**Figure 18.1** The Hierarchical Organisation of Document

The ELINOR database currently only covers the subject areas of business, computing and one European language as required by the BA/BSc Business Information Systems (BIS) course. The database contains documents of various types including textbooks, various examination paper and course handbooks, several issues of three journals, and a limited number of lecture notes, totalling 35,000 pages. The contents pages and the back-of-index pages of a book and every page of other document types are also OCR'ed (OCR stands for optical character recognition) into ASCII text for indexing purposes.

## 18.2.2   Browsing and Reading Documents

Browsing is an important way of discovering information. After studying the information retrieval behaviour of 34 subjects, Chen concluded "it is alarming that the least effective and efficient strategies, namely, the SCREEN-BROWSING and the TRIAL-AND-ERROR strategies, were used overwhelmingly by the subject searchers. over 80used these two strategies" [54]. We are not going to argue about whether browsing is or is not "effective and efficient", but if browsing is used by the majority of users, then it is important to support it efficiently.

Because of the subject-based hierarchical organisation of documents, browsing the database in ELINOR is by descending the subject tree and allows a set of "related" documents to be found in one go. Browsing from the root down to the "BIS Student Course Handbooks" folder in Figure 18.2, for example, revealed several related documents on the subject. Once an interested document is found, it can be viewed on screen. The reader can flip through the pages by clicking the Next or Previous buttons, or use the mouse to pick a page number in the document window, or press the Goto button to select any given page. It is also possible to view multiple pages from several documents at the same time.

## 18.2.3   Searching for Documents

The ELINOR electronic library supports both free text and structured field searching. The free text search is based on neural networks, or more specifically, adaptive pattern recognition processing , which caters for both Boolean and natural language retrieval [82]. The structured field search provides searching similar to that of the library catalogue records in OPACs.

A free text search is done in two steps. A quick preliminary search on the neural network index results in a hit list with a preliminary score indicating the degree of relevance. The hit list can subsequently be rated according to the relevance of the documents to the query. The system allows fuzzy searching regardless of spelling errors in the user's query or OCR errors in the text. Users can adjust the degree of relevance to indicate to what extent the query should match the source patterns in the texts. The free text retrieval interface is illustrated in Figure 18.3. As is illustrated by the example, the query contains a misspelled word "docament" but the system can still find "document image processing" when the search exactness parameter is at 70may be combined to find a relevant document.

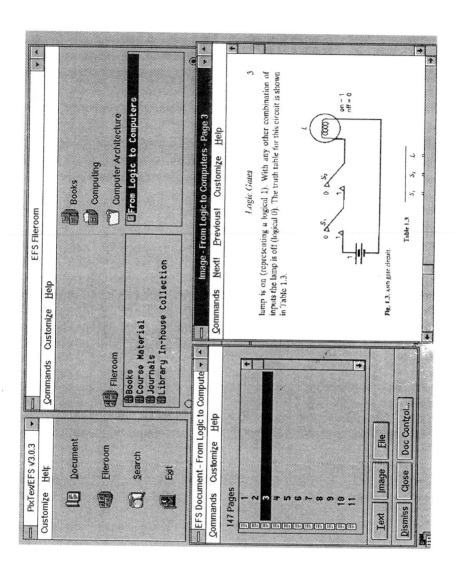

**Figure 18.2** Browsing and Reading in ELINOR

248  Chapter 18  The ELINOR Electronic Library

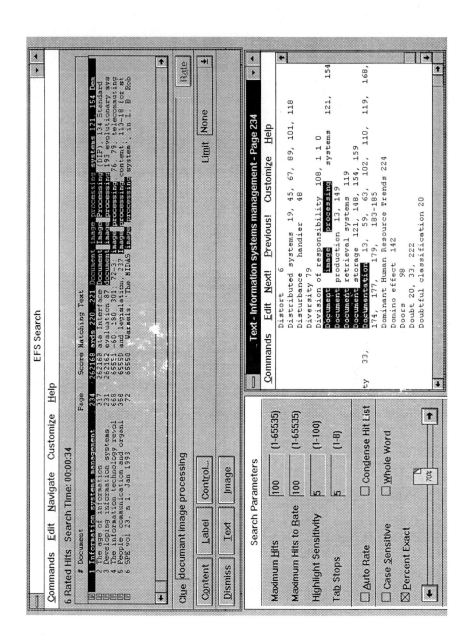

**Figure 18.3** Searching in ELINOR

## 18.2.4  Printing Documents

Technically users can select pages from a document or select a whole document for printing in the ELINOR electronic library system. Politically printing is a quite complicated process. Since most documents in the system are copyright material and different publishers have different requirements on charging and on the number of pages a user can print per day, printing has to be controlled individually on a per publisher basis. De Montfort University also levies a seven pence basic print charge for each page printed.

When a user submits a print request, the request is not actually sent to the printer queue directly but is buffered instead. This avoids the problem of students requesting a print run but not collecting their printouts. When a student comes to collect his printouts, the printing control software checks for the various limits set by publishers, checks whether the user still has any credit left, and finally if all conditions are met, prints out the pages with a copyright cover page. Figure 18.4 shows an example cover page which lists the copyright notice from publishers, and the charging details.

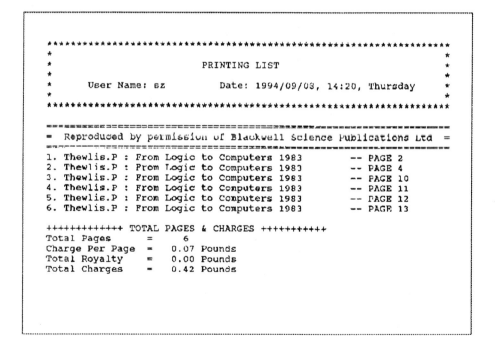

**Figure 18.4** Sample Printing Cover

## 18.3    User Study

A small scale user study was carried out in the Autumn term of 1993 [94]. The objectives of the study were: 1) to gauge objectively the usability of the ELINOR electronic library system by comparing the use of the electronic books with that of printed books; 2) to gauge the subjective reactions to ELINOR from the users, and 3) to establish a coherent methodology which can be employed later for larger scale user studies.

A controlled experiment with two tasks was carried out to compare the use of electronic books with that of printed books. Eight students were selected randomly from 33 first-year BIS students as the study subjects. The first task requires the subjects to find answers for given questions in known books both in a traditional library and in the electronic library. The second task is similar to the first one but without telling the students which books contain the answers. In both tasks, the subjects need to find the books then get the answers from the books. Time taken in finding the books and time taken in finding answers from the books both in the electronic library and traditional library were recorded and analysed. Questionnaires about the usability and usefulness of the electronic library were also handed to the subjects to obtain their personal reactions to the system.

The study found that : 1) it is quicker to locate books containing the answers to the given questions from the electronic library than from the traditional library but it is slower to find an answer from the electronic book than from the printed book; 2) the subjects appreciated the concepts of the electronic library and regarded it as more useful than OPACs. It must be pointed out that the user study is based on the pilot ELINOR electronic library system with a very small subject sample. The findings are preliminary and not conclusive. The speed of reading electronic book, for example, may be improved considerably when hypertext is introduced to the ELINOR electronic library system.

## 18.4    The Systems Aspect of ELINOR

### 18.4.1    The System Architecture

The ELINOR electronic library is based on client/server architecture. As shown in Figure 18.5, the system consists of PC clients, computer networks and the server. The server functions are implemented through the search engine, the document inputting subsystem, the USCM(usage statistics collection and management) subsystem, the printing control subsystem, and the tool box which contains tools for manipulating the databases.

The ELINOR server is hosted on an IBM/RS6000 workstation with 15 Gigabytes of hard disk space. The underlying protocol is the Internet TCP/IP. Since the whole campus runs Novell Netware, the PC clients not only "talk" TCP/IP protocol to access the ELINOR server but also "talk" Netware IPX protocol to access the Novell file servers. A prototype WWW gateway to the system,

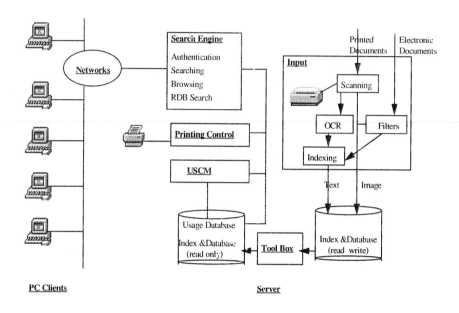

**Figure 18.5** The ELINOR electronic library system architecture

which allows accessing the text files of the ELINOR database and is restricted
to within the university, was also built. Users can use WWW broswers such as
the MOSAIC browser, to access the ELINOR database. The browsing interface
is hierarchical and similar to that of the PixTex/EFS. The searching is fuzzy
and is also through the PixTex/EFS search engine. Figure 18.6 shows the top
page of the interface.

## 18.4.2   Usage Statistics Collection

Usage statistics collection and management (USCM) in the ELINOR electronic
library is concerned with tracking, managing, analysing, and reporting resource
usage by the electronic library users. How many pages of a particular book
are referenced by users in a particular time period, for example, is a usage
statistics figure for copyright management purposes in ELINOR. Usage statistics
collection and management have been largely ignored in most DIP or free text
systems including PixTex/EFS [89]. The first obstacle in implementing a USCM
subsystem in ELINOR is collecting the usage statistics. Usage statistics are not
generated by users intentionally but are by-products of user actions. When a user
displays a page, for example, some sort of usage statistics data are generated and
must be selectively picked up by the statistics collection subsystem. Picking up
the usage statistics data from ELINOR is a problem because the core software
does not provide this facility. The second obstacle in implementing a USCM
subsystem is finding a suitable database structure to store the statistics data.
Usage statistics data are summaries of ordinary usage data obtained by applying
aggregation functions on a set of ordinary data records [7]. Conventional data
modelling methods which focus on "reality" or "facts" may not be suitable for
usage statistics data. In reality, most usage statistics are about the usage of
resources during a particular time period and there is little meaning in talking
about resource usage without a time limit. Time, which is not supported by
most database systems, must also be taken into account.

To overcome the collecting problem, we adopted an approach which takes
advantage of the operating system monitoring functions. Since the operating
system is in charge of all lower level resource management including all the
resources managed by the electronic library database server, it is possible for us
to map between the operating system generated resource usage and that of the
database server.If the operating system can pick up a file read event with a file
name which is also meaningful to the electronic library database server, then
we know this event is also an event of the database server. Events of irrelevant
type are ignored and relevant events are further projected and formatted for
automatic batch processing during the night.

## 18.4.3   Usage Statistics Management

The simplest way to store the usage statistics data is to store the events in flat
files. However, this does not work both from the point of view of storage and from
the point of view of system performance. A busy system can generate a huge

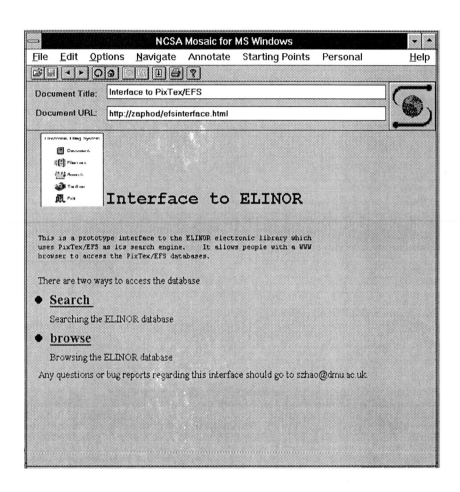

**Figure 18.6** Using MOSAIC to Access ELINOR

amount of events in a short time period thereby overloading the system storage capacities. Unless the stored data is compressed and taken off-line regularly, which means online usage statistics query is not possible, space is going to be a problem. Also, any usage statistics query on any objects may need a whole database search causing unacceptable performance. Decomposing and storing the events in several databases is thus inevitable. Instead of using an ad-hoc approach which may rule out better design alternatives, a modelling approach which aims at a thorough understanding and precise description of the semantics of the usage statistics data and the relations among them is clearly preferred.

Conventional data modelling produces models of "reality" or "situation". However, a data model of the reality (or situation) is not our purpose. We want a model of the summaries of the reality because we are interested in the summaries of events. A two step data modelling approach is thus needed. In the first step, we construct the model of the reality, that is the model of the objects(or entities) and their relationships. Next we summarise the relations as is required by statistics operations by breaking the links between objects and recording the summary information in the object itself. We will use a simplified version of the ELINOR modelling as an example to illustrate the approach. The reality data model (or object model) of ELINOR regarding usage but without considering any statistics requirement is shown in Figure 18.7. The model says "a reader initiates several sessions with each session being a sequence of page references; and a publisher owns several books each consisting of a sequence of pages which can be referenced by several sessions".

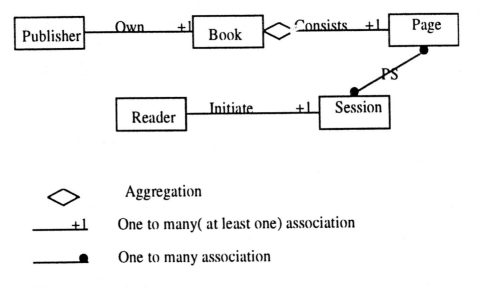

**Figure 18.7** The Model of Reality

However, we do not want to keep such a detailed reality model which is inefficient to process and expensive to store. We are only interested in the required usage statistics information. To be more exact, we are not interested in the details of the individual reader who referenced a particular page, but just in how many times they have referenced the page – a summary of the page-end for the relation PS as shown in Figure 18.7. Similarly we are not interested in which pages make up a particular session, but just interested in summary information of how many pages are in a session. By breaking the relations PS and replacing it with the two count attributes for the objects, we obtain Figure 18.8. The data model in Figure 18.8 captured the logical structures of the usage data and should serve as the basis for database implementation. Because time must also be taken into account, we used a hierarchical time-based storage structure to organise the databases.

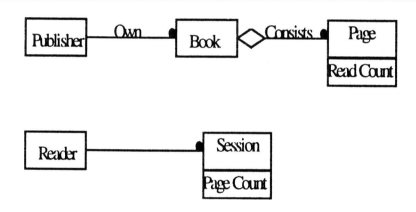

**Figure 18.8** The Model of Usage Statistics Data

## 18.4.4 Usage Statistics Reporting

There are two types of usage statistics report in ELINOR. The first type is concerned with the use of books and the data is taken from the "book" database. By applying filtering or aggregation functions on the "book" database, a variety of queries can be produced. For example, a report showing the summary usage by a publisher "dmu" can be obtained by applying the filter "publisher = dmu". Figure 18.9 is a fraction of a monthly summary report for a publisher named "dmu" (dmu stands for De Montfort University and all our in-house document collections are under the publisher "dmu") for April 1994. The report can also be detailed to page level in which case the heading "page" will be an individual page number instead of total pages.

The second type of report is about the users and is called the transaction report. Again a variety of transaction reports of different detail and different

| Publisher | Author | Book Title | Page | NO-ref | R-time | Prints | Charge |
|---|---|---|---|---|---|---|---|
| dmu | dmu | BIS Examination Paper 1991-1992 | 71 | 167 | 15 | 0 | |
| dmu | dmu | Standard 4 Year Sandwich Route | 73 | 167 | 0 | 0 | |
| dmu | dmu | Student Course Handbook 1992-1993 | 19 | 60 | 0 | 0 | |
| dmu | dmu | Computer Science Course Book | 31 | 98 | 2 | 0 | |
| dmu | dmu | Computer Science Syllabi 1993 | 50 | 121 | 6 | 0 | |
| dmu | dmu | Database Application Programming | 15 | 34 | 2 | 0 | |
| dmu | dmu | BA\BSc BIS Syllabi June 1993 | 74 | 173 | 24 | 0 | |
| Summary | All | | 7 | 333 | 820 | 52 | 0 |

**Publisher**: The name of publishers      **Author**: The name of the author
**Page**     : Pages referenced            **NO-ref**: Total number of references to the book
**R-time**   : Total time spent reading the pages of the book
**Prints**   : Total number of pages printed from the book
**Charge**   : Charge for the printing

**Figure 18.9** Sample Usage Statistics Report for Publisher dmu

groups can be produced by applying filtering and aggregation functions on the
"reader" dtabase. Figure 18.10 is an example report for a user named "sz" for
April 1994. As shown, user reports are only detailed to session level. Since
a printing charge is levied for every page printed, all detailed credit history
information is also kept.

| Date & Time | Transact | User | Logon | Pages | Deposit | Print | Charge | Pub fee | Balance |
|---|---|---|---|---|---|---|---|---|---|
| 01/04-00:00 | Forward | sz | 21 | 53 | 5 | 5 | 0.35 | 0 | 4.65 |
| 19/04-17:17 | Reading | sz | 0 | 5 | 0 | 0 | 0 | 0 | 4.65 |
| 19/04-18:19 | Print | sz | 0 | 0 | 0 | 2 | 0.14 | 0 | 4.51 |
| 19/04-18:20 | Reading | sz | 51 | 7 | 0 | 0 | 0 | 0 | 4.51 |
| 29/04-12:15 | Print | sz | 0 | 0 | 0 | 1 | 0.07 | 0 | 4.44 |
| total | | 6 | 1 | 72 | 65 | 5 | 8 | 0.56 | 0 | 4.44 |

**Figure 18.10** Sample Monthly User Report

The various usage statistics reports have not only provided feedback for the
publishers but also helped us in identifying useful materials and managing the
electronic library database. We found from the statistics report that the most
popular materials are examination paper and short loan books (core reading
material available on daily loan basis). We are thus enlarging the examination
paper collection and extending access to it to another site. We found also that
out of the 140 registered users, 28 used the system and most of the them used it
regularly from October 1993 to April 1994. This probably implies that if a user
used the system once, he or she is likely to use it later again. New user training
is thus an important task.

# Conclusion

This chapter discusses the various aspects of the ELINOR electronic library including the user aspect, system architecture, and usage statistics management.
ELINOR has been in operation since October 1993 for experimenting and exploring the electronic library ideas. The contents of the database and the access
points to the ELINOR server have been increasing. Theoretical works on un-

derstanding the electronic library are also under way. Modelling the electronic library application, including user modelling, price modelling, data modelling, and functional modelling, is an important part of the research. The ELINOR project is working toward a coherent model for future electronic libraries.

## Acknowledgements

The authors wish to thank Professor Mel Collier, the initiator and organiser of the ELINOR project, for his encouragement and support of this work. Thanks also go to Zimin Wu for his work on the user study.

# Chapter 19

## Dienst: Building a Production Technical Report Server

James R. Davis[*], Carl Lagoze[†] and Dean B. Krafft[‡]

## 19.1   Introduction

In this chapter, we describe our experiences with designing, implementing, and distributing Dienst. Dienst [71] is a protocol and implementation that provides Internet access to a distributed, decentralized multi-format document collection. The collection is managed by a set of interoperating Dienst servers distributed over the Internet. These servers manage three basic digital library services: repositories of multi-format documents; indexes into the document collection and search engines for these indexes; and user interfaces to provide front-end services for browsing, searching, and accessing the collection.

In the sections below we give a brief overview of Dienst, we describe a number of areas where Dienst has made a significant contribution to the state-of-the-art, and we then discuss some areas of current research and development. We conclude with a look at our plans for the future of Dienst.

## 19.2   Overview of Dienst

The Dienst architecture was created by a team from the Cornell University Computer Science Department and Xerox Corporation as part of the Computer Science Technical Report (CSTR) project. This project is an ARPA-funded consortium consisting of the computer science departments at UC Berkeley, CMU, Cornell, MIT, and Stanford, under the leadership of Bob Kahn and John Garrett of the Corporation for National Research Initiatives (CNRI), the prime contractor.

From the standpoint of a Dienst user, a document collection consists of a unified space of uniquely identified documents, each of which may be available in a variety of formats. Using publicly available World Wide Web clients, users

---

[*]Xerox Corporation, Design Research Institute, Cornell University, Ithaca, NY 14853, davis@dri.cornell.edu

[†]Computer Science Department, Cornell University, Ithaca, NY 14853, lagoze@cs.cornell.edu

[‡]Computer Science Department, Cornell University, Ithaca, NY 14853, dean@cs.cornell.edu

may search the collection, browse and read individual documents in any of their available formats, and download or print a document. The Dienst system also provides site administrators with tools for managing their document collections, including, among others, automated submission procedures, indexing tools, and format conversion tools.

Dienst servers execute through gateways from any World-Wide Web (WWW) server that supports the Common Gateway Interface. Dienst protocol requests are embedded within HTTP, the WWW protocol. The Dienst protocol includes requests to search for documents, access one or more servers, display particular parts of documents in specific formats, print or download all or parts of documents, and the like. The protocol is designed to support both user-level and program-level queries, making it easy to write automated systems that access collections served by Dienst.

An implementation of Dienst is now being used by CSTR consortium members and a number of other C.S. departments to make their technical reports available over the Internet, providing access to thousands of computer science technical reports[§]. The technology that underlies Dienst is not specific to the computer science technical report domain and can be applied to many other document collections. We should note, however, that the current implementation does not address issues unique to copyrighted commercial materials, such as limiting access to authorized individuals and charging.

## 19.3　Experience Gained

### 19.3.1　Dienst and the World Wide Web

Dienst is implemented as a layer above the architecture of the World Wide Web. This allows Dienst to exploit the functionality of four components of the Web:

- HTTP protocol — Dienst protocol requests are encapsulated within the URL of an HTTP request. Dienst protocol responses are encoded as HTTP responses.

- WWW servers (HTTPD) — Dienst servers are accessed through gateways from any WWW server that supports the Common Gateway Interface (CGI).

- HyperText Markup Language (HTML) — the Dienst user interface is implemented using HTML document markup, most notably the forms feature.

- WWW clients — the three preceding features make Dienst available from any full-featured WWW client.

This integration with the WWW sets Dienst apart from other systems that provide access to online documents. Traditional commercial systems, such as

---

[§]The Cornell Dienst server is accessible at http://cs-tr.cs.cornell.edu.

Dialog and Lexis/Nexis, while available over the Internet, are accessed via terminal interfaces. These systems are often difficult to use, because of limited user interfaces, and deliver only ASCII documents. A number of other systems have been developed based on client/server architecture. Notable among these are the System 33 Document Service [187] from Xerox, the RightPages system [218] from AT&T Bell Laboratories, and the CORE project [87] from BellCore, Cornell University, OCLC, and others. Each of these systems use proprietary clients, servers, and protocols. Finally, there are a number of systems that, while accessed through the World Wide Web, are mostly interfaces to central indexing sites; the actual documents are retrieved using URL's to FTP sites. Two examples of this are the Wide Area Technical Report Server (WATERS)[153] and the Unified Computer Science TR Index (UCSTRI)[228].

Dienst benefits in a number of ways from its use of the World Wide Web:

1. Browsers for the World Wide Web are available, generally for free, for all popular workstations and personal computers. The increasing number of users accustomed to the Web will have little problem using Dienst.

   Current Web browsers provide a number of powerful features. Three of these features are central to the Dienst interface. Browser support for embedded images is used to display document pages in Dienst. The ability of browsers to launch viewers, or helper applications, as a function of document type facilitates Dienst's multi-format document model. Finally, the imagemap feature, whereby the location of a user click in an image is transmitted to the server, is used by Dienst as an aid to document browsing, image zooming, and full-text searching.

2. WWW servers are available for many UNIX platforms and generally are free. The current mainstream servers, NCSA httpd and CERN httpd, provide a number of features that Dienst automatically inherits. These include clickable image support, ability to run as a proxy which provides support for firewalls, and the ability to control access to specific users or groups of users. We can expect that servers will soon include a number of additional features, such as tools for user authentication, payment mechanisms, and support for new graphics standards. The first two features are of importance so Dienst can be used where access to documents must be strictly controlled or cost recovery is important.

   Finally, WWW servers are now installed at a growing number of institutions with Internet access. System administrators are familiar with configuring and maintaining these servers. Running a Dienst server as a gateway from an existing Web server requires few additional administrative tasks.

3. HTTP provides a mechanism for transmitting meta-information such as file format (MIME type) and date separately from actual file contents. Dienst uses this to provide explicit types for documents that it returns, eliminating the need for client programs to guess the type.

4. The forms features of HTML permit the development of a common cross-architecture user interface. Although the user interfaces provided by forms are far from perfect, they are reasonably powerful, as demonstrated by the number of interactive services on the Web.

Dienst's dependence on the Web has some negative aspects. Browsing through multiple page documents does incur high overhead due to the stateless nature of HTTP. The Web has insufficient mechanisms for displaying documents with multiple textual and non-textual parts. We believe that compound documents, especially mixes of text and video, will become more common in the future. Servers are also not aware of the display capabilities of clients, making it impossible to "guess" at the best default format of a document. We expect that many of these issues will be resolved as development of Web technologies continues.

## 19.3.2  Copyright Issues

Traditionally, computer science technical reports have been distributed in hardcopy form with little concern for copyright. Frequently, there would be no explicit copyright notice on the publication, which before March 1989 effectively put the technical report in the public domain [220, chapter 4]. Moreover, authors would typically assign exclusive rights for a journal version of the same paper to another publisher, with both author and publisher ignoring the existence of a technical report version of the paper.

With the advent of Internet distribution of technical reports, concerns over copyright and intellectual property issues have been greatly heightened. When technical reports existed only as a relatively small number of copies with a limited distribution, journal publishers could afford to take the position that they would have little impact on their own sales and subscriptions. When an unlimited number of copies are immediately available over the network to any interested researcher, the impact on the traditional journal is much more significant.

In developing Dienst, whose purpose was to make access to Cornell's technical reports simple and immediate, we therefore had to deal with several issues related to copyright:

1. Technical report authors wished to ensure the rapid dissemination of breaking research results. Typical journal publication was a process that could require two or three years.

2. Since promotion and tenure decisions are based in part on publication in refereed journals, authors were not prepared to have the publication of a paper as a technical report endanger its future publication as a journal article.

3. Users of the technical report server deserved a clear statement of their rights in the reports they were accessing. Could they print a copy? Multiple copies? Could they e-mail it to another researcher? Could they permanently archive a copy for redistribution?

4. The legal status of technical reports distributed over the Internet was (and is) unclear. Does network distribution count as publication, or is it a "performance" of the work [150]? What happens when someone prints a copy? Does fair use apply to reports "performed" over the network?

After extensive discussions with authors, librarians, and lawyers, we devised a scheme for dealing with copyright on Cornell technical reports. The author explicitly licenses full rights to Cornell, including the right to sub-license these rights to others. However, the author retains the right to withdraw this license on sixty days written notice. The exact wording of the copyright notice on the technical report server is:

> You are granted permission for the non-commercial reproduction, distribution, display, and performance of this technical report in any format, BUT this permission is only for a period of 45 (forty-five) days from the most recent time that you verified that this technical report is still available from the Computer Science Department of Cornell University under terms that include this permission. All other rights are reserved by the author(s).

This approach has the following features:

1. If the paper is accepted by a journal, then the author can withdraw the report and turn around and offer full and exclusive copyright to a journal (although the paper will have been previously published as a technical report).

2. The author grants full rights to Cornell, including sub-licensing. This means that Cornell can grant explicit rights to anyone wishing to view, copy, print, or redistribute the report. However, these rights *time-out* after forty-five days.

3. Once the paper has been withdrawn and the rights have timed-out, no further distribution, "performance", or viewing of the on-line version will take place. However, existing paper copies are not affected, and continue to be available on loan from libraries and individuals. Copies can also be made under the *fair-use* provisions of the copyright law.

The issues of copyright for electronically distributed works are still far from clear. The scheme we have proposed here is untested in the courts, and so is subject to the vagaries of future legal interpretations. It also leaves the publisher with a work that has potentially been much more widely distributed than would have been the case with paper preprints. However, since one of the main functions of a university is the dissemination of knowledge, the benefit seems worth the risks. So far, this approach has proved to be acceptable to all the parties involved. It provides a clear legal basis for Cornell's electronic distribution of the technical reports, and it seems to give authors, publishers, and users a compromise that they can live with.

## 19.3.3   Document Submission and Management

Digital library technology will only propagate beyond the technologically savvy if such systems require minimal expert administration and do not burden authors with technical details. Many of the organizations that wish to publish documents digitally (e.g. government agencies, academic departments) have little in-house technical expertise. Authors are concerned with writing documents and getting them published. Submission to a digital library should require little more skill than using a word processor.

We have implemented in Dienst a set of tools that mostly automate the process of adding documents to and managing a digital library. These tools are integrated with the Dienst digital library server. Our goal when creating these tools was to make the digital library maintainable by a document librarian (DL) with low-level computer training. This DL serves four major roles: 1) as the general manager of the collection; 2) as the reviewer of document submissions, to protect against counterfeit document submissions; 3) as the clearing house for copyright issues; and 4) as the archiver of document hardcopy.

The author submits a document to the library in PostScript. Rather than working with a plethora of document formats from a variety of word processors, we determined that PostScript represents a *lingua franca* that can be generated from virtually all word or text processing systems. We recognize that there will be documents that can not be represented in this fashion, but estimate that the number will be very few and that techniques for managing them can be developed as the process matures. The author submits a document to the library by completing an HTML form that contains text fields for bibliographic data about the document. These fields are document title, author(s), pathname of the PostScript file, abstract, and submitter's e-mail address. The submitter can quickly complete this form by "cutting and pasting" text from the document source.

The document librarian, in the role of gatekeeper of the system, learns of each submission through an automatically generated e-mail message. No document actually enters the document database until the DL manually checks the submission. In addition, the DL acts as the legal gateway, ensuring that the authors complete a copyright release form that gives the department permission to make the document available over the Internet. When manual checking and copyright clearing are complete, the DL uses a simple command to assign a unique document identifier (the *docid*) to the document and signal that the document is ready for entry into the database.

The remainder of the submission process is fully automated. Software that is integrated with the Dienst server generates the bibliographic entry from the submitter's entry, checks the validity of the PostScript file, builds the actual database entry, and generates the page images for online viewing and browsing of the document, and the plain text version for full text indexing. Text extraction is performed by rendering the PostScript into images, then performing optical character recognition. Although this is more expensive than simply extracting the strings from the PostScript, it also produces a higher quality output, since the OCR system we use (ScanWorX from Xerox) produces paragraph bounding boxes, which we then use to perform paragraph- level full text search. Figures and graphs are of course lost, but are of no use for full text search in any case. Once in the database the document is searchable and viewable from any interoperating Dienst server.

It is sometimes necessary to withdraw a document from the library due to invalidation of the results in the document, replacement by another document, or submission of the document to a journal. Whereas the decision to withdraw is up to the author, withdrawal from the database is effected via a simple command from the document librarian. When a document is withdrawn, users are unable to see either bibliographic information or contents of the document. The document identifier remains associated with the withdrawn document.

While electronic document delivery is the *raison d'etre* of our system, we recognize that publication quality hardcopy is sometimes needed. The document librarian must be able to produce paper copy for archival storage and for people who do not have electronic access. For this purpose, we have developed an interface between the Dienst database and the Xerox Docutech publishing system [62]. This system can be used to produce very high-quality bound and covered hard-copy of any document in the library database.

Finally, the Dienst software includes an extensive document database checker utility. The document librarian can use this utility to scan the entire document database and determine the integrity of the document files. In the current release of the software this utility only reports integrity errors, and repairs have to be made manually. In future releases, we hope to automate the repair process.

## 19.3.4 Providing Documents in Multiple Formats

Long before we invented Dienst, many sites were distributing technical reports via anonymous FTP. Why not continue to use FTP? Unfortunately, an FTP server appears to the user much like a file system. The user just sees a collection of files, perhaps grouped into trees. If several files jointly constitute a document (for instance, the scanned pages), the relation is not explicitly marked in any way, rather the user must guess from such evidence as similarities in the file name. Not even the file type or format is marked. Related files may be grouped together into a common directory; this would be helpful, except for the lack of standard conventions for the grouping. Even though humans are often able to correctly guess the organization, this is not possible for programs that might want to access the collection. A file system is just too low level an abstraction for a digital library.

A system that provides a higher level interface must somehow understand the storage conventions used at the site. It can try to do this by applying heuristics (which UCSTRI does, to an extent), but file systems are so diverse and chaotic that this can't work for every case. A more reliable approach is for each site to provide definitions that map the common abstraction into the particular conventions of the site. This is the approach used by Dienst.

Each Dienst installation includes specifications that provide a mapping from a *docid* and format name into a local pathname at that site. Thus, users can address Dienst documents in terms of their names and formats, and Dienst translates these automatically into locally meaningful pathnames. This mapping is divided into two parts. The first maps a *docid* into a particular directory in the file system. Dienst requires that all files associated with a document be stored in or under a common subdirectory. This mapping is expressed by a subroutine, which differs at each site. The second mapping takes a format into a file name, and is expressed declaratively.

The actual names of formats are not intended to be seen by end users. Instead, the declaration also includes a "pretty" name to be shown to the user, as well as some further text for explanation. Thus, for example, the "ocr" format includes a disclaimer that "text produced by OCR may have errors". Some commonly used formats are: *thumbnail* — a reduced size image intended for rapid visual browsing; *inline* — an image intended for inline display; *scanned* — a page image as produced by the scanner; *postscript* — PostScript; *ocr*— text as produced by OCR.

The format names are chosen to be useful in describing the intended purpose of the formats, not the actual encoding used, because there might be several alternative encodings capable of meeting a purpose¶. For instance, an inline image is usually stored as in GIF format, but could as well be an X bitmap, or (on some browsers anyway) a JPEG image. There is no reason in principle why TIFF or JBIG encoding could not be used.

## 19.4   Ongoing Issues

### 19.4.1   Interoperability Among Heterogeneous Search Engines

Queries to the existing Dienst digital library may be expressed either as Boolean combinations of keywords in fields (author, title, etc.) or as full text searches. Both forms of search return a list of *docids*; with full text search the list is sorted by relevance. We anticipate that when Dienst is applied in other domains, librarians will add additional fields to the bibliographic records. For example, if one were to use Dienst for a digital art library, one might add a field specifying the nationality of the artist, or the medium used in the original work. At present, we use the bibliographic format defined in RFC 1357, but the Dienst query protocol can be easily adapted to support additional fields or new bibliographic formats.

We further anticipate that some collections might wish to use entirely new query languages, such as the Common Command Language (CCL) used by CMU's Mercury Server. The Dienst protocol is extensible to support other query languages (so long as they can somehow be encoded into a URL), but further work is needed to define the semantics of a search expressed in one formalism when the base records are stored in another. In some cases, the query

---

¶In an earlier version of Dienst, we encoded formats with MIME types. This was a mistake.

languages can be fully translated, but in other cases the mapping will not be complete. In the incomplete cases, is it better to return an error code and no result, or is a partially correct search better than nothing?

More work is also needed in combining results from multiple index servers. Boolean queries produce unordered sets of documents, which can easily be merged, requiring, at most, removal of duplicates, something easily done given that each document has a unique identifier. But full text queries return sorted results, and these are more difficult to merge, as each list is sorted according to statistics of term frequency that are only meaningful in the context of a single collection, not globally across the entire collection. A related problem is merging results from "foreign" servers such as WATERS or UCSTRI, which come in the form of raw HTML. Unless we attempt to parse the HTML and extract document information, the best we can do is to simply list the HTML in a separate section of the display.

## 19.4.2 Heterogeneous Servers and the Dynamic User Interface

An unresolved issue is the extent to which the differing capabilities of each search system should be reflected back to the end user. For example, CCL offers a "proximity" operator which finds words within a specified distance of one another; and relevance feedback requires users to select from all returned documents those that are relevant. This causes a conflict for the future of Dienst's user interface. On the one hand, we'd like to make it simple and uniform; on the other, we'd like to provide access to more powerful features when available.

To make such features available requires a dynamic user interface that changes its appearance depending on the features provided by the search system. This would require that the Dienst user interface server query an index server to determine what features are available before returning a search form to the user. However, this conflicts with another goal of Dienst: to try and hide the existence of multiple index servers from the user. How can we indicate that some searching features may be only partially applied to the document collection?

Whatever decision we take will be difficult to implement gracefully in the WWW, because user selections are available to the server only after the user has completely filled out the form. In more tightly integrated user interface tool kits, every user action is returned to the server as it occurs, thus affording an opportunity to reconfigure the interface. The obvious solution would involve multiple rounds of user submission and the creation of a more targeted query form, but this would needlessly exasperate many users.

## 19.4.3 Reliability

As the number of servers increases, the chances decrease that all will be in operation when a search is requested. How can we make the entire collection useful in such an environment? There are two alternatives open, and we need to explore both. The first is to begin replicating index servers, to increase availability. We may be forced to do this anyway, if Dienst becomes more popular. Many useful Web services are now so heavily loaded that their response time has become unbearably long.

A second alternative is to add persistent search, which continues to attempt to contact non-responsive sites. A persistent search would allow partial search results on the available servers to be returned immediately and the rest of the search to be "held", pending the availability of the remaining index servers. The full results could then either be locally cached for later user access, or mailed to the user. This does have the potential to make the user interface more complex, which is not desirable.

### 19.4.4   Document Structure

Documents have both physical and logical structure. Physical structure is the division into physical pieces, e.g. pages, and is already handled well by Dienst. When a document is stored in paged form (e.g. when it has been scanned from paper) one can request a specific page in a specific format. In the future, as we begin to handle more media types, it may be useful to add additional physical coordinates, e.g. SMPTE time codes for video or rectangular subsets of pages; but these extensions should not be difficult to design.

Logical structure, on the other hand, is only barely present in the current Dienst protocol. One may request the "Body" of a document, but no finer level of logical addressing is supported. Further granularity can be added, but only by extending the protocol as a whole. This won't scale well, as it is likely that there will be many alternative schemes for document structure, and requiring modifications to the entire protocol is too cumbersome. What is needed is some kind of generic addressing, so that any document may have any desired (hierarchical) structure expressed in locally meaningful units. This will require a new message which returns the abstract structural schema for a document (which might be an SGML DTD), and a query which can accept coordinates in any coordinate system. Thus for example, suppose one has a legal document stored in Dienst. One would first determine that the document is structured as numbered sections with numbered paragraphs within, and then ask for paragraph N within section M.

### 19.4.5   Technology Transfer

Dienst servers are currently running at all the CSTR consortium sites and at a number of other computer science departments in the United States. The technology is relatively mature and development of the server and protocol is continuing at Cornell.

We have an ongoing effort to disseminate the technology beyond its current reach. Our strongest effort has been in the computer science domain; we have contacted almost all other Ph.D. degree granting computer science department in the United States. However, Dienst is not specific to computer science technical reports. The technology can be used by any network of sites that wish to provide

Internet access to documents that are freely available and have minimal copyright restrictions. This is an increasingly common goal of other academic departments, government agencies, and corporations. We have made some initial contacts in these other domains, especially government agencies, and expect to see the establishment of other Dienst networks.

The transfer of the technology beyond its research base has met a number of impediments:

- Many sites are justifiably wary of any product of research. They are suspicious of the "industrial strength" of the software. Other sites are not confident that there will be any support for the software once the research effort closes shop.

- Although we have made some effort to simplify the tasks of installing and maintaining Dienst servers, more work is needed. Computer science departments usually have some savvy grad student who is interested in tinkering with new software. This is not true of other departments or agencies. Administering a Unix system, in itself, is an insurmountable task for many sites.

- Many institutions are increasingly wary of committing to any "latest and greatest" technology. They have already had the experience of dedicating resources to some technology, only to see it replaced months later by something else (e.g., the rush to Gopher just a couple of years ago).

- Cost recovery is often an issue even when documents have a history of being available for "free". Many institutions use a small handling fee to cover shipping of paper documents and skim a little off the top of this fee to recover the costs of administering a document library. Providing these same documents electronically eliminates shipping and paper fees, but it does not eliminate administrative costs and even incurs some new ones. Yet with no cost recovery model in digital library servers, the small income stream is lost.

These are some of the many technology transfer issues which need to be examined as digital library research proceeds over the next few years.

## 19.5   Future Plans

In addition to dealing with the problems described in the section above, we plan to continue developing Dienst to extend the functionality, scalability, and robustness of the architecture. In particular, we intend to address the following issues:

**Multiple Domains** Currently, while Dienst supports uniform access to a distributed collection of documents, each such collection is independent. The Dienst servers accessing one information domain, say computer science technical reports, do not interact with the Dienst servers providing agricultural information from cooperative extension sites. A user is expected to deal with a server covering documents in a particular subject area. Search results from multiple collections must be obtained and combined by hand.

We plan to extend Dienst so that such server collections provide information about the subject matter and content of the collection. This information will be available to users through a *server-of-servers* to assist users in finding appropriate information resources.

Moreover, as the number of possibly relevant corpora and Dienst servers gets very large, full searches over all available information become prohibitively expensive. It then becomes critical to identify the "best" servers for any given search. We intend to investigate mechanisms for carrying out this selection and incorporate the most appropriate into Dienst.

**Compound Documents** Dienst currently supports a variety of document formats, at both the page and the complete document level. However, each instance of a format is assumed to be uniform over the document. We intend to extend Dienst to support true compound documents, where a single document may include such elements as text, sound clips, MPEG movies, high-resolution color graphics, program code, and scientific data sets.

**User Studies** Dienst servers are already being widely used to access a number of documents. Moreover, Dienst provides a number of different capabilities for browsing, searching, and viewing documents. By instrumenting Dienst servers, we can collect information on a range of *usability* issues related to document access. Some potential topics are: What is the trade-off between viewing documents on-line and printing a copy? What search facilities are most useful — full-text, boolean bibliographic search, or searching on specific fields? How do different levels of network connectivity affect the usability of the library?

The Dienst architecture provides both an excellent production system for accessing a distributed collection of documents, and a robust platform for future work in document publishing and dissemination. Over the next several years, we plan to continue extensive development and support of Dienst as an easy-to-use "drop-in" system for the publication of on-line documents. Such a system has a wide range of potential applications, ranging from government documents, to research reports, to product marketing information, to on-line documentation. By providing a uniform, integrated, and freely available system for document dissemination, Dienst can have a major impact on network publishing.

# 19.6    Acknowledgements

This work was supported in part by the Advanced Research Projects Agency under Grant No. MDA972-92-J-1029 with the Corporation for National Research Initiatives (CNRI). Its content does not necessarily reflect the position or the policy of the Government or CNRI, and no official endorsement should be inferred. This work was done at the Design Research Institute, a collaboration of Xerox Corporation and Cornell University, and at the Computer Science Department at Cornell University.

# Bibliography

[1] User models: Method, theory, and practice. *IJMMS*, 32:511–543, 1990.

[2] Fgdc newsletter no. 1, publication of the federal geographic data committee, 1991.

[3] Inspec classification, 1992.

[4] Inspec thesaurus, 1993.

[5] Standard reuse library Basic Data Interoperability Model (BIDM). Technical Report RPS-0001, Reuse Library Interoperability Group, 1993.

[6] "Information Retrieval: Application Service Definition and Protocol Specification". ANSI/NISO Z39.50, January 1995. Post Ballot Draft.

[7] Shoshani A. and H.K.T Wong. Statistics and scientific database issues. *IEEE Transactions on Software Engineering*, SE-11:1040–1046, 1985.

[8] C. A. Addison, W. H. Enright, P. W. Gaffney, I. Gladwell, and P. M. Hanson. Algorithm 687: A decision tree for the numerical solution of initial value ordinary differential equations. *ACM Trans. Math. Softw.*, 17(1):1–11, March 1991.

[9] U.S. Defense Mapping Agency. *Digital chart of the world, edition 1*. Defense Mapping Agency, Fairfax, VA, 1992.

[10] R.B. Allen. Two digital library interfaces that exploit hierarchical structure. In *Proceedings of Electronic Publishing and the Information Superhighway*, May 1995.

[11] R. Alonso, D. Barbara, and L. L. Cova. Data sharing in large heterogeneous information networks. *Workshop on Heterogeneous Databases*, Dec. 1989. IEEE-CS Technical Committee on Distributed Processing.

[12] Karen Anderson and Fred Mintzer. "Digital Watermarking of Images". private communication, August 1994.

[13] M. Andreessen. "NCSA Mosaic Technical Summary 2.1". Technical report, National Center for Supercomputing Applications, May 8 1993.

[14] K. Andrews and F. Kappe. Soaring through hyper space: A snapshot of hyper-g and its harmony client. In W. Hezner and F. Kappe, editors, *Proc. of Eurographics Symposium of multimedia/Hypermedia in Open Distributed Environments, Graz, Austria*, pages 181–191. Springer Verlag, 1994.

[15] W. Appelt. *Document Architecture in Open Systems the ODA Standard.* Springer Verlag, Berlin, 1991.

[16] E. Ashton and G. Cruickshank. The newspaper of the future: A look beyond the front porch. In *Proc. of the 14th Nat. Online Meeting*, pages 11–16, 1993.

[17] Bach, Maurice J. *The design of the Unix Operating System.* Prentice-Hall, Engelwoods Cliffs, NJ, 1986.

[18] Richard Barrett, Michael Berry, Tony F. Chan, James Demmel, June Dunato, Jack Dongarra, Victor Eijkhout, Roldan Pozo, Charles Romine, and Henk Van der Vorst. *Templates for the Solution of Linear Systems: Building Blocks for Iterative Methods.* SIAM, 1994.

[19] R. Bayer. OMNIS/Myriad: Electronic administration and publication of multimedia documents. In *Informatik, Wirtschaft und Gesellschaft. 23. GI-Jahrestagung.* Springer Verlag, Dresden, 1993.

[20] R. Bayer, P. Vogel, and S. Wiesener. OMNIS/Myriad document retrieval and its database requirements. In *Fifth International Conference on Database and Expert Systems Applications (DEXA)*. Springer Verlag, Athen, October 1994.

[21] D. Becker. Utf – an sgml standard for the news distribution industry. In *RIAO 94 Conference Proceedings*, pages 631–648, 1994.

[22] H.J. Beker. "Security in an electronic fund transfer system". *Information Privacy*, 2(5):185–189, September 1980.

[23] W. Bender, H. Lie, J. Orwant, L. Teodosio, and N. Abramson. Newspace: Mass media and personal computing. In *Proc. Summer 1991 USENIX Conference*, pages 329–349, 1991.

[24] T. Berners-Lee, R. Cailliau, A. Luotonen, H. F. Nielsen, and A. Secret. The World-Wide-Web. *Comunications of the ACM*, 37(8):76–82, August 1994.

[25] Berners-Lee, T. UR* and The Names and Addresses of WWW objects,. Technical Report http://info.cern.ch/hypertext/WWW/Addressing/Addressing.html, see also RFC 1738, CERN, Geneva, 1994.

[26] Berners-Lee, T. Wide Web Initiative: The Project. Technical Report http://info.cern.ch/hypertext/WWW/TheProject, CERN, Geneva, 1994.

[27] Berners-Lee, T. and Cailliau, R. WorldWideWeb: Proposal for a HyperText Project. Technical Report http://info.cern.ch/hypertext/WWW/Proposal.html, CERN, Geneva, 1994.

[28] Berners-Lee, Tim, Connolly D. Hypertext Markup Language, Internet working draft,. Technical Report http://info.cern.ch/hypertext/WWW/MarkUp/HTML.html, CERN, Geneva, 1994.

[29] P. Bernstein, V. Hadzilacos, and N. Goodman. *Concurrency Control and Recovery in Database Systems*. Addison-Wesley Publishing Company, Reading, MA, 1987.

[30] Michael W. Berry, Jack J. Dongarra, Brian H. Larose, and Todd Letsche. PDS: A performance database server. *Scientific Computing*, 3(2):147–156, 1994.

[31] A. D. Birell, R. Levin, R. N. Needham, and M. D. Schroeder. Grapevine: An exercise in distributed computing. *Communications of the ACM*, 25(4):260–274, April 1982.

[32] W.P. Birmingham, K.M. Drabenstott, C. O. Frost, A. J Warner, and K. Willis. "The University of Michigan Digital Library: This is not your father's library". *Proc. of Digital Libraries*, pages 53–60, 1994.

[33] G.E. Blake, M.P. Consens, P. Kilpelainen, P. Larsen, T. Snider, and F.W. Tompa. "Text/ relational database management systems: Harmonizing SQL and SGML". pages 267 279, March 1994.

[34] K. Böhm and K. Aberer. "Storing HyTime Documents in an Object-Oriented Database". *CIKM'94*, pages 26–33, 1994.

[35] K. Böhm, A. Mueller, and E. Neuhold. "Structured Document Handling - a Case for Integrating Databases and Information Retrieval". *CIKM'94*, pages 147–154, 1994.

[36] Ronald F. Boisvert. Toward an intelligent system for mathematical software selection. In P. W. Gaffney and E. N. Houstis, editors, *Programming Environments for High-Level Scientific Problem Solving*, pages 79–92. North-Holland, Amsterdam, 1992.

[37] Ronald F. Boisvert. The architecture of an intelligent virtual mathematical software repository system. *Math. & Comp. in Simul.*, 36:269–279, 1994.

[38] Ronald F. Boisvert, Sally E. Howe, and David K. Kahaner. The Guide to Available Mathematical Software problem classification system. *Comm. Stat. – Simul. Comp.*, 20(4):811–842, 1991.

[39] A. Bouguettaya. Large multidatabases: Beyond federation and global schema integration. In R. Sacks-Davis, editor, *Proc. of the Fifth Australasian Database Conference*, pages 258–273. Global Publications Service, Christchurch, New Zealand, January 1994.

[40] A. Bouguettaya and R. King. Large multidatabases: Issues and directions. In D. K. Hsiao, E. J. Neuhold, and R. Sacks-Davis, editors, *IFIP DS-5 Semantics of Interoperable Database Systems*. Elsevier Publishers, Lorne, Victoria, Australia, 1993.

[41] A. Bouguettaya, R. King, D. Galligan, and J. Simmons. Implementation of interoperability in large multidatabases. In *Third International Workshop on Research Issues on Data Engineering: Interoperability in Multidatabase Systems*. IEEE Computer Press, Vienna, Austria, April 1993.

[42] Jack Brassil, S. Low, N.F.F. Maxemchuk, and L. O'Gorman. "Electronic Marking and Identification Techniques to Discourage Document Copying". In *Proc. Thirteenth Annual Joint Conference of the IEEE Computer and Communications Societies (IEEE InfoComm'94)*, pages 1278–1287, June 1994.

[43] Francis Bretherton. Reference model for metadata: A strawman. In *Proc. IEEE Workshop on Metadata for Scientific and Technical Data Management*, Washington, DC, May 1994.

[44] Ernest J. Breton. Indexing for invention. *Journal of the American Society for Information Science*, 42(3):173–177, 1991.

[45] M. Brian. *SGML—An Authors Guide to the Standard Generalized Markup Language*. Addison Wesley, Wokingham, 1989.

[46] Shirley Browne, Jack Dongarra, Stan Green, Keith Moore, Theresa Pepin, Tom Rowan, and Reed Wade. Location-independent naming for virtual distributed software repositories. In *ACM-SIGSOFT Symposium on Software Reusability*, April 1995. (to appear).

[47] Shirley Browne, Jack Dongarra, Stan Green, Keith Moore, Tom Rowan, and Reed Wade. Netlib services and resources. Technical Report UT-CS-94-222, University of Tennessee Computer Science Department, February 1994.

[48] Shirley Browne, Jack Dongarra, Stan Green, Keith Moore, Tom Rowan, Reed Wade, Geoffrey Fox, Ken Hawick, Ken Kennedy, Jim Pool, and Rick Stevens. The national HPCC software exchange. *IEEE Computational Science and Engineering*, 1995. (to appear).

[49] P. Buneman, S.Davidson, and A. Kosky. "Theoretical aspects of schema merging". *Advances in DB Technology- EDBT, 3rd International Conference on Extending DB Technology*, Proceedings:152–167, March 1992.

[50] F.J. Burkowski, C.R. Watters, and Michael A. Shepherd. Delivery of electronic news: A broadband application. In *Proceedings of CASCON'94*, pages cd–rom, 1994.

[51] F.J. Burkowski, C.R. Watters, and Michael A. Shepherd. Electronic News Delivery. Technical Report PR-94-01, University of Waterloo, Dept. of Computer Science, 1994.

[52] K.A. Butter. "Red Sage: The next step in delivery of electronic journals". *Medical Reference Services Quarterly*, 13(3):75–81, Fall 1994.

[53] R. G. G. Cattell and T. Atwood, editors. *"The Object Database Standard, ODMG-93"*. M. Kaufmann, 1993.

[54] H. Chen and V. Dhar. Cognitive process as a basis for intelligent retrieval systems design. *Information Processing and Management*, 17:405–431, 1991.

[55] M. Christel, T. Kanade, M. Mauldin, R. Reddy, M. Sirbu, S. Stevens, and H. Wactlar. "Informedia Digital Video Library". *Communications of ACM*, 38(4):57–58, April 1995.

[56] V. Christophides, S.Abiteboul, S.Cluet, and M.Scoll. "From Structured Documents to Novel Query Facilities". *SIGMOD '94*, Proceedings:313–323, May 1994.

[57] A. Clausnitzer, P. Vogel, and S. Wiesener. A WWW interface to the OMNIS/Myriad literature retrieval engine. In *Third International World Wide Web Conference*, Darmstadt, April 1995.

[58] Danny Cohen. A format for e-mailing bibliographic records. Internet RFC 1357, July 1992.

[59] U.S. Federal Geospatial Data Committee. *Content standards for digital geospatial metadata*. U.S. Geological Survey, Reston, VA, 1994.

[60] W. W. Conhaim. Maturing french videotext becomes key international tool. *Information Today*, 9(1):28, January 1992.

[61] P. Constantopoulos and E. Pataki. A browser for software reuse. In *Advanced Information Systems Engineering, 4th International Conference CAiSE '92, Porceedings*, pages 304–326. Springer-Verlag, Berlin, Germany, May 12–15 1992.

[62] Cornell Information Technologies, Ithaca, NY. *How to Use EZ-PUBLISH and the Docutech Printer at Cornell Information Technologies*, November 1993.

[63] Infoseek Corporation. InfoSeek. Technical Report none, none, http://www.infoseek.com:80/Home, April 1995.

[64] Netscape Communications Corporation. Internet Search. Technical report, none, http://home.mcom.com/home/internet-search.html, April 1995.

[65] W. B. Croft, A. Smith, and H. R. Turtle. "A loosely-coupled integration of a text retrieval system and an object-oriented database system". *15th. Ann. Int'l SIGIR Conference*, Proceedings:223–232, 1992.

[66] G. Cruz and R.D. Hill. Capturing and playing multimedia events with STREAMS. In *ACMMM*, pages 193–200, Nov. 1994.

[67] C. Damier and B. Defude. "The Document Management Component of a Multimedia Data Model". *11th Int. Conf. on Research and Development in IR*, pages 451–464, 1988.

[68] Ron Daniel and Michael Mealling. URC scenarios and requirements. Internet Draft draft-ietf-uri-urc-req-00.txt, November 1994.

[69] P. B. Danzig, S-H. Li, and K. Obraczka. Distributed indexing of autonomous internet services. *Computing Systems*, 5(4):433–459, Fall 1992.

[70] James R. Davis and Carl Lagoze. Dienst, a protocol for a distributed digital document library. Internet Draft accessible at http://cs-tr.cs.cornell.edu/Info/dienst_protocol.html, July 1994.

[71] James R. Davis and Carl Lagoze. A protocol and server for a distributed digital technical report library. Technical Report TR94-1418, Computer Science Department, Cornell University, 1994.

[72] M. Davis. Media Streams: Representing video for retrieval and repurposing. In *ACMMM*, pages 478–479, Nov. 1994.

[73] Dorothy E.R. Denning. *"Cryptography and Data Security"*. Addison-Wesley, 1982.

[74] Desai, Bipin C. WebJournal: Visualization of Web Journey. Technical Report http://www.cs.concordia.ca/WebJournal.html, Concordia University, Montreal, CANADA, August 1994.

[75] Aldus Developers Desk. *TIFF revision 6.0*. Aldus Corp., Seattle, WA, 1992.

[76] Dialog Information Services, Inc. *"DIALOG Basics: A Brief Introductory Guide to Searching"*, October 1988.

[77] W. Diffie and M. Hellman. "New Directions in Cryptography". *IEEE Transactions on Information Theory*, 22(6):644–654, November 1976.

[78] N. Dimitrova and F. Golshani. Rx for semantic video database retrieval. In *ACMMM*, pages 219–226, Nov. 1994.

[79] Michael A. Domaratz. Content standards for digital spatial metadata. In *Proc. IEEE Workshop on Metadata for Scientific and Technical Data Management*, Washington, DC, May 1994.

[80] Jack Dongarra, Tom Rowan, and Reed Wade. Software distribution using XNETLIB. *ACM Trans. Math. Softw.*, 21(1), 1995 1995.

[81] Jack J. Dongarra and Eric Grosse. Distribution of mathematical software via electronic mail. *Communications of the ACM*, 30(5):403–407, May 1987.

[82] J. Dowe. Neural networks in text retrieval. *EDMS(Electronic Document Management Systems) Journals*, 2, 1991.

[83] E.L. Elliot. Watch-grab-arrange-see: Thinking with motion images via streams and collages. Master's thesis, Visual Studies, MIT, Feb. 1993.

[84] David Ely. The handle management system. Technical report, Corporation for National Research Initiatives, January 1995.

[85] A. Emtage and P. Deutsch. Archie: An electronic directory service for the internet. *Proc. Winter 1992 Usenix Conf.*, pages 93–110, 1992.

[86] Richard Entlich, Lorrin Garson, Michael Lesk, Lorraine Normore, Jan Olsen, and Stuart Weibel. "Making a Digital Library: The Chemistry Online Retrieval Experiment". *Communications of ACM*, 38(4):54, April 1995.

[87] Richard Entlich, Lorrin Garson, Michael Lesk, Lorraine Normore, Jan Olsen, and Stuart Weibel. Making a Digital Library: The Contents of the CORE Project. *Communications of the ACM*, March (forthcoming) 1995.

[88] K. Erhardtdomino, T. Pletcher, W. Wilson, D. Atkins, and W.B. Panko. "The Internet - Will this highway serve the digital library". *Bulletin of the Medical Library Association*, 82(4):426–433, October 1994.

[89] A. Ramsden et al. Selection criteria for a document image processing system for the elinor electronic library project. *Program*, 27:371–387, 1993.

[90] K.J. Arnold et al. Electronic library for higher education - an experiment at de montfort university milton keynes. *Journal of Information Networking*, 1:117–135, 1994.

[91] M. W. Collier et al. The electronic library: Virtually a reality? In A. H. Helal, editor, *Opportunity 2000: Understanding and Serving Users in an electronic library*, pages 135–146. Universitatsbibliothek Essen, 1992.

[92] T. Berners-Lee et al. World -wide web: The information univers. *Electronic Networking: Research, Application, and Policy*, 1:52–58, 1992.

[93] T. R. Smith et al. *Towards a distributed digital library with comprehensive services for images and spatially-referenced information.* http://alexandria.sdc.ucsb.edu/proposal.html, 1994.

[94] Z. Wu et al. The user perspective of the elinor electronic library. In *Aslib Proceedings*, pages 13–22. Aslib, 1995.

[95] S. Feiner. Seeing the forest for the trees: Hierarchical display of hypertext structure. In *ACM Conference on Office Information Systems*, pages 205–212, Mar. 1988.

[96] R. Ferguson. Info highway will soon travel almost anywhere. *The Chronicle-Herald*, page B7, April 22 1994.

[97] National Science Foundation. Research on digital libraries. Technical Report NFS 93-141, National Science Foundation, September 1993.

[98] E. A. Fox. Digital libraries of the future. In *Proceedings of the First ACM International Conference on Multimedia*, Anaheim, California, August 1993.

[99] E.A. Fox and L.F. Lunin. "Perspectives on Digital Libraries". *J. American Society for Information Science*, 44(8):441–443, September 1993.

[100] Edward A. Fox. "Digital Libraries". *IEEE Computer*, 26(11):79–81, November 1993.

[101] Geoffrey Fox, R. D. Williams, and Paul Messina. *Parallel Computing Works.* Morgan Kaufmann, 1994.

[102] William B. Frakes and Thomas P. Pole. An empirical study of representation methods for reusable software components. *IEEE Trans. on Software Engineering*, 20(8):617–630, August 1994.

[103] J. C. French, A. K. Jones, and J. L. Pfaltz. Summary of the final report of the NSF workshop on scientific database management at the university of virginia on march 12-13, 1990. *SIGMOD RECORD*, 19(4):32–40, December 1990.

[104] et.al. G. Salton. Automatic analysis, theme generation, and summarization of machine- readable texts. *Science*, 264:1421–1426, 1994.

[105] D. K. Gapen. The virtual library: Knowledge, society and the librarian. In L. Saunders, editor, *The Virtual Library: Vision and Realities*, pages 1–14. Meckler, 1993.

[106] J.R. Garrett. "Text to Screen Revisited: Copyright in the Electronic Age". *ONLINE*, pages 22–24, March 1991.

[107] Henry M. Gladney et al. Digital library: Gross structure and requirements: Report from a march 1994 workshop. In *Proceedings of Digital Libraries '94*, pages 101–107, 1994.

[108] H.M. Gladney, E.A. Fox, Z. Ahmed, and et al. "Digital Library: Gross Structure and Requirements". In *Proc. First Annual Conference on the Theory and Practice of Digital Libraries (Digital Libraries '94)*, pages 101–107, June 1994. A longer version is available as IBM Almaden Research Center Report RJ9840, May 1994.

[109] C. F. Goldfarb. *The SGML Handbook*. Oxford University Press, 1992.

[110] C.F. Goldfarb. *"The SGML Handbook"*. Clarendon Press, Oxford, 1991.

[111] U.S. Government. High Performance Computing and High Speed Networking Applications Act of 1993. Technical Report H.R. 1757, 103d Congress, 1st Session, Washington, D.C., none 1993.

[112] Eric Grosse. A catalogue of algorithms for approximation. In J. Mason and M. Cox, editors, *Algorithms for Approximation II*, pages 479–514 (of 514), London, England, 1990. Chapman and Halll.

[113] Eric Grosse. Repository mirroring. *ACM Trans. Math. Softw.*, 21(1), March 1995.

[114] Joint Photographic Experts Group. *Digital compression and coding of continuous-tone still images, ISO/IEC 10918-1,-2.* 1993.

[115] The Stanford Digital Libraries Group. "The Stanford Digital Library Project". *Communications of ACM*, 38(4):59, April 1995.

[116] F. Halasz and M. Schwartz. The dexter hypertext. *Communications of the ACM*, 37:30–39, 1994.

[117] F. Halasz and M. Schwartz. The dexter hypertext reference model. *Communications of the ACM*, 37(2), February 1994. also: NIST Hypertext Standardization Workshop, Gaithersburg, January 1990.

[118] F. Halasz and M. Schwartz. The Dexter reference model. *CACM*, 37:30–39, 1994.

[119] K. A. Hawick. High Performance Computing and Communications glossary. Technical report, Northeast Parallel Architectures Center at Syracuse University, July 1994.

[120] D. Heimbigner and D. McLeod. A federated architecture for information systems. *ACM Transactions on Office Information Systems*, 3(3):253–278, July 1985.

[121] M. Hoffman, L. O'Gorman, G.A. Story, and J.Q. Arnold. "The RightPages Service: An Image-based Electronic Library". *J. American Society for Information Science*, 44(8):446–452, September 1993.

[122] Hypertext markup language (HTML). http://www.w3.org/hypertext/WWW/MarkUp/MarkUp.html.

[123] J. Steven Hughes and Ann M. Farny. The management of metadata within the planetary data system. In *Proc. IEEE Workshop on Metadata for Scientific and Technical Data Management*, Washington, DC, May 1994.

[124] Carol Hunter and Rebecca Springmeyer. Using metadata to create library guides for scientific analysis. In *Proc. IEEE Workshop on Metadata for Scientific and Technical Data Management*, Washington, DC, May 1994. Intelligent Archive Project, Lawrence Livermore National Laboratory.

[125] K. Hunter and J. Zijlstra. "TULIP - The University Licensing Project". *J. Interlibr. Loan Doc. Deliv. Inf. Supply*, 4(3):19–22, 1994.

[126] Environmental Systems Research Institute Inc. *ArcView 2.0c software, Alpha/OSF1 version*. Environmental Systems Research Institute Inc., 1994.

[127] International Business Machines Corporation. *"ADSTAR Distributed Storage Manager General Information"*, July 1993. Publication No. GH35-0114.

[128] International Business Machines Corporation. *"DATABASE 2 AIX/6000 Information and Planning Guide"*, October 1993. Publication No. GC09-1569.

[129] International Business Machines Corporation. *"IBM ImagePlus VisualInfo General Information and Planning Guide"*, February 1994. Publication No. GK2T-1709.

[130] International Business Machines Corporation. *"SearchManager/6000 Overview"*, 1994. Publication No. GK10-2032.

[131] ISO8879. "Information Processing-Text and Office Systems-Standard Generalized Markup Language (SGML)". 1986.

[132] B. Kahle and A. Medlar. An information system for corporate users: Wide area information servers. *Connexions - The Interoperability Report*, 5(11):2–9, November 1991.

[133] B. Kahle and A. Medlar. An information system for corporate users: wide area information servers. *Connexions – The Interoperability Report*, 5:2–9, 1991.

[134] Robert Kahn and Robert Wilensky. Accessing digital library services and objects: A frame of reference. Draft 4.4 for discussion purposes, February 1995.

[135] M. S. Kamel, K. S. Ma, and W. H. Enright. ODEXPERT: An expert system to select numerical solvers for initial value ODE systems. *ACM Trans. Math. Softw.*, 19(1):44–62, March 1993.

[136] Ephraim Katz. *The Film Encyclopedia*. Fireside Press, second edition, 1989.

[137] D. Knuth. *Sorting and Searching*, volume 3 of *The Art of Computer Programming*. Addison-Wesley, 1973.

[138] W. Kowarschick, Ch. Roth, P. Vogel, S. Wiesener, and R. Bayer. OMNIS/Myriad on its way to a full hypermedia system. In *European Information Technology Conference (EITC), First Workshop on Human Comfort and Security*. Springer Verlag, Brussels, June 1994.

[139] R. Larson. Evaluation of advanced retrieval techniques in an experimental online catalog. *Journal of the American Society for Information Science*, 43(1):34–53, 1992.

[140] Ray R. Larson. Design and development of a network-based electronic library. In *Proc. ASIS Mid-Year Meeting*, pages 95–114, Portland, Oregon, May 1994.

[141] A.J. Lee, E.A. Rundensteiner, and S.W. Thomas. "Active OODB System for Genome Map Assembly". *Information Systems, Special Issue on Scientific Databases, to appear Spring 1995*.

[142] M. Lesk. The core electronic chemistry library. In *Proceedings of the ACM Special Interest Group on Information Retrieval Conference*, 1991.

[143] V. I. Levenshtein. Binary codes capable of correcting deletions, insertions and reversals. *Soviet Physics Doklady*, 10(8):707–710, February 1966.

[144] T.D.C. Little, et al. A digital on-demand video service supporting content-based queries. In *ACMMM*, pages 427–436, Aug. 1993.

[145] W. Litwin and A. Abdellatif. Multidatabase interoperability. *IEEE Computer Magazine*, 19(12):10–18, December 1986.

[146] Bede Liu, Wayne Wolf, Sanjeev Kulkarni, Andrew Wolfe, Hisashi Kobayashi, Fred Greenstein, Ira Fuchs, Arding Hsu, Farshid Arman, , and Yiqing Liang. The princeton video library of politics. In *Proceedings, Digital Libraries '94*, pages 215–216. Texas A&M University, 1994.

[147] Michael Lucks and Ian Gladwell. Automated selection of mathematical software. *ACM Trans. Math. Softw.*, 18(1):11–54, March 1992.

[148] C. A. Lynch. Information retrieval protocol: An overview and status report. *ACM SIGCOMM*, 21:58–70, 1991.

[149] C.A. Lynch. The development of electronic publishing and digital library collections of the nren. *Electronic Networking*, 1(2):6–22, 1991.

[150] Patrice A. Lyons. Interactive access to computer programs over telecommunications pathways: Some copyright implications. Submitted for publication as part of ASIS Monograph, The MIT Press.

[151] et.al. M. Schwartz. A Comparison of Internet Resource Discovery Approaches. Technical Report none, none, ftp://wais.think.com/, none 1992.

[152] Y. Malhotra. "Controlling Copyright Infringements of Intellectual Property: The Case of Computer Software". *Journal of Systems Management*, 45(6):32–35, June 1994.

[153] Kurt J. Maly, Edward A. Fox, James C. French, and Alan L. Selman. Wide area technical report server. Technical Report TR-92-44, Old Dominion University, 1992.

[154] E. Mangan. *Crosswalk between USMARC and CSDGM, 9/29/94*. Library of Congress, Geography and Map Division, Washington, DC, 1994.

[155] G. Marchionini and G. Crane. Evaluating hypermedia and learning: Methods and results from the Perseus project. *tois*, 12:5–34, 1994.

[156] Roger D. Masters. Individual and cultural differences in response to leaders: nonverbal displays. *Journal of Social Issues*, 47(3):151–165, 1991.

[157] M. Mauldin. Lycos: The Catalog of the Internet. Technical Report none, Carnegie Mellon Univeristy, http://lycos.cs.cmu.edu/, April 1995.

[158] N.F. Maxemchuk. "Electronic Document Distribution". *AT&T Technical Journal*, 1994.

[159] M. McCahill. The internet gopher protocol: A distributed server information system. *Connexions - The Interoperability Report*, 6(7):10–14, July 1992.

[160] M. McCahill. The internet gopher protocol: a distributed servers information system. *Connexions – The Interoperability Repor*, 6:10–14, 1992.

[161] C. McKnight. "Electronic journals, past, present, and future?". *ASLIB Proc*, 45(1):7–10, January 1993.

[162] C. McKnight. "Electronic Journals". In *AGARD Conference Proceedings 544: International High Speed Networks for Scientific and Technical Information*, 1994.

[163] M. F. McTear. User modelling for adaptive computer systems: a survey of recent developments. *Artificial Intelligence Review*, 7:157–184, 1993.

[164] R.C. Merkle. "Protocols for Public Key Cryptosystems". In *Proc. IEEE Computer Society Symposium on Security and Privacy*, pages 122–133, April 1980.

[165] S. Milliner and M. Papazoglou. Reassessing the roles of negotiation and contracting for interoperable databases. In *ADBIS'94*, pages 144–157, Moscow, May 1994.

[166] E. Mittendorf, P. Schäuble, and P. Sheridan. Applying probabilistic term weighting to ocr text in the case of a large alphabetic library catalogue. In *(to appear): Proceedings of the SIGIR'95, Seattle*, 1995.

[167] S. Muckherjea and J.D. Foley. Visualizing the world-wide web with the navigational view builder. *Computer Networks and ISDN Systems*, 27:1075–1087, 1995.

[168] NASA. NASA's Strategic Plan for Education, A Strategy for Change: 1993-1998. Technical Report EP-289, NASA, Washington, D.C., none 1992.

[169] NCSA. Mosaic. Technical Report http://www.ncsa.uiuc.edu/SDG/Software/Mosaic/NCSAMosaicHome.html, NCSA, Urbana, IL, 1994.

[170] S.R. Newcomb. The HyTime hypermedia/time-based document structuring language. *CACM*, 34:67–83, 1991.

[171] Newspaper Association of America. *IPTC-NAA Universal Text Format*, 0.8 edition, 1994.

[172] A. Nica and E. A. Rundensteiner. "A Constraint-based Object Model for Structured Document Management". *Electrical Engineering and Computer Science Dept., Computer Science and Engineering Division, University of Michigan, Ann Arbor, Tech. Rep.*, 1995.

[173] Sibylle R. Noras. All the news that's fit to screen – the development of fulltext newspaper data bases. *Australian Library Journal*, 38:17–27, 1989.

[174] Andrew M. Odlyzko. "Tragic loss or good riddance? The impending demise of traditional scholarly journals". AT&T Bell Laboratories, preliminary paper, December 30, 1993.

[175] M. Oezsu and P. Valduriez. *Principle of Distributed Database Systems*. Prentice-Hall, Englewood Cliffs, NJ, 1991.

[176] Library of Congress. MARC Development Office. *Maps: a MARC format.* Library of Congress Information Systems Office, Washington, DC, 1976.

[177] U.S. Bureau of the Census. *TIGER/Line 1992, the coast-to-coast digital map data base.* U.S. Bureau of the Census, Washington, D.C., 1992.

[178] T. Okuda, E. Tanaka, and T. Kasai. A method for the correction of garbled words based on the levenshtein metric. *IEEE Transactions on Computers*, pages 172–178, February 1976.

[179] J. Ousterhout. *Tcl and the Tk Toolkit*. Addison-Wesley, Reading, MA, 1994.

[180] Thomas Pack. Electronic newspapers – the state of the art. In *Proc. of the 14th National Online Meeting*, pages 331–335, 1993.

[181] U. Pfeifer, T. Poersch, and N. Fuhr. Searching proper names in databases. In R. Kuhlen and M. Rittberger, editors, *Hypertext – Information Retrieval – Multimedia, Proceedings HIM '95, Konstanz, Germany*, pages 259–275. Universitätsverlag Konstanz, 1995.

[182] Richard Pollard. A hypertext-based thesaurus as a subject browsing aid for bibliographic databases. *Information Processing and Management*, 29(3):345–357, 1993.

[183] M. Poppelier and H. Van Der Togt. "Documentation of the Elsevier Science Article DTD". April 1994.

[184] R. Price. MHEG: An introduction to the future international standard for hypermedia object interchange. In *ACMMM*, pages 121–128, Aug. 1993.

[185] R. Prieto-Diaz. Implementing faceted classification for software reuse. *Communications of the ACM*, 34(5):88–97, May 1991.

[186] T.A. Phillips P.T. Baffes, R.O. Shelton. NETS User's Guide: Version 3.0 of NETS. Technical Report JSC-23366, NASA, Johnson Space Center, none 1991.

[187] Steve Putz. Design and Implementation of the System 33 Document Service. Technical Report ISTL-NLTT-93-07-01, Xerox Palo Alto Research Center, 1993.

[188] Wolfgang Putz and Erich J. Neuhold. is-news: A multimedia information system. *IEEE Data Engineering*, 14:16–25, 1991.

[189] M. R. Quillian. Semantic memory. In M. Minsky, editor, *Semantic Information Processing*. MIT Press, Cambridge, 1968.

[190] S. V. Rice, J. Kanai, and T. Nartker. An evaluation of ocr accuracy. In K. O. Grover, editor, *UNLV Information Science Research Institute 1993 Annual Report*, pages 9–34. Information Science Research Institute, Universtity of Nevada, Las Vegas, 4505 Maryland Parkway, Box 454021, Las Vegas, Nevada 89154-4021, 1993.

[191] S. V. Rice, J. Kanai, and T. A. Nartker. The third annual test of ocr accuracy. In K. O. Grover, editor, *Information Science Research Institute — 1994 Annual Research Report*, pages 11–38. Information Science Research Institute, University of Nevada, Las Vegas, 4505 Maryland Parkway, Box 454021, Las Vegas, Nevada 89154–4021, USA, 1994.

[192] R. Rivest, A. Shamir, and L. Adelman. "A Method for Obtaining Digital Signature and Public Key Cryptosystems". *Communications of ACM*, 21:120–126, 1978.

[193] M.E. Rorvig. Psychometric measurement and information retrieval. In M.E. Williams, editor, *Annual Review of Information Science and Technology*, pages 157–189. ASIS, 1988.

[194] M.E. Rorvig and R.O. Shelton. An Intelligent Filter for Visual Documents. Technical Report MSC-22093-1, NASA, Johnson Space Center, none 1992.

[195] Jeff Rothenberg. "Ensuring the Longevity of Digital Documents". *Scientific American*, pages 42–47, January 1995.

[196] D.E. Rumelhart. Notes on a schema for stories. In D. Bobrow and A. Collins, editors, *Representation and Understanding*, pages 211–236. Academic, New York, 1975.

[197] E.A. Rundensteiner, L. Bic, J. Gilbert, and M. Yin. "Set-Restricted Semantic Groupings". *IEEE Transaction on Data and Knowledge Engineering*, 6:193 – 204, April 1994.

[198] N. A. Kipp S. R. Newcomb and V. T. Newcomb. The hytime hypermedia /time-based document structuring language. *Communications of the ACM*, 34:67–84, 1991.

[199] Marc E. Salomon and David C. Martin. "An Electronic Journal Browser Implemented in the World Wide Web", 1994.

[200] G. Salton and M. J. McGill. *Introduction to Modern Information Retrieval*. McGraw Hill Computer Science Series. McGraw Hill Book Company, New York, 1983.

[201] J.H. Saltzer. *"Technology, Networks, and the Library of the Year 2000"*, pages 51–67. Lecture Notes in Computer Science. 1992.

[202] Pamela Samuelson. "Copyright and Digital Libraries". *Communications of ACM*, 38(4):15, April 1995.

[203] P. Schaeuble. "SPIDER: A multiuser information retrieval system for semi-structured and dynamic data". *ACM-SIGIR '93, Pittsburgh, PA*, June 1993.

[204] B.R. Schatz and J.B. Hardin. Ncsa mosaic and the world-wide web: Global hypermedia protocols for the internet. *Science*, 265:895–901, 1994.

[205] M. F. Schwartz. Internet resource discovery at the University of Colorado. *IEEE Computer Magazine*, 26(9):25–35, September 1993.

[206] Scientific American. "Special Issue on Communications, Computers and Networks", September 1991.

[207] P. Sellers. The theory and computation of evolutionary distances: Pattern recognition. *J. Algorithms*, pages 359–373, 1980.

[208] R.O. Shelton. Hybrid Feed-Forward Neural Network with Conditionally Instantiated Connections Controlled by a Decision Tree Based on Logic Linear Discriminants. Technical Report MSC-22533-1, NASA, Johnson Space Center, none 1994.

[209] Amit P. Sheth and James A. Larson. Federated database systems and managing distributed, heterogeneous, and autonomous databases. *ACM Computing Surveys*, 22(3):183–226, September 1990.

[210] G.J. Simmons. "Symmetric and Asymmetric Encryption". *Computing Surveys*, 11(4):305–330, December 1979.

[211] E.A. Smith and R.J. Senter. Automated Readability Index. Technical Report AD 667 273, Clearinghouse for Federal Scientific and Technical Information, Wright-Patterson Air Force Base, Ohio, none 1967.

[212] J. M. Smith, P. A. Bernstein, U. Dayal, N. Goodman, T. Landers, K. W. T. Lin, and E. Wong. Multibase – integrating heterogeneous distributed database systems. *AFIP, National Computer Conference*, pages 487–499, 1981.

[213] S. Smith and C. Stanfill. An analysis of the effects of data corruption on text retrieval performance. Technical report, Thinking Machines Corporation, Cambridge, MA, 1988.

[214] T. R. Smith, D. P. Peuquet, S. Menon, and D. Agrawal. Kbgis-ii: A knowledge-based geographical information system. *International Journal of Geographical Information Systems*, 1987.

[215] T. R. Smith, J. Su, A. El Abbadi, D. Agrawal, A. Alonso, and A. Saran. Computational modeling systems. *Journal of Information Systems*, 19 (4), 1995.

[216] Karen Sollins and Larry Masinter. Functional requirements for uniform resource names. Internet RFC 1737, December 1994.

[217] G.A. Story, L. O'Gorman, D. Fox, L. Schaper, and H.V. Jagadish. "The RightPages Image-Based Electronic Library for Alerting and Browsing". *IEEE Computer*, 25(9):17–26, September 1992.

[218] Guy A. Story, Lawrence O'Gorman, David Fox, Louise Levy Schaper, and H.V. Jagadish. The RightPages Image-Based Electronic Library for Alerting and Browsing. *IEEE Computer*, pages 17–25, September 1992.

[219] P.D. Stotts and R. Furuta. Petri-net-based hypertext: Document structure with browsing semantics. *tois*, 7:3–29, 1989.

[220] William S. Strong. *The Copyright Book*. The MIT Press, Cambridge, Massachusetts, fourth edition, 1993.

[221] P. Suppes. Some theoretical models for mathematics learning. In *Journal of Research and Development in Education*, volume 1, pages 5–22, 1975.

[222] E. Tanaka and Y. Kojima. A high speed string correction method using a hierarchical file. *IEEE Transactions on Pattern Analysis and Machine Intelligence (PAMI)*, 9(6):806–815, November 1987.

[223] TransAction Software GmbH, Munich. *Myriad System and Administration Guide, Myriad Fulltext Database System Version 3.0.*, 1992.

[224] W. Turner. The document architecture for the Cornell Digital Library. Internet RFC 1691, August 1994.

[225] Carnegie Mellon University. The mercury electronic library and library information system ii. the first three years. Technical Report no. 6, Carnegie Mellon University, Feburary 1992.

[226] U.S. Geological Survey Reston VA. *1:100,000-scale Digital Line Graph (DLG) data, hydrography and transportation; area 12, central Pacific states. Optional format.* U.S. Geological Survey, 1993.

[227] C.J. van Rijsbergen. *Information Retrieval.* Butterworths, 2nd edition, 1979.

[228] Marc VanHeynigen. WWW page. http://cs.indiana.edu/cstr/search.

[229] N.R. Wagner. "Fingerprinting". In *Proceedings of the 1983 Symposium on Security and Privacy*, pages 18–22. IEEE Computer Society, April 1983.

[230] Wais Inc. WAIS for UNIX, technical description. http://www.wais.com/newhomepages/techtoc.html, Thinking Machines.

[231] C. Warlick and C. Stout. Wide Area Instantiation, Deployment, and Management of Autonomous Knowledge Robots: An unsolicited proposal for a research grant to the National Aeronautics and Space Administration. Technical Report JSC-4-94-9304, University of Texas at Austin, Austin, Texas, Office of Sponsored Projects, April 1994.

[232] R. Watson. Identifiers (naming) in distributed systems. In B. W. Lampson, M. Paul, and H. J. Siegert, editors, *Lecture Notes in Computer Science: Distributed Systems - Architecture and Implementation*, pages 191–210. Springer Verlag, New York, 1981.

[233] Stuart Weibel, Eric Miller, Jean Godby, and Ralph LeVan. "An Architecture for Scholarly Publishing on the World Wide Web", 1994.

[234] Robert Wilensky. "UC Berkeley's Digital Library Project". *Communications of ACM*, 38(4):60, April 1995.

[235] ICDE Workshop on Active DBMS Systems. "Research Issues in Active Databases". *ACM*, 1994.

[236] S. Wu and U. Manber. Fast text searching with errors. Technical Report TR 91-11, Department of Computer Science, University of Arizona, 1991.

[237] X/Open Company Limited. "*X/Open Backup Services API, Preliminary Specification*". to appear.

[238] T.W. Yan and J. Annevelink. "Integrating a structured-text retrieval system with an OODB system". *Proceed. of 20th VLDB Conf., Santiago, Chile*, 1994.

[239] Minerva Yeung, Boon-Lock Yeo, Wayne Wolf, and Bede Liu. Video browsing using clustering and scene transitions on compressed sequences. In *Proceedings, 1995 SPIE Conference on Multimedia Computing and Networking*. SPIE, 1995.

[240] Young, Douglas. *The X Window System, Programming and Applications with Xt*. Prentice-Hall, Engelwoods Cliffs, NJ, 2nd edition, 1994.

[241] P.T. Zellweger. Scripted documents: A hypermedia path mechanism. In *ACM Hypertext '89*, pages 1–14, Nov. 1989.

[242] D. G. Zhao. Usage statistics collection and management in the elinor electronic library. *Journal of Information Science*, 21:1–9, 1995.

# Springer
# and the
# environment

At Springer we firmly believe that an international science publisher has a special obligation to the environment, and our corporate policies consistently reflect this conviction.

We also expect our business partners – paper mills, printers, packaging manufacturers, etc. – to commit themselves to using materials and production processes that do not harm the environment. The paper in this book is made from low- or no-chlorine pulp and is acid free, in conformance with international standards for paper permanency.

Springer

# Lecture Notes in Computer Science

For information about Vols. 1–1081

please contact your bookseller or Springer-Verlag

Vol. 1116: J. Hall (Ed.), Management of Telecommunication Systems and Services. XXI, 229 pages. 1996.

Vol. 1117: A. Ferreira, J. Rolim, Y. Saad, T. Yang (Eds.), Parallel Algorithms for Irregularly Structured Problems. Proceedings, 1996. IX, 358 pages. 1996.

Vol. 1118: E.C. Freuder (Ed.), Principles and Practice of Constraint Programming — CP 96. Proceedings, 1996. XIX, 574 pages. 1996.

Vol. 1119: U. Montanari, V. Sassone (Eds.), CONCUR '96: Concurrency Theory. Proceedings, 1996. XII, 751 pages. 1996.

Vol. 1120: M. Deza. R. Euler, I. Manoussakis (Eds.), Combinatorics and Computer Science. Proceedings, 1995. IX, 415 pages. 1996.

Vol. 1121: P. Perner, P. Wang, A. Rosenfeld (Eds.), Advances in Structural and Syntactical Pattern Recognition. Proceedings, 1996. X, 393 pages. 1996.

Vol. 1122: H. Cohen (Ed.), Algorithmic Number Theory. Proceedings, 1996. IX, 405 pages. 1996.

Vol. 1123: L. Bougé, P. Fraigniaud, A. Mignotte, Y. Robert (Eds.), Euro-Par'96. Parallel Processing. Proceedings, 1996, Vol. I. XXXIII, 842 pages. 1996.

Vol. 1124: L. Bougé, P. Fraigniaud, A. Mignotte, Y. Robert (Eds.), Euro-Par'96. Parallel Processing. Proceedings, 1996, Vol. II. XXXIII, 926 pages. 1996.

Vol. 1125: J. von Wright, J. Grundy, J. Harrison (Eds.), Theorem Proving in Higher Order Logics. Proceedings, 1996. VIII, 447 pages. 1996.

Vol. 1126: J.J. Alferes, L. Moniz Pereira, E. Orlowska (Eds.), Logics in Artificial Intelligence. Proceedings, 1996. IX, 417 pages. 1996. (Subseries LNAI).

Vol. 1127: L. Böszörményi (Ed.), Parallel Computation. Proceedings, 1996. XI, 235 pages. 1996.

Vol. 1128: J. Calmet, C. Limongelli (Eds.), Design and Implementation of Symbolic Computation Systems. Proceedings, 1996. IX, 356 pages. 1996.

Vol. 1129: J. Launchbury, E. Meijer, T. Sheard (Eds.), Advanced Functional Programming. Proceedings, 1996. VII, 238 pages. 1996.

Vol. 1130: M. Haveraaen, O. Owe, O.-J. Dahl (Eds.), Recent Trends in Data Type Specification. Proceedings, 1995. VIII, 551 pages. 1996.

Vol. 1131: K.H. Höhne, R. Kikinis (Eds.), Visualization in Biomedical Computing. Proceedings, 1996. XII, 610 pages. 1996.

Vol. 1132: G.-R. Perrin, A. Darte (Eds.), The Data Parallel Programming Model. XV, 284 pages. 1996.

Vol. 1133: J.-Y. Chouinard, P. Fortier, T.A. Gulliver (Eds.), Information Theory and Applications II. Proceedings, 1995. XII, 309 pages. 1996.

Vol. 1134: R. Wagner, H. Thoma (Eds.), Database and Expert Systems Applications. Proceedings, 1996. XV, 921 pages. 1996.

Vol. 1135: B. Jonsson, J. Parrow (Eds.), Formal Techniques in Real-Time and Fault-Tolerant Systems. Proceedings, 1996. X, 479 pages. 1996.

Vol. 1136: J. Diaz, M. Serna (Eds.), Algorithms – ESA '96. Proceedings, 1996. XII, 566 pages. 1996.

Vol. 1137: G. Görz, S. Hölldobler (Eds.), KI-96: Advances in Artificial Intelligence. Proceedings, 1996. XI, 387 pages. 1996. (Subseries LNAI).

Vol. 1138: J. Calmet, J.A. Campbell, J. Pfalzgraf (Eds.), Artificial Intelligence and Symbolic Mathematical Computation. Proceedings, 1996. VIII, 381 pages. 1996.

Vol. 1139: M. Hanus, M. Rogriguez-Artalejo (Eds.), Algebraic and Logic Programming. Proceedings, 1996. VIII, 345 pages. 1996.

Vol. 1140: H. Kuchen, S. Doaitse Swierstra (Eds.), Programming Languages: Implementations, Logics, and Programs. Proceedings, 1996. XI, 479 pages. 1996.

Vol. 1141: H.-M. Voigt, W. Ebeling, I. Rechenberg, H.-P. Schwefel (Eds.), Parallel Problem Solving from Nature – PPSN IV. Proceedings, 1996. XVII, 1.050 pages. 1996.

Vol. 1142: R.W. Hartenstein, M. Glesner (Eds.), Field-Programmable Logic. Proceedings, 1996. X, 432 pages. 1996.

Vol. 1143: T.C. Fogarty (Ed.), Evolutionary Computing. Proceedings, 1996. VIII, 305 pages. 1996.

Vol. 1144: J. Ponce, A. Zisserman, M. Hebert (Eds.), Object Representation in Computer Vision. Proceedings, 1996. VIII, 403 pages. 1996.

Vol. 1145: R. Cousot, D.A. Schmidt (Eds.), Static Analysis. Proceedings, 1996. IX, 389 pages. 1996.

Vol. 1146: E. Bertino, H. Kurth, G. Martella, E. Montolivo (Eds.), Computer Security – ESORICS 96. Proceedings, 1996. X, 365 pages. 1996.

Vol. 1147: L. Miclet, C. de la Higuera (Eds.), Grammatical Inference: Learning Syntax from Sentences. Proceedings, 1996. VIII, 327 pages. 1996. (Subseries LNAI).

Vol. 1148: M.C. Lin, D. Manocha (Eds.), Applied Computational Geometry. Proceedings, 1996. VIII, 223 pages. 1996.

Vol. 1149: C. Montangero (Ed.), Software Process Technology. Proceedings, 1996. IX, 291 pages. 1996.

Vol. 1150: A. Hlawiczka, J.G. Silva, L. Simoncini (Eds.), Dependable Computing – EDCC-2. Proceedings, 1996. XVI, 440 pages. 1996.

Vol. 1151: Ö. Babaoğlu, K. Marzullo (Eds.), Distributed Algorithms. Proceedings, 1996. VIII, 381 pages. 1996.

Vol. 1153: E. Burke, P. Ross (Eds.), Practice and Theory of Automated Timetabling. Proceedings, 1995. XIII, 381 pages. 1996.

Vol. 1154: D. Pedreschi, C. Zaniolo (Eds.), Logic in Databases. Proceedings, 1996. X, 497 pages. 1996.

Vol. 1155: J. Roberts, U. Mocci, J. Virtamo (Eds.), Broadbank Network Teletraffic. XXII, 584 pages. 1996.

Vol. 1156: A. Bode, J. Dongarra, T. Ludwig, V. Sunderam (Eds.), Parallel Virtual Machine – EuroPVM '96. Proceedings, 1996. XIV, 362 pages. 1996.

Vol. 1157: B. Thalheim (Ed.), Conceptual Modeling – ER '96. Proceedings, 1996. XII, 489 pages. 1996.

Vol. 1158: S. Berardi, M. Coppo (Eds.), Types for Proofs and Programs. Proceedings, 1995. X, 296 pages. 1996.